Palgrave Studies in Gender and Education

Series Editor

Yvette Taylor
School of Education
University of Strathclyde
Glasgow, United Kingdom

This Series aims to provide a comprehensive space for an increasingly diverse and complex area of interdisciplinary social science research: gender and education. Because the field of women and gender studies is developing rapidly and becoming 'internationalised' – as are traditional social science disciplines such as sociology, educational studies, social geography, and so on – there is a greater need for this dynamic, global Series that plots emerging definition and debates and monitors critical complexities of gender and education. This Series has an explicitly feminist approach and orientation and attends to key theoretical and methodological debates, ensuring a continued conversation and relevance within the well-established, interdisciplinary field of gender and education. The Series combines renewed and revitalised feminist research methods and theories with emergent and salient public policy issues. These include pre-compulsory and post-compulsory education; 'early years' and 'lifelong' education; educational (dis)engagements of pupils, students and staff; trajectories and intersectional inequalities including race, class, sexuality, age and disability; policy and practice across educational landscapes; diversity and difference, including institutional (schools, colleges, universities), locational and embodied (in 'teacher'–'learner' positions); varied global activism in and beyond the classroom and the 'public university'; educational technologies and transitions and the (ir)relevance of (in)formal educational settings; and emergent educational mainstreams and margins. In using a critical approach to gender and education, the Series recognises the importance of probing beyond the boundaries of specific territorial-legislative domains inorder to develop a more international, intersectional focus. In addressing varied conceptual and methodological questions, the Series combines anintersectional focus on competing – and sometimes colliding – strands of educational provisioning and equality and 'diversity', and provides insightful reflections on the continuing critical shift of gender and feminism within (and beyond) the academy.

More information about this series at
http://www.springer.com/series/14626

Firdevs Melis Cin

Gender Justice, Education and Equality

Creating Capabilities for Girls' and Women's Development

palgrave
macmillan

Firdevs Melis Cin
Department of Psychology
Istanbul Ticaret Universitesi
Istanbul, Turkey

Palgrave Studies in Gender and Education
ISBN 978-3-319-39103-8   ISBN 978-3-319-39104-5   (eBook)
DOI 10.1007/978-3-319-39104-5

Library of Congress Control Number: 2016959269

Cover Image © Tom Wang/Alamy Stock Photo

Printed on acid-free paper

This Palgrave Macmillan imprint is published by Springer Nature
The registered company is Springer International Publishing AG
The registered company address is: Gewerbestrasse 11, 6330 Cham, Switzerland

Acknowledgements

There are so many people who have inspired and supported me during this research. It has been an enjoyable and enriching journey for me. It is impossible to thank all the people I have come across during this period. To start with, I would like to express my gratitude, first and foremost, to my parents, Belgin Cin and Mesut Cin, and to my brother, Mehmet Melih Cin, for their constant encouragement and support.

I am gratefully indebted to Professor Melanie Walker and Professor Monica McLean for their guidance and for being a source of inspiration throughout this project. No words could express my appreciation of them. I would also like to express my gratitude to University of Nottingham, School of Education, for offering funds and scholarship to undertake this project.

I would like to thank my aunt, Yelda Baba, and my uncle, Professor Dr. Fevzi Baba, for their support and encouragement during my studies.

As for my friends, I cannot pay back the emotional and intellectual support I got from Julia Long, Ecem Karlıdağ, Aurora Lopez-Fogues, Görkem Altınörs, Francesca Silvestri, Earl Kehoe, Tham Ngyuen and Rahime Süleymanoğlu-Kürüm. I am also hugely grateful to Dimitrios Anagnostakis for the encouragement, invaluable support and intellectual debates. He has given his time to read over various versions of this book and provide feedback.

My special thanks go to my colleagues Prof. Dr. Gökhan Malkoç, Dr. Ela Arı, Dr. Aydın Karaçanta and Gizem Cesur for their encouragement and support during the writing of this book. Thanks for listening to me going on about this research and this book.

My thanks to all my participants who have enthusiastically joined in this study and opened their lives and hearts to me.

CONTENTS

LIST OF TABLES

CHAPTER 1

Introduction: Conceptualising Gender Justice

This book elaborates on the capabilities approach, developed by Amartya Sen (1999) and Martha Nussbaum (2000), engaging with the study of education, gender and development by looking into women's lives and giving them the opportunity to speak for themselves. In so doing, it takes Turkey as a case where women are located at the crossroads between embracing modernity and living under traditional and cultural norms (Göle 1997). The book explores women's positioning, survival, resistance, freedoms, well-being and agency through the clash of multifaceted, socio-logical phenomena, such as: religion/secularism, modernism/tradition, ethnicity, multilingualism and the paradoxes of culture and generations, both in the public sphere and in their private lives. It analyses the everyday expression and narratives of women who have variously defined them-selves as nationalist, feminist, modern, activist, submissive and traditional. Through the collective voices of three different generations of women teachers, I voice women's experiences of being a woman and becoming a teacher in socio-culturally diverse Turkey. Turkey, as a developing context, provides an interesting site to explore how the issues of gender, education and development interweave with its diverse socio-cultural setting—mid-way between the values and systems of the West and the East.

Located at the intersection of gender and education, the book also looks into how education can be transformative in women's private and public lives, and distribute justice. At the same time, it examines how gender inequalities can be reproduced through education and aims to explore

© The Editor(s) (if applicable) and The Author(s) 2017
F.M. Cin, *Gender Justice, Education and Equality*, Palgrave Studies in Gender and Education, DOI 10.1007/978-3-319-39104-5_1

1

the potentialities of using the capabilities approach and feminist theories to better understand gender and education and to make recommendations to policy-makers in order to improve educational policies. A feminist lens applied through the capabilities approach is used as an overarching theoretical framework to address women's individual experiences in relation to wider societal and educational issues. I use Nussbaum's capabilities approach as a feminist theory of justice, serving as a space for evaluating women's real opportunities in life. At the same time, using the capabilities framework, I focus on fundamental concepts of gender justice, and intrinsic and subjective freedoms for human development, such as how we address the real lives of women subject to gender discrimination or the oppression of culture and tradition, or which valuable freedoms are necessary to provide women with lives they value and choose. However, Martha Nussbaum's capabilities approach is not enough to illuminate the freedoms and opportunities in women's lives. What matters as much as freedoms is agency—that is, to what extent are women capable of enacting their agency, having freedom to pursue and achieve their valued goals, being active participants of social change or helping people to expand their capabilities. Therefore, I take an agency-oriented capabilities approach and utilise Amartya Sen's (1999) approach to agency to explain women's capacities and potentials to initiate change or to commit themselves to an action and pursue their objectives.

The book aspires to illuminate the broader issues in an arena of gender justice by focusing on Turkey. Therefore, it does not restrict itself to a specific context, but offers necessary lenses and empirical implications to think about gender justice, education and human development in broader terms. This introductory chapter provides a contextual and methodological framework for the book. It begins by focusing on the current debates on gender, education and development, and it problematises the ways current debates approach gender equality. Then it introduces the Turkish context in relation to issues of gender and education, teasing out how the capabilities approach coupled with feminist theories can offer a better understanding of gender and education in Turkey. Finally, the chapter sets out the feminist methodology employed in this book to reach women's voices.

GENDER, EDUCATION AND DEVELOPMENT

Gender affects a broad range of inequalities in our world, particularly in relation to education and schooling. Across the world, around 65 million girls are not schooled and two-thirds of the world's 774 million illiterate adults are female (see UNESCO Statistics 2013). To address these issues, the Education for All (EFA) campaign (initiated in Dhaka in 2000) set out to provide basic education for all children across the world and identified six goals—including the goal of eliminating gender disparities and inequalities—to be met by 2015. The recently published EFA 2015 report by UNESCO shows that there has been some notable progress in relation to ensuring that girls have equal access to basic education. Nevertheless, in 2015, only 69 % of countries are estimated to have reached gender parity at the primary education level, and this figure drops to 48 % in secondary education. This shows there is still a long way to go towards achieving gender equality.

Such inequality and injustice is not only a question of lack of funds, but also related to ensuring access, providing quality of education, culture, sustainability and governance; all of which could be framed around the concept of gender as they usually involve lack of representation, distribution or recognition of the interests of women and girls. All these issues are central to development, particularly to the development of women and girls, and thus to the themes in this book. As McCowan and Unterhalter (2015) state, education and development are two closely related and interdependent themes, and education is an integral part of development. Yet, while the kind of development we are speaking of here is a positive change, it should be noted that education can also restrict the development of marginalised or socially excluded groups, and therefore the nature and quality of education is a contentious issue, and one to be addressed in the field of development studies.

Until very recently, traditional human development approaches have remained at a macro perspective throughout the years, being concerned solely with measuring economic growth as an important indication for assessing development. Development has been considered only in terms of economic development and has undervalued a focus on women and their dignity (Nussbaum 2003a). The gross domestic product (GDP), the utilitarian approach and the resource-based approach have all proven to be inadequate means of analysing the quality of women's lives and the challenges they face (Nussbaum and Sen 1993). Furthermore, they do not provide any information on other aspects of life, such as education, freedoms and opportunities (Nussbuam 2011). These approaches have failed to explain how well people are doing, especially those within marginalised or subordinated groups. They lack a gender perspective, have a limited focus on merely concentrating on income and wealth as the basis of assessment, or measure the quality of life according to people's own feelings about their lives, looking at overall satisfaction without taking into account individual differences or the real opportunities women have. Gender justice has remained a secondary issue, but without gender equality and justice, any attempts or strategies towards development are likely to fail.

Like gender equality, education is also central to human flourishing and development, yet it has been given little space in development approaches and studies. Gender is an underpinning rationale with which one approaches education and development. The frameworks of Women in Development (WID), Gender and Development (GAD), post-structuralism, normative approaches of human capital theory, the human rights-based approach, and the capabilities approach (human development) form the core debates on gender, education and development with their distinctive concerns for addressing gender equality. The human capital theory is an instrumentalist way of viewing development or empowerment in terms of economic growth or social cohesion. It has a superficial and descriptive understanding of gender. Gender is understood as a biological category and the education of girls and women is identified as important because it contributes to economic growth, helping create more educated families or reducing infant and child mortality so that women can better serve the national economic growth and interests (Unterhalter 2007a). It offers an essentialised account of gender differences and a depoliticised account of gender inequality, and fails to promote gender equality substantively (Unterhalter 2007a; Vaughan 2010). Within this approach, gender equality is limited to equality in numbers—equal numbers of boys and girls in education—and closing the gender gap.

The human rights-based approach associates development and empowerment mostly with legal documents and equal citizenship, and women's education is seen as a fundamental right. This approach addresses gender equality both in formal and substantive dimensions, and recognises the existence of socially constructed gender differences (Vaughan 2010). Gender equality is understood to involve transformation and reforms in social institutions that perpetuate gender-based inequalities. However, equal rights do not necessarily mean gender equality or empowerment, because women are not always considered as equal partners with men in democracies (Pateman 1988); and granting rights does not challenge the power and gender inequalities deeply embedded in institutions. Although the human rights-based approach provides strong language and directives for legislative tools to advocate gender equality at the international and national level, it does not necessarily follow that laws and treaties which exist to advance women's claims will create a more moral social order or redistribute resources and power in alignment with notions of gender equality (Unterhalter 2007a).

The capabilities approach distinguishes itself from other approaches in that it provides a moral and ethical philosophical lens to examine the nature of rights and human dignity, and establishes a normative theory to look into gender equalities. It focuses on substantive freedoms and the widening of opportunities, particularly for girls and women. In this approach, education is central to women's empowerment (Nussbaum 2003a). For example, education can empower women by: revealing the way to leave an abusive marriage; ensuring their freedom of mobility outside of the home; creating the possibility of work; developing the ability to form social networks; and providing them with a means of access to discover their political and legal processes and rights. The capabilities approach builds on the human capital and human rights-based approaches. It recognises the socially constructed nature of gender differences (Unterhalter 2007a). Unlike human capital theory, gender equality in education is seen as intrinsically good and as a 'necessary condition to allow reflection on capabilities, the conversion of resources into capabilities for differently situated people and to enable the development of further capabilities' (Unterhalter 2007a: 81). In achieving gender equality in education, it assigns responsibility not only to governments, institutions or individuals, but also to society, and calls for a redistribution of resources and power.

Capabilities also focus on women's agency, which is a neglected area of development studies and development theories (Sen 1999). For Sen, addressing gender inequalities is important because it is an important barrier that affects what women can do and be. The necessity of addressing how women's opportunities can be expanded to allow them to achieve what they value, bring about change and work to expand the capabilities of other people is a central concern of capability theorists. However, the agency concept needs to be conceptualised in an integrated way, to delineate it from empowerment and to offer a robust account of how both are relevant ways to challenge gender inequalities. Many theorists offer a nuanced understanding of empowerment in relation to agency and the capabilities approach. Murphy-Graham (2012: 15) defines empowerment as the process of recognition of women's subordination, building their capability and developing their inherent worth 'to take action towards personal and social transformation'. Kabeer (1999) sees empowerment as the ability to make strategic choices. She ascribes three important structures to empowerment: resources (material and social resources); agency (the ability to define one's goals); and achievements (well-being outcomes). These structures refer to the following concepts of Sen's capabilities: people's desire to do what they want; and their achievement of valued ways of 'being and doing'. Stromquist (1995) proposes a framework which regards empowerment as the development of self-confidence and self-esteem, and argues that women need the necessary conditions for development of personal and collective levels of agency to lead public actions. Likewise, Mosedale (2005) argues for an empowerment process that leads women to redefine their potentials and expand the possibilities of what they can achieve and what is available. She argues that her empowerment differs from Kabeer's in two ways: Mosadale focuses on a process of change initiated by women to expand not only their own individual options, but also those of other women. Thus, she argues for collectivist actions. Secondly, she emphasises the gendered nature of disempowerment and expresses the need for women to challenge their gender roles in order to initiate a collective struggle. All these definitions underpin the philosophical understanding provided by the capabilities approach. As such, Raynor (2007) refers to capabilities as an empowerment approach to development and Unterhalter (2011) argues that capabilities align with empowerment and sees empowerment as a normative concept. So, as has been seen, capabilities and empowerment are used interchangeably by some scholars. However, Sen's account allows an understanding of whether people in particular contexts and specific conditions can enact their agency and achieve their own well-being. Thus, he focuses on the provision of political, economic and social resources to expand one's agency to achieve both self-desired and altruistic goals. Yet Koggel (2013) and Drydyk (2013) criticise Sen for failing to provide an analysis of how political, economic and social resources and institutions are entrenched in the norms, relationships and practices that form a barrier to gender equality. They argue for an empowerment account that places relationships—instead of individuals—at the heart of analysis and they link empowerment with power relations. However, my framing of empowerment, drawing on Nussbaum and Sen's concepts, argues that it is a process that equips women with the capabilities to pursue opportunities they value; to expand the capabilities of others, and to initiate social change. Thus, it is a process that leads to women's development and it is at the same time an important outcome, often provided by education or access to information, to avoid the risk of falling into adaptive preferences (i.e. adapting what is valuable to oneself according to the norms and conditions one lives in).

By and large, in both empowerment and capabilities literature, education is seen as a way to expand women's opportunities; to empower women; to improve women's rights; and—most importantly—to achieve gender equality. Education, however, does not always result in women's empowerment, due to the socio-economic context in which women's lives are situated (Murphy-Graham 2012), or to processes and norms and learning practices dominated by power and gender relations, historical contradictions (Walker and Unterhalter 2007) and the dominant state ideologies. These processes may not always necessarily enhance freedoms, but may rather cause capability deprivation (Unterhalter 2003a). A growing body of research using a capabilities framework shows that schooling could limit the opportunities of individuals through interacting with cultural and economic contexts and with forms of gendered discrimination. Particularly, the gendered relations in the social, physical and relational environment, and the gendered regimes and power structures in education and at school, negatively affect girls' educational opportunities and learning (through, for instance, the narrow content of the curriculum and the policing of gender, race and class relations), and impede their access to schools (Aikman and Unterhalter 2013; Arends-Kuenning and Amin 2001; Raynor 2007; Unterhalter 2005b). Such gendered regimes include gender biases in curricula, gendered beliefs about girls' learning and education, gendered stereotypes in school and textbooks depicting traditional gendered roles (Ames 2005; Fennel an Arnot 2008; Stromquist 2007; Skelton et al. 2009; UNICEF and UNGEI 2008). Thus, the education one receives may not be transformative in the sense that it may not challenge gender roles and gender-based identities and norms at school and in society.

Therefore, the limiting factor of education and the wider structural coercion against the empowerment of girls raise an issue regarding the quality and the content of education. Researchers (Aikman et al. 2011; Aikman and Unterhalter 2013; Goetz 2007; Monkman 2011; Murphy-Graham 2012; Robeyns 2010a; Unterhalter 2007a, b) emphasise that a quality education requires gender equality and equity in guiding women to challenge traditional gender roles, norms and stereotypes. Assessing the quality of education should involve addressing questions of how schooling articulates labour market opportunities, how the media depicts gender, how women's exclusion inside and outside the school is addressed, and how the social, cultural, political and economic processes that cause gender discrimination in the public sphere and in labour markets are challenged (Aikman and Unterhalter 2013). Stromquist (2006), for example, suggests that education, in order to achieve gender equality and to offer a transformative agenda, requires the support of other sectors of society besides the state—such as the mass media or the participation of civil society.

As can be seen, education does not always necessarily empower, lead to the expansion of capabilities, or ensure freedoms in one's life; yet it is often forgotten that education from a capabilities-based feminist perspective can empower women, give them the ability to make strategic life choices and develop the capacity for self-determination. Most educational systems reflect social inequalities and prejudices, and do not challenge the social status quo (Stromquist 1995). Expecting that education per se will lead to empowerment or development is an optimistic perspective, as educational initiatives throughout the world are often weak in addressing change at societal levels (Stacki and Monkman 2003) and educational programmes often fail to challenge sexual and ethnic stereotypes and deeply embedded sexism in society. Therefore, a feminist and capabilities perspective to design initiatives and policies that could truly lead to gender awareness and gender equity is needed, as it can help to identify inequalities in education, evaluate whether education distributes justice in women's lives and leads to empowerment, and gauge the obstacles that stand in the way. So far, I have briefly presented the discussions around gender, development and education and highlighted how the capabilities approach is set apart from other approaches and how it is linked with the concept of empowerment and agency. The next section looks into the context of gender equality in education in Turkey and teases out the lack of gender perspective in the design and implementation of education policies.

The Context of Gender Equality in Education in Turkey

The main concern of Turkey in relation to gender equality has been gender parity. The Ministry of National Education (MoNE) has launched various campaigns to expand girls' education, to increase the number of girls at secondary and primary schools and to achieve numerical equality in education. These campaigns have mostly focused on Eastern Turkey, which is the least economically and socially developed region of Turkey. Campaigns have been initiated in collaboration with the World Bank, UNICEF and the EU, but they are also supported by powerful government educational policies and legislation.[1] For instance, the Social Assistance and Solidarity Fund (SYDF) of monthly conditional cash transfers (CTT) under the World Bank project of Social Risk Mitigation; and The Girls Education Campaign, launched in 2003 with the collaboration of the MoNE and UNICEF; whereas government policies have been aimed at distributing free textbooks; door-to-door campaigns visiting every household to persuade fathers to permit their daughters to attend school; imams giving Friday sermons stressing the importance of girls' schooling; and the support of electronic and print media through publications and the broadcast of free spots on the significance of girls' education. In addition to these policies, national campaigns such as 'Snowdrops', 'Daddy, Send Me to School', and 'I have a daughter in Anatolia and she will be a teacher' were influential in increasing girls' schooling and enrolment. The 'Project for Increasing Enrolment Rates, Especially For Girls', introduced by MoNE, was launched to enhance investment in human capital by increasing girls' enrolment rates and improving the links between education and the labour market (Velibeyoglu 2013). The project aims to decrease the dropout rates in primary and secondary education and increase vocational school enrolment rates to increase the existing labour force. Lastly, the 'Promoting Gender Equality in Education Project' was launched by MoNE in 2015 to promote gender equality in schools and to increase the awareness of gender equality among students, parents and teaching and non-teaching staff.

These campaigns have also sought to meet EFA[2] and MDG (Millennium Development Goals)[3] goals number 2 and number 3 to expand primary school participation globally. Although these campaigns and policies have, to a large extent, achieved numerical equality in enrolment rates, they have failed to engage with the structural problems girls face at schools. As argued by Cin and Walker (2016) and McCLure (2014), these initiatives focused on a distributional justice of scholarship and cash transfers, or on building more classrooms and employing more teachers in disadvantaged regions of Turkey. They have paid little attention to girls' schooling experiences within and outside of schools, gender and social relations within and around the school, the quality of education girls receive, or how market and family relations impact on girls' schooling. They only touch the surface of a greater problem in girls' education by focusing on increasing gender parity or providing funding and resources and increasing access to education without any gender concerns.

Although these campaigns can be argued to have achieved some level of numerical success by increasing the enrolment rate of girls (see Table 3.5) and financially assisting some disadvantaged girls—through following policies similar to school stipend programmes and free primary education programmes in Malawi, Uganda, Tanzania, Pakistan and Bangladesh or cash transfers in Brazil and Chile (Chaudhury and Parajuli 2010; Filmer and Schady 2008)—these enrolment rates do not reveal the problems of attendance, completing studies or low levels of learning, and do not necessarily mean that there is equality in terms of challenging social, economic and gender inequalities (Aikman and Rao 2012). Therefore, stipends alone are not enough when the learning processes that make the educational experience empowering for girls are absent.

This implies that the Ministry of Education in Turkey views gender inequality mainly as a problem concerning the gender gap between boys' and girls' attendance of school or girls' attainment. Their involvement is limited to renovating classrooms, supplying learning materials and filling schools with students. It does not extend to encouraging girls' participation in learning; eliminating gender differences in class; addressing inequities; or creating more girl-friendly schools (McCLure 2014). There is no mention of educational quality, gendered structures, relations or pedagogies within the school, or of the social relations outside the school which prevent equal participation in social life. No attention has been given to girls' schooling experiences within and outside the schools, gender and social relations within and around the school, the quality of education girls receive, or how market and family relations impact girls' schooling. No concern is demonstrated for ameliorating gendered social forces (the social factors shaping girls and boys differently both in school environment and at home) or gendered educational forces (such as identifying what girls and teachers have reason to value in education). Rhetorically, a good level of net schooling enrolment rate has been achieved, but nothing has been done towards the structures and relations that discriminate against girls. There is no space to analyse how gender justice can be redefined and contested.

I therefore argue that education requires a gender justice approach in which equality for girls and boys extends beyond numbers to norms, relationships and practices in both education and society, if it is to empower girls and women. Listening to women teachers' voices critically could reveal structural gender inequalities infusing education across the generations and guide us to evaluate the extent to which education distributes gender justice and leads to development of girls and women. The capabilities approach can offer significant guidance towards finding out which opportunities matter for them. Therefore, in the next section, I focus on what capabilities can offer as a feminist framework for gender justice, which is essential for human development and the expansion of women's capabilities.

CAPABILITIES APPROACH AS A FEMINIST FRAMEWORK

The humanly rich aspect of the capabilities approach is attractive for feminist research. As Robeyns (2003a) outlines, firstly, the ethical (or normative) individualism of the capabilities approach rejects any attitudes that could underestimate women's well-being under market and non-market settings. The inclusion of people's well-being both in market settings, such as comparisons of income, or job-holdings, and non-market settings, such as care work, household work, or social networking, plays an important role in addressing women's inequalities. This is an important aspect because feminist economics (Folbre 1994; Knobloch 2014) highlights that a market economy often ignores women's duties within the household and community entities. Women spend more time taking care of gender-related tasks, which in return affects their well-being or capability sets. Secondly, the capabilities approach acknowledges human diversity (race, gender and ethnicity) and criticises the fact that equality is measured in male terms and that men's lives form the standard, which tends to ignore and overlook the impact of gender on women's lives through gendered institutions, power, ideologies and norms, or the biological differences between sexes, which all subsume gender inequality in women's lives. It offers a normative theory of justice which makes it possible to treat each person as being of moral worth and value and in evaluating sources of inequalities.

Additionally, feminist research and theories in the field mostly use habitus or discourse to analyse women's lives or to look into gender inequalities. Yet the capabilities approach could offer more to this research in comparison with these theoretical frameworks. To briefly state the case for habitus (by Bourdieu), which has also been used widely in feminist research and taken as gender habitus (Reay 1997; Skeggs 1997), it offers researchers an opportunity to understand the complexity of human interactions.

Particularly for feminist research, habitus offers a way of understanding relations, identity and the cultural and social practices of gender. It offers an alternative to focus on economic, cultural and social inequalities, and a method to analyse how the socially disadvantaged and privileged are structured in a social system via everyday life experiences. Furthermore, it elaborates on how inequalities lived in daily practice intertwine with race and gender, and are inscribed on women's bodies or played out in their social interactions. However, habitus is not always consistent with change and accords little value to individual agency and the act of choice, whereas the capabilities approach takes agency and change as an important aspect of human life in evaluating the needs of individuals. As Madeline Arnot (2002: 49) suggests, 'it is hard to establish the nature of its [habitus] existence and the forms it may take in different historical junctures (...) offers no account of social change in the cultural arena.' This is because habitus does not take into account the possibility of change through recognising one's own habitus of thought, perception and action, which could potentially lead to an action that breaks the sexual and economic divisions of labour instead of restructuring them (Arnot 2002).

On the other hand, discourse theory is vague in providing solutions for gender justice. It argues that power is everywhere and diffused/distributed throughout society, creating injustices while making it difficult to locate the cause or origin of a problem and take action against it. In this sense, it could also underestimate nuanced differences in relation to where inequalities are enacted. Additionally, discourse based on the work of Foucault takes humanism as an episteme (way of thinking) of the moment and rejects the value judgement. Although the deconstruction in the discourse approach is a useful means of explaining how things (such as power and gender) are (and are not), it does not engage in saying how things ought to be. In this sense, it is at the level of abstraction and fails to offer a pathway towards rethinking what is needed to maximise gender equality in society, unlike the capabilities approach, which relies on the concept of a good life and value judgement and draws out some *sine qua non* entitlements for gender equality. All these factors add to the argument that, for this particular study, I first needed a normative theory of justice, one which is individualistic and takes individual differences into account, considering the diverse socio-cultural setting in Turkey. Secondly, a theory with a strong focus on the aspect of agency could better illuminate the extent to which women teachers in this study could use their agency for change. Likewise, I was not only interested in determining the sources of inequality, but also wanted to find out which freedoms matter for women in the Turkish context and how these could be addressed. Therefore, using the capabilities approach as an overarching theoretical framework, with feminist lenses, allowed me to reconsider the questions of justice in relation to gender equality, between school and the labour market, non-market settings, institutions and pedagogies (Walker and Unterhalter 2007).

METHODOLOGY

This book provides a multi-generational study and displays how gender (in)justice is politically and culturally constructed and circulated within society, and in women's professional, personal and educational lives, referring to both public and private spheres at different times in the history of Turkey. The focus is directed at women teachers for several reasons. First, in Turkey, teaching has predominantly been recognised as a feminine occupation because of patriarchal cultural values (such as being able to spare time for domestic responsibilities) and gender-based stereotypes (such as women being viewed as patient, understanding, and 'motherly') (Griffiths 2006; Sari 2012). Nonetheless, women teachers continue to be hidden and historically long-neglected actors working for social change, not only in Turkey, but also across the world. While there is a great deal of research about women teachers and their teaching practices (Acker 1994, 1995; Moreau et al. 2007; Sari 2012), there is little research that focuses on the lives and quality of life of women teachers. Little is known about their lives and aspirations although, since Republican times, Turkish women have been represented in the teaching profession as the initiators and active agents of social change. Secondly, I believe an important share of the responsibility falls on women teachers—with regard to contributing to development, promoting gender equality and breaking the traditional structures seeing woman as less autonomous actors in Turkey. Women teachers, having themselves been educated by teachers in the past, strive to educate girls, women and students in general and to improve the lives of other people. In this sense, it is significant to examine to what extent these teachers could use their agency towards the aim of gender justice and to enhance other people's capabilities. Thirdly, the narratives of the women teachers in this study insert their voices into our knowledge of education in Turkey and enable us to engage with the question of the extent to which education in Turkey is liberating. The feminist perspective I take examines what it means to be a woman and a woman teacher from a relational account in comparison to men, diverse women, society, state and culture. It also reveals the long-standing injustices and undemocratic attitudes women in Turkey face, by voicing and studying the lives of ordinary women teachers.

METHODS

This book reframes gender and education issues from a feminist perspective through a multi-generational study of women as teachers, and also as daughters, wives and mothers. It takes a closer look at these women's recollections, in order to understand how gender roles were created, negotiated and contested, and how the transition to modern ways of socialising and existing was shaped and women's emancipation was guided by women teachers as social actors, rather than as passive onlookers or oppressed individuals. As such, the research draws upon life history as a feminist methodology based on the capabilities approach. The capabilities approach is compatible with feminist methodology in that it gives a role to the importance of the real lives of individuals, each of whom is of ethical importance and a unit of moral concern. At the same time, it provides a normative framework to assess the institutional environments, gendered constraints, the processes and the socio-economic and political circumstances that affect or facilitate conversion factors for capability achievement. So, in focusing on the basic capabilities of women and understanding the circumstances of women experiencing inequality and exclusion—which is essential in development initiatives—feminist methodology works as an epistemological and ontological ally of the capabilities approach in guiding us on the power imbalances that treat men and women differently, and work unfavourably towards women by thwarting the opportunities and capabilities available to them. On the other hand, the use of a life history approach can connect specific personal stories to a macro perspective (the cultural, historical and political context of their lives) of how an individual understands herself and her life experiences in relation to the world in which she exists. Epistemologically, the use of life history as a feminist methodology establishes an interactional relationship and exchange between researcher and respondent, seeks to reveal the silence of women through a historical record, and focuses on women's constantly shifting, neglected and excluded position to make their experiences visible and meaningful (Reinharz and Davidman 1992).

I conducted semi-structured interviews with 15 women teachers from three different generations. In total, 45 interviews were carried out with women, including the pre-interviews and follow-up interviews (see Appendix A). I did not set out to find a large or representative sample of teachers in Turkey, but rather to purposively establish a sample which would enable me to theoretically explore capability formation across three key generations of educated women. I also made the conscious decision to recruit women teachers who were born and raised in the Aegean province (Western Turkey), who were working at public schools (and therefore, were civil servants) and who were sent to rural and economically less-developed provinces to complete their hardship posts—a government policy and requirement for all new teachers since the establishment of Turkey. I explain the hardship posts in detail in Chap. 4 when introducing the participants.

The capabilities approach also shaped the questions that I asked. I carried out semi-structured interviews to elicit material that would allow me to explore social structures and institutions in terms of the causal importance they have for women's well-being and agency, and to explore the women's perceptions of gender and of being a woman and a teacher; their stories of freedom or restriction, hopes, disappointments; and their experiences as a woman teacher in society. Semi-structured interviews offered flexibility and allowed me and the women I interviewed to expand, shift or elaborate on answers in an interactional manner (Kvale 1996). Although I had a ground I wanted to cover, the women themselves shaped how the interview unfolded and made choices about which elements of their stories they wished to recount. The interview questions were formulated to explore the extent to which the women had freedoms and opportunities to achieve their valued functioning and capabilities covering their life trajectories from childhood to today. They covered a wide range of topics and, in some instances, I asked follow-on questions to clarify the points they made.

In exploring the extent to which women, in reality, are full agents in their own lives and can use their democratic rights, the extent to which they have access to opportunities and basic capabilities, and what they have reason to value, the book seeks to answer a number research questions:

1. How have the capabilities and agency of three generations of interviewed women teachers been expanded and restricted throughout their lives from the Republican Era to contemporary times in the Turkish context?

   (a) How have their capabilities and agency been restricted or expanded in the private sphere of their personal lives (natal families) and marriages?
   (b) How have their capabilities and agency been restricted or expanded in the public sphere of their educational and professional lives?

2. How do these women make their way up to become teachers, in contrast to the majority of Turkish women?
3. To what extent has education in Turkey been liberating for them?
4. To what extent were these women capable of being agents of social change and justice?

These questions are intended to furnish an understanding of the professional, social, personal and educational lives of women, and to examine the ways gender has interfered with women's use of agency and enactment of freedoms. By giving voice to women's experiences, the book provides a good basis for critically considering how their lives have been shaped by gendered and cultural norms in family and in social institutions (such as the education system and workplace) which systematically subordinated them, and restricted their capabilities and agency. It presents a shifting account of women in Turkey and of their vigorous struggle for rights in public and private spheres, as well as their often passive, powerless and silent positions within these spheres.

STRUCTURE OF THE BOOK

The book draws upon a range of literatures along with the analysis of the empirical data. Chapter 1 establishes the intellectual context, including this introduction chapter and Chap. 2 presents an integrated understanding of education, gender justice and human development; conceptualises gender justice drawing on the approaches of various feminist political philosophers; and explains in detail how the capabilities approach allowed me to build a frame-of-justice lens developed for this study to view women's lives, opportunities, freedoms and agency. The stories the women told are the products of particular social, political and historical contexts. Accordingly, Chap. 3 takes a closer look at Turkey's past in terms of political, feminist and education history. This chapter has three sections. In the first section, I present the relevant historical context of Turkey, which helps us to contextualise the women's lives within the three eras through which they have lived. In the second part of the chapter, I highlight the historical circumstances and gender politics of Turkey that are most relevant to this study. I also present the literature on gender issues in Turkey. The third part offers a brief explanation of the provision of education throughout different periods. Chapter 4 presents detailed accounts of participants to help readers contextualise their lives and grasp the rigour of each woman's dynamics, and also describes the interviewing procedure, sampling method, data collection process and analytical process of data analysis. The next three chapters present an analysis and interpretation of the life histories in light of the conceptual framework. In accordance with the key premises of the data analysis method employed in the study, particular emphasis is given to the voices of the women, highlighting the importance of listening to how they speak about themselves *before* I speak of them, which (in the book) refers to the adaptation of the capabilities approach as an analytical tool and conceptual frame. In Chap. 5, I focus on an analysis of all three generations of the women's experience in the private sphere by highlighting the cycle of reproduced gender inequalities, drawing generational comparisons. This private sphere includes the women's personal lives and experiences in their natal families and women's intimate relations within marriage for the married participants. For the unmarried participants, the chapter presents the reasons for their choosing not to marry and the expectations they have of marriage. The main argument in this chapter focuses on how the private domains in women's lives act as a restrictive space upon their capabilities and aspirations. In Chap. 6, I present an analysis of all three generations of the women's educational experiences by illuminating the continuities and discontinuities in the way (gender) inequalities are configured in their lives and the way education works as a tool for (dis)empowerment and reproduction. Chapter 7 focuses on women's professional experiences. The main argument in this chapter is that whereas the private sphere produced limitations on women's lives and freedoms, women's experiences in the public sphere opened up a space for them to achieve their valued functioning and capabilities, and gave them an opportunity to deconstruct the gendered teaching and expectations formed in the private domain. Chapter 8, as the conclusion, argues how the direction of change in women's lives gives good guidance towards reconsidering gender justice and education now and in the future, and opens a dialogue to compromise on the ideas and freedoms that could provide women with equal respect and dignity as men, by virtue of both being human. It analytically draws together the three empirical chapters, revisits the research question and sums up the arguments of the thesis. This chapter also makes suggestions to policy-makers to tailor education and social policies according to cultural and gender sensitive issues in an effort to improve women's lives, and women teachers' working conditions.

Notes

1. See Cin and Walker (2016) for a detailed list and analysis of these campaigns.
2. See UNESCO (2015) for further information and analysis on EFA.
3. MDG goals 2 and 3, respectively, aim to achieve universal primary education and to promote gender equality and empower women.

CHAPTER 2

Understanding(s) of Education, Gender Justice and Human Development

Revisiting Gender Justice

In the 1990s, with the emergence of new social movements emphasising the diversity and complex identities and subjectivities of the postmodern era, feminist political theorists in the UK and USA started to criticise the application of the same principles of evaluation and distribution to all people regardless of their social positions and question whether this approach was sufficient to promote justice, as it did not address differences such as gender, race, sexuality and disability (Arnot 2006). The particular importance of 'difference' as a complementary component of equality for gender justice is that most modern societies contain multiple cultural groups which may dominate the state and social institutions, and may leave little place for minority groups or cultures, including women, to live a meaningful life, to participate in society and to benefit from the equal rights they hold. To address this concern, feminist philosophers (Fraser 2013; Nussbaum 2000; Okin 1999; Young 1990) have developed different perspectives to redress the structural, cultural and political inequalities arising from difference and misrecognition of women and suppressed groups. Here, I focus on three different approaches to thinking about gender justice, which are recognition and redistribution, democratic participation and representation and a (social) contract with the aim of establishing a universally applicable yet contextually gender-sensitive gender justice approach based on diversity, which could be applied to education.

© The Editor(s) (if applicable) and The Author(s) 2017
F.M. Cin, *Gender Justice, Education and Equality*, Palgrave Studies in Gender and Education, DOI 10.1007/978-3-319-39104-5_2

In examining gender justice and difference, Nancy Fraser (2013) and Iris Marion Young (2004) engage with the idea of distribution and recognition. Young (1990) proposes a politics of difference, which is constituted of two forms: the politics of positional difference and the politics of cultural difference. The former elaborates on the groups and individuals constituted through structural social processes such as gender, disability, race, class and how these individuals are differently positioned in society. The latter emphasises the value of cultural distinctness and elaborates on how dominant groups limit the rights of cultural minorities. Both versions imply that there is a lack of recognition of certain groups. Young (1990) emphasises an institutional critique of capitalist, sexist, racist and heterosexist formations, and argues for five interlocking faces of oppression (exploitation, alienation, marginalisation, cultural imperialism and violence) that underpin the sources of domination experienced by the above-mentioned groups in every society, including women. The problem of gender injustice arises from being blind to the structural processes of the social division of labour (such as women doing the unpaid care work) and public and private institutional policies/practices failing to accommodate the needs of women (such as pregnant and breastfeeding women, harassment and discrimination of women) (Young 2004). In her account, distributive injustice begins with the concepts of domination and oppression and involves social structures and relations (Young 1990). Promoting justice requires recognising social and cultural differences and paying attention to processes of creating inequalities in social and economic institutions and practices (Young 2004).

For her part, Fraser (2003) has argued for a two-dimensional categorisation of redistribution (economic) and recognition (cultural), while more recently, Fraser (2007, 2013) advocates a three-dimensional categorisation including the representation principle, on the basis of parity of participation (political). This entails that all members of society interact with each other as peers. Thus, she aims to cover inequalities related to both socio-economic and socio-cultural perspective, as well as to a socio-political perspective through the principle of who is included and excluded from justice claims. She proposes the restructuring of society via institutions. Both Young's and Fraser's perspectives intersect on the point that addressing the inequalities requires recognising the different, marginalised and oppressed groups; and such inequalities are multi-dimensional and intersecting, and contribute to distributive injustice.

Young's politics of difference (1990) and Fraser's (2013) three-dimensional justice framework (redistribution, recognition and representation) are also applied to discuss gender inequality problems in education, such as girls' deprivation of education opportunities, unequal distribution of resources in education, and discriminatory structures and relations. Several authors (e.g. Eisenberg 2006; Enslin 2006; Gewirtz 2006) apply Young's multi-dimensional account of injustice to education, arguing that a reallocation of resources alone can do little to address structural barriers which exclude girls (and suppressed groups). These scholars argue that Young's ideas might be used to challenge domination by creating curricula reflecting the diversity of the multi-cultural and multi-lingual nature of society; raising awareness against racism and sexism; ensuring that the voices of parents, teachers and community are included in decision making; examining exploitative relationships within educational institutions and processes of marginalisation; and by looking into violent practices within or around education and schools.

On the other hand, Arnot (2006) has used Fraser's discussion of the redistribution–recognition dilemma to look into gender inequality issues in education in the UK. Drawing from this discussion, she highlights a new concept of transformative pedagogy of difference and argues how this could help both female and male students from diverse cultures and socio-economic backgrounds to use their capacity and confidence to have a say in their learning experiences. Similarly, Aikman (2011) uses Fraser's analysis of social justice to examine indigenous peoples' rights to education in Africa and highlights a valued way of life that is different from those valued and given in national school systems. Thus, it raises the importance and need for recognition of different education systems, skills and bodies of knowledge based on the culture and values of people, and a possible reframing of education for indigenous distributive and representative justice. Dejaeghere et al. (2015) use Fraser's multi-dimensional approach to look into how ethnicity is discursively formed in education policies in China and Vietnam to understand inequalities. The study of DeJagehere and Wiger (2013) in Bangladesh draws on ideas from Fraser to show teachers' discourses of gender equality. Dyer (2010), for example, conceptualises Fraser's parity of participation as a framework to explore the relationship between education and economic, social and political justice for pastoralist children in India. Bozalek and Boughey (2012) use Fraser's framework to explore (mis)representation in apartheid and post-apartheid policies of higher education in South Africa. Such ideas could equally be applied to girls' education. For instance, in Turkey, education of girls and that of ethnic minorities are still problematic because policies and processes do not recognise and acknowledge gender, ethnic (Kurds) and religious (non-Muslims and Alawites) differences in the society. In this respect, the perspective of recognition and redistribution becomes relevant to this research in examining how women are left beyond the boundaries of political, social, economic and educational opportunities.

The second approach to gender justice I focus on here is democratic participation (representation) and forms of deliberative democracy. Benhabib (1996, 2002) and Phillips (1998) argue that deliberative democracy is important for collective decision-making in diverse societies to reach a consensus on the problems of the public good. It addresses differences and frames the gender issue from a perspective of intercultural dialogue. Benhabib (2002) argues that an open cultural dialogue, openness of one culture to another and negotiation among different cultural traditions in a democratic civil society can bring about sexually egalitarian norms and moderate tensions between gender equality and cultural difference. Everyone who has been affected can have a voice in deliberations (Benhabib 1996), whereas some feminist philosophers (Fraser 1989; Young 2002) are sceptical about deliberation and point out that in the process of trying to reach consensus, those who have been historically silenced may not be able to voice their views, and the untrained voices of women and others who have been marginalised may not be heard. This is because a rationalist, male and hegemonic polity ignores the differences in articulation of voice and ideas of the public. To redress this feminist critique, Young (2002) in her work on 'Inclusion and Democracy' develops a model of communicative democracy, which requires individuals to attend to one another's differences such as class, gender, race and religion through the different forms of communications such as greeting, rhetoric and narrative for genuine inclusion. According to Young, women, disadvantaged groups and untrained voices could better express themselves through these forms of communication rather than formal political debate, which is based on assumptions about rational procedures.

Similarly, Anne Phillips (1998) argues that debate and discussion can lead to discovering significant common ground and a recognition of principles of justice in particular historical contexts. Democratisation can be one way of enabling different groups to articulate an understanding of cultural groups' rights and sexual equality. However, this process necessitates a guarantee of the heterogeneity of the citizens who partake in discussions and recognition of human differences because, from a feminist perspective, women have been excluded from the process of decision-making and democratic deliberation. In this respect, the mobilisation of alternative voices, the full representation of women (as well as suppressed identities) in discussion and decision-makings are important to address the gender inequality all spheres of social, economic and political life. Deliberation can dislodge hierarchies of power and male hegemony (Phillips 1998). In her later works, Phillips (2007) also highlights the substantive conditions such as education, political and civil redress that could enable women to voice an objection in deliberation and give them an exit option from the coercive cultural practices.

Some authors (Englund 2000; Enslin et al. 2001; Gutman 1987; Gutman and Thompson 1996) used the idea of deliberative democracy as an education process to promote a democratic culture, which implies that education and schools should develop students' capacities and create the opportunity to question traditional authorities (religious ideas, social norms) that could impede the freedoms or interfere with the lives of women and girls. Schools should provide every student with critical thinking in order to develop children's political capacity to enter critical discussions, so that students can learn to produce mutually acceptable decisions. This process of developing critical understanding could be activated not only by formal curriculum but also by extramural activities such as clubs or societies working as a plurality of modes of associations. These ideas form resonance with Tikly's (2011) three-dimensional principles of quality education: inclusion (active participation of every group in education), relevance (well-being valued by communities), and democracy (linked with public debate and accountability). A deliberative democracy perspective on education can also fix the shortcomings in Tikly's (2011) approach. Aikman and Unterhalter (2013) critique how the relevance and democracy dimensions in education can lead to unwanted outcome of promoting powerful voices who are actually interested in preserving practices undermining women's well-being. For instance, in a community where women's primary role is recognised as homemaking and childcare, public discussion is likely to determine the content and aim of education serving to these needs and thus forming gendered forms of education. Raising deliberative citizens can form a pre-condition of Tikly's (2011) democracy and relevance principle so that citizens can question conventional views. Women in particular could realise, discuss and oppose the challenges that limit their widest possible capability sets. In relation to my work, it is important that education should provide women with the skills to develop critical reasoning so that they are able to voice their demands and challenge discriminatory structures excluding them from decision-making on the issues concerning their lives and opportunities.

Finally, the third perspective of gender equality addressed in this section is the (social) contract model. Pateman (1988) theorises cycles of gendered vulnerability based on three sexual contracts: marriage, employment and prostitution contracts, and argues that these three paradigmatic contemporary contracts hold the patriarchal control of women through gestational services, labour power and sexual services, respectively. Her sexual contact theory is a feminist critique of social contract theories. She criticises that the idealised contract theories (specifically John Rawls' Theory of Justice or John Locke's contract theory) ignore relations of subordination between men and women in which the former, as a super-ordinate power, command and dominate the latter in the aforementioned three contracts (also see Fraser 1993). Her theory points out that a contract is not always a path to freedom or equality, and stresses that further exploration of power relations in contract theories is needed to avoid the constitution of modern patriarchy. Drawing from Pateman's insights and sexual contract, Goetz (2007) proposes that we look into how social sources of power that illegitimately interact with state institutions limit the capacities of women's claims to their rights and deny the constitutional rights they have. She highlights that state actors or agencies based on prejudices and cultural norms may well be reluctant to advocate women's rights and causes. Therefore, she suggests a form of social contract (accountability model) to assess gender inequalities built into different institutions, and the extent these inequalities are carried over into other private institutions (such as family, marriage and religious practices). In the accountability model, power holders in the state, family and institutions are held responsible if they impede women's access to resources and their capacity to make choices. They should answer to those who have delegated power to them and should face penalties if they are found to be guilty.

Aikman and Unterhalter (2013) suggest that Goetz's accountability model is helpful for addressing gender-based violence in schools, households and communities. Particularly at an educational level, these ideas can be used to look at how decision-makers or school managers, as power holders, deal with girls' subordination and exclusion in schools. Likewise, such an approach can be transferred to the quality of education to regulate gender relations which are excluding and discriminating girls at schools (such as gendered attitudes of teachers towards girls' learning).

In the same vein, Onora O'Neill (2000) argues for an idea of social contract in the form of the consent and agreement of the governed. For her, principles of justice and structures that affect vulnerable people can be refused or renegotiated. O'Neill (2000), in attempt to engage with a critique of approaches to justice that are blind to differences and particular contexts such as histories of political and cultural communities, argues that justice should include principles all people adopt, agree and consent to. For instance, she criticises the principles of justice that attempt to generate universal equality, such as Convention on the Elimination of All Forms of Discrimination against Women (CEDAW) or rights-based approaches, because these falsify the position of the socially weak or idealise conceptions of human agents, rationality, family or national sovereignty which are often feasible for men rather than women and also for developed societies. She is not completely against universal justice and suggests that there could be a universal adoption of principles by all agents as long as the principles are stripped away from deception, violence, coercion or victimisation. Taking disadvantaged and vulnerable individuals, who cannot benefit from non-coercive arrangements, into consideration, she argues that any policy or institutional arrangement should deal with the structures of vulnerability and understand that structures constrain and limit the lives of the vulnerable. The consent is real only when these arrangements can be genuinely negotiated. Indeed, her ideas provide a good entry point for looking into girls' education in communities where there is a cultural prohibition on schooling of girls. Her approach was put into practice in northern Kenya, where teachers and members of the community gathered to negotiate on policies to increase schooling of girls until a consensus had been achieved and a single sex primary school was established which increased the enrolment of girls (Unterhalter et al. 2005). In relation to my research, her ideas can also be helpful to form a consensus with community, family and girls to increase the girls' schooling in Eastern Turkey, where girls' education is culturally prohibited.

The implications of these three perspectives (recognition and distribution; deliberative democracy and representation; and contract model) for gender justice in relation to education underpin the importance of addressing diversity and the inclusiveness of rearranging the principles of justice to the disadvantaged through recognition and distribution; encouraging democratic participation of all groups, seeing gender justice as an outcome and process; and forming an institutional and state obligation towards citizens. All three constitute important aspects of gender justice and form a robust frame of justice. However, the capabilities approach of Martha Nussbaum (2000) and Amartya Sen (1985, 2009) works as an umbrella gender justice approach covering all these three perspectives mentioned above. The capabilities approach offers a normative and a global framework that is concerned with widening opportunities and freedoms so that individuals can convert resources at their disposal into valuable achievements. First of all, it is an ethically individualistic approach and therefore, incorporates recognition of each person as an end in themselves and accommodates differences such as gender, disability and the socioeconomic conditions of individuals. For instance, the approach argues that a disabled person may need more resources and opportunities to go to school than a fully abled person. Thus, it covers the concern of recognition and redistribution.

Secondly, Nussbaum's (2000) thinking on gender justice takes a political direction, arguing for entitlements and positive freedoms and conditions secured for each citizen by a state constitution. She ascribes responsibility to institutions and governments which then have a political responsibility to secure capabilities (in her case, her list of ten universal capabilities) to all citizens at a minimum threshold. She thus argues for a form of contract between institutions, the state and its citizens. She also suggests a global form of justice and obligations by suggesting that rich nations should help poorer nations to promote human freedoms and that disadvantaged people in each nation or region should be addressed.

Sen's interpretation of gender justice resonates to a large extent with Nussbaum's, but, in addition to legal obligations that institutions need to follow, Sen (1985, 1999) approaches the protection of freedoms and rights from an ethical position and advocates imperfect obligations (which may not be legally binding) to improve lives or freedoms based on the fulfilment of our ethical responsibility to humanity. This could be interpreted as a contract wherein an individual has an imperfect moral obligation to help a person in need.

Thirdly, Sen (1999), unlike Nussbaum's prescriptive list, advocates that capabilities in each community should be determined through dialogue and public discussion. For Sen, gender justice would emerge from inclusive public reasoning and scrutiny of public policy, whereas Nussbaum, sharing similar concerns with Fraser and Young, prescribes a list to avoid the exclusion of women's voices and demands in these public discussions.

Nussbaum (2000) claims that she has formed her list as the results of years of cross-cultural discussion. Therefore, her list has the input of the voices of the disadvantaged, women, the marginalised and the suppressed. Broadly then, gender justice for Nussbaum is securing for all women her list of capabilities.

For both Sen and Nussbaum, education is a fundamental entitlement, and crucial to women's freedoms and development; yet for Nussbaum, gender equality in education is a central aspect for one to develop critical reflection and cultivation of mind, and for Sen, it has an intrinsic importance because it prepares the conditions for freedoms and a wider capability set. Thus, the capabilities approach addresses all the perspectives outlined above and offers a practical and robust framework not only in terms of analysing gender inequalities in women's everyday lives, but also looking into the education processes. Therefore, in the next section, I set out to present how education can be located in relation to different theories of development, gender and social justice approaches.

APPROACHES TO GENDER EQUALITY IN EDUCATION

This section critically and briefly presents the contrasting frameworks for conceptualising gender equality in education; human capital theory, human rights theory and human development theories (mainly capabilities). In addition, post-structuralism, although not a frame in quite the same way, has been influential in feminist writing on issues of identity formation. As such, it can be seen in some ways to infuse approaches to rights and capabilities, but not to human capital, which does not take identity and difference into account per se. Each framework has a different understanding of gender and proposes different action for gender equality in education.

The Women in Development (WID) framework emerged in the early 1970s with the aim of bringing women and girls to education and development. This framework associates development and empowerment with economic growth and focuses largely on the gap between girls and boys in enrolment and achievement and distribution of opportunities and sources for access to education (such as teachers, books, transportation facilities and stipends). WID is often linked to the theory of human capital (Unterhalter 2005a), which similarly elaborates the economic value of schooling with an emphasis on delivering individuals for the labour market (Unterhalter 2009). It is critiqued for being instrumentalist and economist in explaining inequalities in education and failing to address non-market relations, the complexity of human lives and gender and power relations that lead to exclusion and marginalisation (Robeyns 2006; Tikly 2011). It also little addresses the structural problems girls come across such as access to school, how they engage with schooling, how they are treated at schools, what or how they learn at schools, or the continuing gender inequalities after schooling is completed (Unterhalter 2005a). It is effectively a limited view of the purposes and outcomes of education for girls and women. Thus, as an opposition to WID, the Gender and Development (GAD) framework emerged in late 1980s and was primarily targeted at gendered power structures of inequality, the sexual division of labour both in and outside the household, unfair laws or unequal distribution of time, money and schooling (Unterhalter 2005a; Aikman et al. 2011). GAD argues that gender inequality in education is related to power structures and is concerned with the removal of structural barriers (Vaughan 2010). However, it little addresses the formal schooling and gendered relations within education settings because GAD was interested primarily in the design of education policies, the transformation of institutions and processes of gender mainstreaming (Unterhalter 2005a).

Post-structuralism and post-colonial theory emerged from the 1980s onwards and raised questions about the experiences of colonised people, post-colonial states' discourses on education and identity formation, power relations and difference. The approach is helpful for exploring identity formation and adapts a recognition politics arguing for multiple subordinate and shifting identities (Unterhalter 2009). However, it does not provide a full normative framework to look into how justice and equality is distributed, nor does it extensively deal with rights and needs or address the improvement of disadvantage in education settings, the content of education and structural causes of gender injustice (Unterhalter 2005a, 2009).

In contrast to economic growth emphasised by human capital theory, the human rights approach to education emerged in the 1980s with three principles. First, free access to education and equality of educational opportunities: the approach advocates the right of free access to education at all levels and equality of opportunity to attend school as stated in the EFA 2015 goals of entitling all children to free primary education (Manion and Menashy 2013). Second, quality education: the approach argues that everyone has the right to quality education. Third, respect for identity and participation rights: the approach upholds the right to respect for the individual, participation right and identity within education (UNESCO and UNICEF 2007). Unlike the human capital approach or WID, the rights approach stresses the equality of education opportunity as an intrinsic value (Robeyns 2006; Unterhalter 2008) and sees gender equality as legal and constitutional provisions (Vaughan 2010). For instance, studies of Tomasevski (2003) and Subrahmanian (2002) show how the human rights approach was effective in gaining legal access to girls' education in the context of education denial, contributing to transform schooling into a more learner-centred and activity-based tradition of teaching. Still, the approach is critiqued for ignoring the conditions that do not operationalise the rights despite countries having legally and rhetorically granted the right to education (Unterhalter 2003a; Robeyns 2006). Most of these countries do not look into the extent to which people benefit from the rights or which factors limit access to education. The approach focuses on legalistic solutions to inequalities, and fails to foster sustainable change and address local realities and complexities (Unterhalter 2009). It has an 'ontologically individualistic' approach to learners (Robeyns 2003a: 65), which means it does not look into social, economic or political forces that influence gendered experiences within classrooms, or who has access to a quality education (Tikly and Barrett 2011). Tikly and Barret's work (2011, 2013) on the quality of education in low-income countries in particular shows that the rights approach, which is widely used by UN agencies, regards schools without considering the local contexts they are situated in, and thus does not act responsively to the lived realities of learners in specific contexts (such as ignoring the needs of communities and students marginalised on the basis of race, caste, tribe, language and religion). Therefore, it fails to look into the fundamentally political nature of education quality. It is more interested in the enactment of negative freedoms such as protection from abuse (e.g. the violence towards girls in South Africa) and less with positive rights and freedoms such as one's rights to learn in one's mother tongue, to have one's identity reflected in the curriculum of schools (e.g. lack of reference to Kurdish identity in curricula in Turkey) or to participate in democratic structures and debates (Tikly and Barrett 2011). Therefore, the rights approach, in general, is not sufficiently supported by political and financial commitments (Robeyns 2006).

Furthermore, for an individual to be able to claim their rights to education, they need to know what their rights are. People need critical thinking, knowledge, reasoning, responsibility and agency to enact their claims, which can be provided by capability building (McCowan 2011).

Capabilities can fruitfully expand the notions of rights, be more precise about how moral and ethical dimensions should be realised and be more concerned with the socio-political and economic circumstances infusing schools and education systems. Therefore, it can supplement these aspects of the rights approach (Unterhalter 2005a).

The capabilities approach, with its focus on human freedoms and well-being, sees education as comprehensive, and as referring to both the economic and intrinsic value of education underpinned by the human capital and rights approach, respectively, including non-economic instrumentalist roles of education (Robeyns 2006; Unterhalter 2007a, b). In this respect, unlike the rights-based approach, the capabilities approach views gender equality in education both as a legal and moral obligation and a necessary condition to widen opportunities and to lead development of further capabilities (Unterhalter 2007a). The approach is concerned with promoting positive freedoms as opportunities and with looking into conditions of being educated and how being educated influences the functionings that each person values (Unterhalter 2007a; Tikly and Barrett 2011). It addresses the multiple perspectives of gender (equality) in education such as intersectionality, gender discrimination related to learning, the impact of curriculum and textbooks on the reproduction of stereotypes about women and men and gender inequalities inside the household, the workplace and the state. These different perspectives must be addressed because these inequalities are infused into schools and education (Aikman et al. 2011; Unterhalter 2007a, 2012a). Capabilities can also allow us to reconsider the questions of justice in relation to gender equality, between school and labour market, non-market settings, institutions and pedagogies (Walker and Unterhalter 2007). Gender equality in education, in this approach, is concerned with the nature of education valued by individuals to see if they could achieve their valued beings and doings through education (Unterhalter 2007b). Thus, the capabilities approach offers a potentially strong framework for promoting gender justice in education, one which takes account of human capital and rights, which can accommodate diversity of identities, but which also goes beyond all of these in framing justice in an expansive way for girls' and women's well-being and agency.

So far, I have outlined some of the main frameworks and approaches to the issues and challenges around gender, education and development. Each has different concerns and identifies different perspectives regarding gender equality in education. The human capital approach, often associated with WID, emphasises the economic benefits of education and argues for equal numeracy in access to schooling or equal distribution of resources. Post-colonial theory aspires to raise questions about identity and how the concept of gender is subjected to fluid, shifting and changing processes of meanings, and rejects the fixed gendered structures that GAD scholars engage with. The rights approach relies on the ethical and moral principles of justice but gives little considerations to how institutions or socio-cultural contexts foster discrimination against women. The capability approach values human diversity and the achievement and enlargement of freedoms one has reason to value in diverse social settings.

Below, I turn to the capabilities approach, which is used as an overarching framework to analyse women's lives and the contexts of education offered to these women.

A CAPABILITIES-BASED GENDER JUSTICE APPROACH

The capabilities approach was developed by Sen (1985, 1999, 2009) and by Nussbaum (2000, 2011). It is a broad normative approach based on the ideas of human dignity and social justice. It is an alternative way of thinking about human well-being. The central question that the capabilities approach asks is: 'What are people actually able to do and be?' In doing so, it looks into people's capabilities to function and their opportunities to act and be who they want to be. Capabilities approach is thus formed of two major concepts: functionings and capabilities. Functionings are the beings and doings of a person—such as working, resting or being healthy. Capabilities are the combinations of functionings that a person holds the possibility of achieving (Sen 1993)—such as having the conditions for freedom of speech or having the conditions (hospital, healthcare workers) to recover from an illness.

For instance, two girls from Turkey sitting for the university entrance exams fail to get a placement. One comes from a wealthy family from Western Turkey where she has access to teachers, private courses and books. The other comes from a poor background from Eastern Anatolia and needs to manage the household and look after her younger siblings. In addition, she has no access to private courses or necessary books, and cannot attend school regularly due to her domestic responsibilities. The former failed because she was not interested in studying whereas the latter was deprived of necessary resources and had little time for preparation. This example shows that the functionings of both girls are the same but the capabilities are different. Therefore, the evaluation of equality should focus on the freedom in opportunities and choices. Both Sen (1999) and Nussbaum (2000) stress the importance of looking into capabilities because one may have the functionings, but may not necessarily have the resources or social and political context to turn the capabilities into functionings. At this point, the approach makes interpersonal comparisons and scrutinises whether the circumstances in which people make choices are just. In such a case, the capabilities approach pays attention to resources, economic growth, social cohesion, social institutions and the availability of commodities and legal entitlements, stressing that these are means to well-being.

Additionally, the concepts of choice and adaptive preferences also require elucidation to understand how capabilities work. Unequal circumstances can lead to unequal capacities to choose, because the choices we make are shaped by the opportunities available to us and the context we are situated in (Nussbaum 2000). For instance, a deeply religious person may have the capability of being well-nourished, but prefer to engage in strict fasting because of his/her own beliefs, whereas a person who is starving cannot be placed in the same category because he/she does not have access to the resources necessary to fulfil the capability and is therefore deprived of the freedom of making a choice. On the other hand, adaptive preferences are formed without one's control or awareness of opportunities and the existence of other options, by a casual mechanism that is not of one's own choice (Nussbaum 2000). For example, in an environment where women are treated as underdogs and men are prioritised, a girl may accept that she does not need and deserve education, because she considers that her duties are to look after children and do housework. Therefore, equality should not be evaluated with regard to preferences. Such preferences can limit not only choices and capabilities but also aspirations for the future.

Therefore, it is important to question to what extent people have genuine access to the operationalisation of their capabilities. In the process of converting resources/opportunities into functionings, the conversion factors play an important role. Sen (2009) identifies four factors that affect one's choices and conversion of capabilities: personal heterogeneities (age, gender, disability, proneness to illness), physical environment (environmental conditions, including climatic circumstances, such as temperature ranges or flooding), social climate (social conditions, public healthcare, community resources, policies and practices, public educational arrangements) and relational perspectives (patterns of behaviour in a community that can affect one's choices and capabilities). Each individual may vary greatly in their needs for resources or abilities to achieve their valued capabilities (Nussbaum 2000).

These are the fundamental ideas Nussbaum and Sen share regarding capabilities approach, yet they have taken their own capabilities theories in different directions. I will now present the differences in their approaches and justify why I have followed Nussbaum's conception of capabilities and Sen's agency concept.

Nussbaum's Conception of Capabilities

Sen and Nussbaum had different goals in developing the capabilities approach. Sen's work focuses more on economic reasoning and poverty in developing countries. Nussbaum's work focuses more on moral, legal and political philosophy, arguing for the political principles that should underlie a constitution to secure the rights of citizens. Her approach engages with narratives and texts to better understand people's lives (Robeyns 2005a) and advocates that each person has the right to live their life as they choose and is responsible for their own determined values. Therefore, it pays more attention to people's actions, aspirations and desires which makes it more individualistic and humanistic than Sen's approach.

Nussbaum's conceptualisation of the capabilities approach has an Aristotelian philosophical perspective largely based on 'a good political arrangement' and 'capabilities to have a fully flourishing life' (Nussbaum 2000: xiii). Inspired by Rawls' list of primary goods,[1] she argues for a list of central human capabilities based on the idea of social justice. Unlike Rawls' theory of justice, her approach asks for a constitutional guarantee of rights. In this respect, her formulation of capabilities begins with ethical individualism, which takes every individual as a subject of their own lives and looks into each individual's needs, functionings, capabilities and freedoms. There are ten central capabilities in Nussbaum's list, each of which is noted as an important fundamental entitlement for a life with full human dignity. These are as follows (Nussbaum 2000: 78–80):

1. Life. Being able to live to the end of a human life of normal length; not dying prematurely, or before one's life is so reduced as to be not worth living.

2. Bodily Health. Being able to have good health, including reproductive health; to be adequately nourished; to have adequate shelter.

3. Bodily Integrity. Being able to move freely from place to place; to be secure against violent assault, including sexual assault and domestic violence; having opportunities for sexual satisfaction and for choice in matters of reproduction.

4. Senses, Imagination, and Thought. Being able to use the senses, to imagine, think, and reason – and to do these things in a 'truly human' way, a way informed and cultivated by an adequate education, including, but by no means limited to, literacy and basic mathematical and scientific training. Being able to use imagination and thought in connection with experiencing and producing works and events of one's own choice, religious, literary, musical, and so forth. Being able to use one's mind in ways protected by guarantees of freedom of expression with respect to both political and artistic speech, and freedom of religious exercise. Being able to have pleasurable experiences and to avoid non-beneficial pain.

5. Emotions. Being able to have attachments to things and people outside ourselves; to love those who love and care for us, to grieve at their absence; in general, to love, to grieve, to experience longing, gratitude, and justified anger. Not having one's emotional development blighted by fear and anxiety. (Supporting this capability means supporting forms of human association that can be shown to be crucial in their development).

6. Practical Reason. Being able to form a conception of the good and to engage in critical reflection about the planning of one's life. (This entails protection for the liberty of conscience and religious observance).

7. Affiliation.

   A. Being able to live with and toward others, to recognise and show concern for other human beings, to engage in various forms of social interaction; to be able to imagine the situation of another. (Protecting this capability means protecting institutions that constitute and nourish such forms of affiliation, and also protecting the freedom of assembly and political speech).

   B. Having the social bases of self-respect and non-humiliation; being able to be treated as a dignified being whose worth is equal to that of others. This entails provisions of non-discrimination on the basis of race, sex, sexual orientation, ethnicity, caste, religion, national origin.

8. Other Species. Being able to live with concern for and in relation to animals, plants, and the world of nature.

9. Play. Being able to laugh, to play, to enjoy recreational activities.

10. Control Over One's Environment.

A. Political. Being able to participate effectively in political choices that govern one's life; having the right of political participation, protections of free speech and association.
B. Material. Being able to hold property (both land and movable goods), and having property rights on an equal basis with others; having the right to seek employment on an equal basis with others; having the freedom from unwarranted search and seizure. In work, being able to work as a human being, exercising practical reason, and entering into meaningful relationships of mutual recognition with other workers.

For Nussbaum, this list represents the most universal set of basic political principles needed for human development. The capabilities in the list cannot be reduced or one capability cannot be traded for another. Among them, 'practical reasoning' and 'affiliation' are afforded greater focus because they organise and expand all other capabilities and stand out as the concepts for empowering individuals, groups or communities (Nussbaum 2011).

Nussbaum's list is not rigid and definite, but 'open-ended and humble' and 'can always be contested and remade' (Nussbaum 2000: 77) or adjusted to different legislatures and courts. It can be adopted according to cultural needs, which makes it sensitive to cultural differences and pluralism. Nussbaum (2000) argues that her list is a consensus of cross-cultural discussions and debates on the international platform about how a life with full human dignity can be maintained, and it is free of any metaphysical, religious, political or ethical views.

The list does not force individuals, nations or cultural communities to achieve every functioning, but ensures that individuals should have the freedom to choose the functionings they value and wish to achieve within the conception of the good and without harming or limiting others' freedoms. Therefore, Nussbaum suggests that governments should constitutionally guarantee and deliver to their citizens the social and minimum basis of these capabilities. Once the stage for capabilities is set and available to individuals, it is the decision of citizens to achieve valuable functionings.

A significant criticism that Sen (2004) brings to Nussbaum's approach is whether a list of capabilities is needed and, if a list is to be formed, how are the capabilities to be selected? Sen (2004) and Robeyns (2005b) criticises Nussbaum's list for being fixed and restricting agency to specified norms proposed by her. According to Sen, the list suggests one type of choice to communities for ideal human flourishing and does not give the freedom of making the choice, instead acting in a paternalistic manner by deciding what is good for them, although he accepts that there are certain specific capabilities that are non-negotiable (such as health and education). His conception suggests that if the capabilities approach is used for policy work, then people who will be affected by the policy should decide on what are valuable functionings and capabilities. Endorsing a defined list will not create an opportunity for deliberative democracy, public deliberation and participation. In addition to Sen's criticism, some authors (Okin 2003; Robeyns 2005b) question the legitimacy of the list and argue that Nussbaum does not specify whose voices are involved in the list. For Robeyns (2003a), without criteria on selection of capabilities, the approach remains tentatively suggestive as to how a just society could be formed and leaves many dilemmas and questions about how such an approach can be effectively and empirically applied.

To defend the above-mentioned criticisms, it could be argued that Sen's avoidance of a list and claims about the significance of democratic procedures and social choice in the selection of capabilities holds the danger of biases (Nussbaum 2003b). In a society and a community where cultural practices subordinate and exclude women (such as in Turkey), the compilation of a list of principles is most likely to exclude freedoms for women. Therefore, Nussbaum's list avoids these kinds of biases and social positioning by clearly stating the central capabilities one should possess. Concerning the debates of formation of the list, Nussbaum (2000) argues that her list could be defended as a part of Rawlsian overlapping consensus between diverse groups of people who have different views on what the good life is.

Nussbaum and Sen's confrontation on a list of capabilities also arises from their fields of expertise and use of capabilities. Sen works on social choice and therefore seeks democratic dialogues, debates and procedures. Nussbaum, on the other hand, has a philosophical approach which is clearly expressed in her understanding of capabilities and focuses on a life with dignity and constitutional design, inevitably leading her on a quest to form a list that could serve all humanity (Robeyns 2003a).

Nussbaum's approach and list offers a feminist framework for researchers because the theory starts from the experience of gender injustices around the globe. Her list includes all the fundamental entitlements that are central to women in developing countries as to Western women. It is universalist, sensitive to cross-cultural norms of justice, local particularity and differences (Nussbaum 2000). Her list also addresses intra-household inequalities in non-market labour such as care responsibilities, unequal distribution of domestic responsibilities or domestic violence, and integrates the private sphere as well the public sphere into her list of capabilities. These aspects give me as a researcher freedom to uncover the multiple dimensions of inequalities in the lives of women who are situated in different historical, cultural and political contexts. Although Nussbaum's list and version of capabilities offers a feminist framework for looking into women's lives, it lacks the aspect of agency, which is a vital concept to understand women's lives, both individually and collectively, and to evaluate the political, social and cultural control mechanisms in their freedom and life choices. The concept of agency is very thinly drawn in Nussbaum's approach, and, the research also draws from Amartya Sen's (1993) capabilities-based notion of agency to complete this overarching framework. Therefore, the next section elucidates Sen's concept of agency.

Capabilities-Based Agency

Agency has a central role within the capabilities approach and it is heavily stressed in the works of Sen (1993, 1999). Sen presents an agency-oriented capability approach and argues that it is not enough to ask people which capabilities are valuable for them or how well they are doing, but that it is also essential to look at the agency of individuals to see whether they decide on what matters to them. Agency matters when people are 'active participants in change rather than…passive and docile recipients of instruction or of dispensed assistance' (Sen 1999: 281). Thus, an agent is an individual who is willing to have a shared responsibility for building a process that ensures everyone's capabilities to decide, to self-determine and to bring about change in the world (Crocker 2008). Concretely, capabilities can be generated through individual efforts and collective processes and, similarly, agency can be individual as well as collective (Ibrahim 2006). Here, the collective agency means individuals responsible for the development and empowerment of their own community and country (Crocker 2008).

Agency can have both self-regarding and other-regarding motivation:

> If individuals, do, in fact, incessantly and uncompromisingly advance only their narrow self-interests, then the pursuit of justice will be hampered at every step by the opposition of everyone who has something to lose from any proposed change. If, on the other hand, individuals as social persons

have broader values and objectives, including sympathy for others and commitment to ethical norms, then the promotion of social justice need not face unremitting opposition at every move. (Sen 1990: 54)

This means that individuals are not only driven by their self-interests or achieving the goals that matter to them, but also engage in goals related to community good and social change. In this light, Sen conceptualises 'the agent' as someone who not only pursues their interests and goals, but also cares for others, and can sacrifice their health, life or well-being for valued objectives.

Nussbaum (2000, 2011) rejects this distinction and sees agency as part of the capability/functioning distinction: If an individual has the capability to achieve functioning X, then they have the autonomous agency to decide to act to achieve capability X. Thus, the achievement of capability X is a display of agency and creates a change in her life. Instead, Nussbaum refers to practical reasoning, namely the act of choosing, when she speaks of agency (Robeyns 2003b). She refers to human beings as agents of their lives who have freedom through the following items on her list of central capabilities: 'critical reflection about the planning of one's life'; 'control over one's political and material environment' (Nussbaum 2000: 78)— which stands for one's ability to plan, act and initiate change in the world. In doing so, she places well-being and agency in the same normative frame and does not follow Sen's distinction.

However, we need Sen's deeper conception of agency because it claims that people can make choices even if these are disadvantageous to their well-being. His conception prioritises individuals' ability to run their lives, rather than leading lives controlled by others. Without a distinction between well-being and agency, it is hard to justify people's lives who do not hesitate to make other lives better, and lead the kinds of lives they pursue for themselves. This idea resonates with the 'imperfect obligations' that are associated with the recognition that one can help the realisation of another person's freedoms (Sen 2009).

Overall, Sen's framework stresses that one's life should matter beyond being healthy, literate, working, resting or taking care of family and that capabilities and functionings cannot explain everything about human life. Therefore, we need the concept of agency to contemplate women's individual or collective actions and motivations which lead them to act beyond their self-interests. In this feminist study, there is a need for a strong agency concept to address and analyse the agency of women both within the private sphere in removing inequalities, and also in the public sphere as teachers who are seen as active agents of social change, who work to improve the lives of others and reject their status as passive recipients. Therefore, the concept of agency is a perfect ally of capabilities in studying the freedoms and opportunities of women's lives and in highlighting the importance of expanding freedoms to understand women's development and empowerment.

THE LIST OF CAPABILITIES PROPOSED FOR THIS STUDY

In this study, I tailored Nussbaum's list for the context of Turkey—a secular, yet conservative society, with many different ethnic and cultural values. Some philosophers, concerned with the evaluative dimension of the capabilities approach, developed an assessment of quality of life or human development. For instance, Alkire (2002), Biggeri et al. (2006), Robeyns (2003a) and Walker (2007) generated a list for empirical research in social sciences to their contextual settings and needs. Among them, only Robeyns' list was developed for gender equality analysis and her list does not fulfil the scope of my research. First of all, Robeyns (2003a) argues that her list[2] is more appropriate for policy-related issues, measurement of individual advantage and the design of socio-economic policies, which is not the focus of my research. This research is a qualitative analysis of how women can cultivate their capabilities, and I aim to look into gender equality by evaluating a range of spheres in women's lives. Second, she proposes a methodology to select relevant capabilities and uses this to form a list of capabilities for the conceptualisation of gender inequality in only Western societies. She concentrates on developed countries and draws her list from the empirical literature in Western European/US context. Her approach therefore restricts itself to a certain context. Considering that Turkey is not a developed country but a developing one situated between the East and the West, Robeyns' list is inadequate for examining the actual lives of the women in this research.

For a politically polarised society like Turkey, there is a need to adapt and establish a new list by considering the political and social context of the country. I find it essential to draw up a list similar to Nussbaum's for Turkish context. This is because in a highly patriarchal society like Turkey, deciding the valued capabilities through public deliberation is likely to suppress the voice of culturally and politically suppressed groups such as women, disabled, ethnic and religious minorities. Also, I believe that any gender justice analysis should be based on moral-legal-political philoso-phy arguing political principles ensured by a government to its citizens. Therefore, I compiled a specific list for this research. My list draws partly from Nussbaum (2000) and also takes into account the socio-cultural/ political context of Turkey and draws from the empirical literature and research in the Turkish context. I propose five capability sets: physical capability, social capability, economic capability, intellectual capability and political capability. These capabilities form the core concepts for this study under which I analyse and interpret the lives of women.

Physical Capability draws the following items from Nussbaum's list of capabilities: life, bodily health and bodily integrity. This capability is related to poor nutrition, shelter and living conditions, poor reproductive health, poor emotional well-being, domestic violence, sexual harassment (both inside and outside the house), not being in a position of bodily safety, not having access to health care facilities and the lack of safe mobil-ity. In other words, it is related to all the conditions that are needed to lead a physically, emotionally and mentally healthy life.

This capability has many gendered dimensions with regard to Turkey. Turkey may seem to have made progress in terms of legislation improving women's rights. However, nationwide surveys show that 38% of women in Turkey experience physical and sexual violence in their life (KSGM 2015). Forty-three per cent of them are uneducated or women with no schooling who are exposed to more physical and sexual violence. Forty-four per cent of women are exposed to emotional violence (KSGM 2015). Additionally, maternal mortality ratio is 23% (UN Women 2012). These figures show that women in Turkey suffer from violence and from the lack of accessible or good quality health care service which in return affect women's well-being.

In relation to poverty, Turkey has no extreme poverty as a middle-income country, but 13 million people (out of 75 million) are poor. As far as gender is concerned, the poverty rate for women is 19.03% as of 2009 (Turkish Statistical Institute [TUIK], 2013b). In particular, the literature on feminisation of poverty (Ecevit 2013; Gokovali 2013) in Turkey argues that the unequal wage and employment opportunities and the low edu-cational level of women in Turkey combined with care responsibilities in the private realm push them to work in the informal sector such as unpaid family work (mainly agriculture) and daily paid jobs with no social secu-rity. As a result of this huge participation in the informal sector, women are more prone to poverty and to being denied access to health care and retirement benefits. Therefore, it is not surprising to see that 70% of people who apply for social aid in Turkey are women (Gokovali 2013). This poverty affects many aspects of women's lives such as dignity and self-esteem, and it causes them to remain silent about the inequalities and violence they face in their lives.

Social Capability includes capabilities of 'emotions and affiliation', 'other species' and 'play' from Nussbaum's list. In addition to the capabilities mentioned above, I added two more items to this list taking the Turkish context into account: sharing an equitable amount of household activities and being free from neighbourhood pressure.

This capability set refers to the following freedoms: engaging in different social activities and (mixed gender) interactions, networking with other people, freedom of communication and associations, organising social events, taking social responsibility for one's own society without facing oppression and harassment, participating in social, economic, and political arenas, and being treated as a dignified human being without any sort of discrimination.

To argue for the capabilities I added to the list, first, I included the functioning of sharing household tasks equitably. Women in Turkey are culturally seen as responsible for household and care work inside the house, regardless of whether they are engaged in paid work outside the house (although, presently a low percentage are engaged in paid work outside the house). Therefore, they face significant inequality regarding the distribution of tasks within the family, and spend long hours in unpaid domestic work. The Organisation for Economic Co-operation and Development (OECD) (2013a) results for work and life balance in Turkey show that Turkish women spend between 4.3 and 5 hours more than men working on domestic chores, which is over the OECD average (which is 2.5 hours). This is a burden not only upon women's physical and psychological well-being (namely on their physical capability set) but also an impediment on their social and personal activities such as having personal time and space to pursue their interests, taking up hobbies and engaging in daily life.

Second, I incorporated the functioning of being (or leading a life) free from neighbourhood pressure, which is a very specific concept in the Turkish context, developed by Serif Mardin (2007) in a public discussion. It stands for the pressure and monitoring coming from the neighbourhood causing an individual to adapt herself to the dominating or expected social norms, and for the lack of tolerance for individual differences. Nationwide surveys (Altinay and Arat 2009; KSGM 2015) and research (Toprak et al. 2009) show that women in Turkey suffer from social monitoring and pressure, and this restricts largely their ability to socialise in the public sphere. Women feel uncomfortable in engaging in mixed gender relations in their neighbourhood, they cannot act freely, and they find it hard to go out of the house, to walk around, and in general, to participate freely in public life. One dimension of this functioning is also related to being free from religious pressure. Turkey is a country with deep-seated religious values, and with the increasing conservatism in the last decade, repression related to religion became widespread. The research of Toprak et al. (2009) shows that there is an increasing pressure on secular people who do not practice religion. This pressure can sometimes take the form of beating, humiliation or exclusion or even the form of pressuring women to cover their hair. Especially in the small central and Eastern Anatolian villages, there is a strong religious and social pressure on women which forces them to adapt to religious lifestyles. Thus, it affects women more than men by restricting their choice of lifestyle.

Intellectual Capability comprises the capabilities of senses, imagination, thought and practical reason from Nussbaum's list. In addition, I included the functioning of having self-confidence and recognising one's own self-worth under this capability set.

It is associated with an individual's right to have adequate education, and any opportunity and skill that education could form in the cultivation of the mind and expanding horizons, such as developing critical reasoning to make choices, enjoying literature and music, developing world knowledge, being able to voice one's demands and ideas and being able to plan one's own life. Education as an intellectual capability plays a role in opening up broader opportunities for women and in leading to the expansion of other capabilities. Therefore, it has a central role in this capability set.

Regarding the situation in Turkey, education is a critical issue. Statistics show that the female illiteracy rate is 9.4%, while it is 1.9% for men. Only 14.2% of women are graduates of high school, and 10.7% of women are graduates of higher education as of 2014 (TUIK 2014a). Furthermore, 33.8% of women in Turkey do not have any education or have not completed the primary level. When we look at the regional differences, this percentage increases to 57% for the women living in Eastern Turkey, whereas it is 25.1% for women in Western Turkey (Jansen et al. 2009). These figures show that how receiving education is crucial and a missed capability for the women in Turkey.

The functioning of self-confidence is often violated at many aspects of the women's life. At the household level, the common practice of girls' non-attendance to school in Eastern Turkey leads girls to lose their self-confidence and self-worth because boys' schooling opportunities are being prioritised whereas girls are being kept for domestic duties (Tansel 2002). Although there is no study on girls' self-confidence and worth in educational setting of Turkish context, the wider literature shows that gender discrimination within the school decrease girls' self-worth/confidence (Walker 2007). Likewise, studies in labour market (Bacak 2010; Toksoz and Gulay 2004) show that women in Turkey lose their self-confidence or feel themselves insignificant in the work place environment because they are not given a chance to express their ideas, to take initiatives and to play an active role in the decision-making processes. They also experience bad treatment and they are not promoted with the same frequency as their male counterparts. This functioning shows that being devalued because of one's gender in different dimensions of life could easily lead to the exclusion of women from becoming full members of society, and the lowering of their self-confidence as well as their aspirations and capability sets.

Economic Capability includes the capabilities of material aspects of control over one's environment in Nussbaum's list. It is the ability of an individual to generate an income, own property, inherit property and to control their own earnings.

This capability has particular importance for women, as, without economic independence, personal autonomy is impossible. It also plays an important role, particularly in the Turkish context: The participation of labour force is 30.5% for female whereas this increases to 71% for male (TUIK 2014b). Such a gender gap may be read as an indication of low financial independence among women. This may result in lack of seeing oneself as an active participant in working society. Yet, it should be noted that participation portrays only a partial picture of women's work. More important is quality of women's work and understanding the employment outcomes for women. Including Turkey, in most developing countries, women tend to earn less (gender wage gap); they are pushed to work in less productive job; or they are overrepresented in vulnerable work (including unpaid family work) (Verick 2014). This means vulnerable employment is less likely to make women financially independent or lead them to economic empowerment.

In addition to the low education level of women, the care responsibilities, the gender discrimination in labour market and the low participation of women in the labour force is also associated with economic violence. The studies on violence (Altinay and Arat 2009; KSGM 2015) in Turkey also show that women's lack of economic freedom is the main reason why women cannot leave an abusive marriage. Twenty-four per cent of women in Turkey are forced to quit their job or they are prevented from working by their partners or by family members. Even if they work, they feel obliged to hand in their salaries to their husbands or partners (KSGM 2015).

Political Capability involves the capabilities concerning the political aspect of control over one's environment (also Nussbaum's list). It is related to one's freedom to express political ideas and to engage in politics. I added two more items to this list: the ability to protest and being free from state repression.

Firstly, one's ability to join protests (strikes/demonstrations) or to act as a political/social activist with regard to civil and political liberties in Turkey have historically been at a minimum level comparing with Western European Countries. Governments in Turkey have generally been repressive, aiming to create a political culture of passivity and a citizenry that is obedient and politically docile. A Freedom House 2015 Report categorises Turkey as a 'partly free' country where political and civil liberties are not fully respected, people and the media have limited freedom to express themselves, and there is an intolerance towards political activism or towards the civic engagement of people. All these cases show that governments in Turkey can be repressive towards the people who wish to express their dissatisfaction and engage in public debate.

The second item I added to the political capability list is freedom from state repression, which takes the form of violence against civilians who do not conform to the dominant state ideology. Although this could easily be grouped under the physical capability set of having bodily integrity too, the point I want to emphasise is that state repression and state violence deprive people from exercising the freedom of political participation, the freedom of assembly and the freedom of speech. This functioning of state repression and political violence is closely associated with the socio-political context of Turkey, where violence against the voices that challenge the dominant state ideology is common. The gender dimension of this capability set can be seen in light of the treatment of women activists. Repression against the women activists is even more violent than the repression against men activists; this is because women activists not only challenge the dominant political ideology but also challenge the broader gender norms that place women's role in the house. Therefore, the state/police reply against this double challenge is even harsher (Hurriyet 2013).

The list I have formulated draws from Nussbaum's list as its point of reference, but it is adapted to the Turkish socio-cultural and political context, from which the analysis of gender inequality in Turkey is conducted in Chaps. 5, 6 and 7. Thus, the five dimensions of capabilities presented above were developed generating my own groupings of capability dimensions (e.g. being exposed to gender discrimination would be failing to achieve social capability), which helped me to track between Nussbaum's list and my own analysis.

CONCLUSION

This chapter presented different conceptualisations of gender justice, drawing from feminist philosophers, and outlined normative understandings of gender equality. Then, it argued the case for capabilities approach as a human development perspective to provide the conceptual lenses for rethinking gender equality and education from a feminist perspective. As noted above, capabilities offers a powerful and expansive evaluative framework for approaching and assessing equality, well-being and injustices in society and women's lives and mediating the value of women and the conditions influencing their choices. Therefore, the list I propose here is crucial for operationalising analyses and interpretations of the lives of women. The next chapter presents the historical history, gender politics and education context of Turkey so that women's lives in this study can be better contextualised.

NOTES

1. Rawls' list of primary goods are: basic rights and liberties; freedom of movement and free choice of occupation against a background of diverse opportunities; powers and prerogatives of offices and positions of responsibility in the political and economic institutions of the basic structure; income and wealth; and the social bases of self-respect (Rawls 2013: 181).
2. Robeyns' list has 14 capabilities: Life and physical health; Mental well-being; Bodily integrity and safety; Social relations; Political empowerment; Education and knowledge; Domestic work and non-market care; Paid work and other projects; Shelter and environment; Mobility; Leisure activities; Time-autonomy; Being respected and treated with dignity, and Religion (Robeyns 2003a: 71–72).

CHAPTER 3

Understanding Context: Political History, Gender Politics and Education Provision in Turkey

THE POLITICAL HISTORY OF TURKEY

The Republic of Turkey was established in 1923 as a secular and democratic country. With its establishment, Mustafa Kemal Atatürk initiated a number of reforms, ranging from everyday life issues to constitutional changes. These reforms were part of the founding ideology of Turkey known as Kemalism.[1] This ideology aimed at overcoming the Ottoman past and building a new modern and secular nation compatible with Western norms. The Islamic Ottoman laws and Islam were perceived as conservative, oppressive and backward forces which impeded the road to modernisation (Arat 2000; Kasaba 1997). Therefore, the Kemalist reforms excluded Islam from the new political order and aimed at building a Turkish nation-state framed on the basis of common language, culture, history and territory. The new state was inclusive only in the sense that the people who shared the aforementioned characteristics were considered to be 'Turkish' and 'Turkish citizens'. Since the formation of the Turkish nation-state, all other national identities such as Kurd, Circassian, Laz, Pomak and other Muslim groups are considered to be Turkish and have full citizenship rights according to the law. Only the non-Muslim groups of Armenians, Greeks and Jews are officially recognised as minorities after the 1923 Lausanne Treaty. This narrow and homogenous conceptualisation of the nation-state left no space for ethnic diversity or the expression of different ethnic identities (Yavuz 2001).

© The Editor(s) (if applicable) and The Author(s) 2017   47
F.M. Cin, *Gender Justice, Education and Equality*, Palgrave Studies
in Gender and Education, DOI 10.1007/978-3-319-39104-5_3

The period between 1923 and 1950 is labelled 'the Republican period' in the history of Turkey because many reforms aiming towards modernisation were completed during this era (Keyder 2008). The Republican People's Party (RPP) remained in power from the establishment of the Turkish Republic until 1949, when the ascendancy to power of the Democrat Party (DP) ushered in the multi-party era in Turkish politics.

The DP was a right-wing pro-Islamist party which stood for conservative religious values and represented Muslim peasants (White 2008). The DP governments' (1950–1960) favourable attitudes towards Islam became more obvious when they changed the language of ezan[2] from Turkish to Arabic and established the first religious school of the Republic. These conservative attitudes did not please the Kemalists and the military (which had traditionally taken the task of safeguarding Republican and Kemalist values). The military coup of 27 May 1960 overthrew the government and banned the DP under the accusation of undermining the secular character of the state through its Islamist programme (White 2008). After the military coup and the fall of the DP government, the 1924 constitution was changed and a more liberal and democratic constitution was adopted, guaranteeing freedom of expression, freedom to organise in political or non-political associations and respect for human rights. The 1961 constitution was the most democratic constitution Turkey ever had (Ahmad 2008).

The freedoms secured by this constitution served as a legal basis for the emergence and organisation of leftist activism in the 1970s (Neyzi 2001). In 1968, the communist movements had already made their appearance, in parallel with the social movements in Europe and Latin America.[3] The right-wing parties in Turkey started to use Islam as a political tool to counter the communist threat. The fight between the secular left on the one hand and the Islamists and fascist right on the other soon escalated into a violent confrontation. As a result, on 12 March 1971 the military asked for the resignation of the government, claiming that the President could not control the political violence (Neyzi 2001).

The 1961 constitution also opened the way for the involvement of many Kurds[4] in left-wing movements and activism during the 1960s and 1970s. By the mid-1970s the Kurdish left started to form student organisations and cultural and political groups which emphasised Kurdish identity and called for the recognition of Kurdish cultural rights. Some groups demanded an independent Kurdish state (namely Kurdistan) and established the Partiya Karkerên Kurdistanê (PKK or Kurdistan Workers'

Party),[5] a left-wing organisation, under the leadership of Abdullah Öcalan (Gunter 2008). The PKK boosted Kurdish nationalism, which emerged as a threat to Turkish nationalism and, in particular, to 'the unitary character of Turkish state' and 'the indivisibility of the state with its territory and nation' (Gunter 2008: 5).

Until the 1980s, Turkey faced political and economic instability. Various political movements (communists, nationalists, fascists, Islamists) clashed violently, causing political conflict, social unrest and chaos. Thus, the 1970s took their place in Turkish history as a period of bloodshed and hostility. The political and economic instability and the violence between the Kurds and the Turks as well as right and left brought the second military coup on 12 September 1980 (Neyzi 2001). As a response to the left/right divisions and the emergence of Kurdish nationalism, the new 1982 constitution emphasised the indivisibility of the state and declared Turkish to be the only official language, banning the use of Kurdish (including giving Kurdish names to children and songs in Kurdish) (Gunter 2008). Moreover, the 1982 constitution limited personal freedom, but not the power of the state. It is the current constitution of Turkey and it was established under military rule, also adopted a framework of 'Turkish-Islamic synthesis' in order to unify people around Turkish nationalism and Islam, and to restrain left-wing Kurdish movements. These policies, however, led to further politicisation of Kurdish identity (Yavuz 2001).

In 1984, the PKK created a military branch and initiated an armed campaign against the Turkish state with the purpose of establishing an independent Kurdistan. Kurdish militants aimed at economic, military and civilian targets in Turkey (Yavuz 2003). Militants raided villages, focusing especially on educational infrastructure, killing teachers and burning down schools, on the basis that the Turkish state 'was using its national education system to assimilate the Kurds' (Kirisci and Winrow 1997: 128). The PKK not only targeted Turkish people, but also pro-government Kurds. In 1987, the state declared emergency rule in the eastern and southeastern provinces and suspended the civil rights of people in Kurdish-populated villages. In 1990, the Anti-Terror Law was introduced, according to which all forms of propaganda (including demonstrations) that may threaten the unity of Turkey were banned. In the mid-1990s, the armed Kurdish attacks reached their peak. The Turkish state responded with a military counter-offensive in order to weaken the PKK influence in eastern provinces and destroy the organisation's bases in northern Iraq. With the capture and trial of Abdullah Öcalan in 1999, the PKK announced its withdrawal from

Turkey and the organisation's attacks diminished (Gunter 2008). The violent clashes between the PKK and the Turkish military in eastern Turkey caused around 37,000 deaths; more than 3000 villages were destroyed; and around 3,000,000 people were internally displaced (Gunter 2008).

The 'Kurdish question' emerged in the 1980s, and until the 1990s the Turkish state denied the existence of a distinct Kurdish identity. Even in the 2000s, most state officials denied that a Kurdish problem existed, claiming instead that the issue was one of terrorism (Bozarslan 2008). The terrorist tactics used by the PKK politicised the Kurdish issue and it became difficult to distinguish between the Kurdish question and the terrorism of the PKK. With the election of Justice and Development Party (JDP) in 2002, the Turkish parliament passed a series of reforms to recognise the cultural rights of Kurds in order to meet EU entry requirements. These laws lifted the ban on broadcasting and publishing in Kurdish and allowed the teaching of the Kurdish language in private courses (Gunter 2008). State television began broadcasting news in Kurdish, and Kurdish literature and language departments were established in universities (Bozarslan 2008). Thus, the 'Kurdish question' has been officially acknowledged and some initial steps towards its solution have been taken.

A process aimed at dialogue and securing Kurdish people's rights under the constitution started in the summer of 2009. The peace process and negotiations between PKK and Turkish government, however, has come to a halt as of summer 2015, when armed attacks by the PKK in eastern Anatolia increased. Attacks continuously occur today in the eastern provinces (as well as in metropolitans), with Turkish soldiers and civilians being the predominant targets.

In this section, I have briefly presented the historical and political contexts of Turkey that are relevant to this research. In the next section, I move onto the historical context of women's movements and rights and gender issues in Turkey.

Gender Politics and the Women's Movements in Turkey

In this section I briefly describe the multiple layers of gender politics in Turkey, putting the lives of women into a historical context and presenting the ongoing and recent discussions on women's issues and equality in Turkey. Women's movements in Turkey are categorised under three eras.

The first era is the Republican era (1923–1950), when many social, political, economic, legal and constitutional reforms were initiated to improve the status of women both in public and family life. The second era is the feminist silence (1950–1980) when there was no involvement of women's groups in politics. The third era is the awakening of feminism in Turkey from 1980s until the present.

Feminism and Women in the Republican Era

During the Republican era, reforms of Kemalists and Republican elites to secularise the nation and to create a new Turkish identity (Kandiyoti 1989; Tekeli 1981) created fertile ground for the first steps towards the introduction of feminism in Turkey. The modernisation process in Turkey did not follow the same route as it had in other countries. In post-colonial states, nationalism and modernity were not linked to the West, since their modernisation process was part of the revolt against the Western cultural (and general) hegemony (Chatterjee 1993). Turkey, however, was never colonised; thus the Turkish modernisation project was predominantly based upon Western concepts, norms and legal codes. The caliphate was abolished in 1924, and in 1925 the dress code was rearranged, with women being granted permission to remove the veil. Unveiled women became a symbol of the new modern nation and the new outlook of Turkish women (Arat 1997). The reforms continued with the abolishment of Islamic family codes and the adoption of the Swiss civil code in 1926. The new civil code outlawed polygamy, recognised both men's and women's right to divorce, also giving both equal rights to inheritance. These rights were followed in 1934 by the granting of suffrage to women (Arat 2000). Lastly, in 1937, a secularist[6] clause was incorporated into the constitution, making Islam a secondary identity in Turkey. Thus, women were granted legal equality in civic and political rights. However, their agency and activism was restricted. In 1923, attempts to establish the Women's People's Party were refused for fear that it might detract attention from the RPP, which was the only party in the country at that time (Arat 2008). The feminist movements, under the leadership of Nezihe Muhittin, established the Turkish Women's Union in 1924. In 1935, the collaboration of the Union with feminists from various parts of the world to host the congress of feminism in Turkey and its declaration against Nazism, were not welcomed (Arat 2000) and led to the closure of the Union. Such a decision revealed the state's belief that women did not need to organise themselves given that it had granted them full political and social rights (Arat 1997).

Hence, feminism in this period was under the control of the state. Legal rights did not bring complete gender equality and the basic rights of women were still in the hands of men. For instance, the 1926 civil code contained several patriarchal aspects; men were legally declared as the heads of the household; guardianship of children was given to men in case of a disagreement between parents; fathers had the right to benefit from the income of their children; and women required their husbands' permission to work outside the home (Arat 2010a). This showed that the state's initiatives for the emancipation of women were still carried out under the influence of patriarchal norms.

While Kemalism cannot be said to have altered traditional norms and conservatism, it created a space in the public sphere for women to express themselves (Durakbasa 1998). The rights given to women during the Republican era were not the demands of women, but the ideals of male elites who sought to meet the basic standards of parliamentary democracy (Kadioglu 1998). Therefore, the reforms could be described as 'state feminism' (Tekeli 1986: 193).

Despite the limitations noted above, Kemalism represented a major step forward, offering women many social, political and cultural rights and making them equal to men in many aspects. The old patterns disappeared more swiftly in urban Turkey than in rural areas (Ahmed 1982). The women who benefited most from Kemalist reforms were urban, educated, middle- and upper middle-class women. Such women became staunch supporters of secularism and Kemalism. On the other hand, the traditional role of women continued, especially in rural areas. The new economic and political rights were like a closed book to many people living in rural areas. Turkey was still under the influence of Islamic tradition, making it hard for women to be critical of the prevalent culture and ideologies (Ahmed 1982). It is due to this contrast between rural and urban areas that the modernisation process and its reforms are often described as having been a top-down process, trying to transform a traditional society into a modern society (Arat 1999). At the same time, reforms signalled a positioning of the state vis-à-vis women and women were integrated in the nation-building project.

Nationalism and Feminism

The questions related to women were important in the modernisation process. How should women be placed in society in a way that did not disturb conservative culture and conservative rural dwellers, who constituted the majority of the new Republic? What role should be assigned to women in order for them to have an appropriate place in public life? Placing women, who had been suppressed for seven centuries of Ottoman rule, at the centre of public, economic and social life, was not something which would be accepted quickly. Therefore, the nation-building project became the main catalyst for the integration of women into the social and public spheres, thus legitimising women's roles as good citizens and mothers, while simultaneously concealing their sexuality and femininity. Durakbasa (1998) defined this new positioning of the state vis-à-vis women as follows:

> an educated-professional woman at work; a socially active organizing woman as a member of social clubs, associations, etc., a biological functioning woman in the family fulfilling reproductive responsibilities as a mother and wife, a feminine woman entertaining men at the balls and parties...If the first two images implied a change in women's place in society, the last two asserted a boundary that assured that the new roles would not alter a woman's subordinate position as a —female in the male–female relationship. (Durakbasa 1998: 148)

Through reforms, women were encouraged to take part in social and economic life, yet, paradoxically, were simultaneously asked to retain their domestic family duties (Arat 1994b). Nation-building was a project through which women could make their voices heard and stand side by side with men in the public sphere. However, the state's aim was to educate women as teachers and create educated wives and mothers who would educate the nation. Women who worked in services such as teaching or nursing embodied a nationalist spirit and were proud to serve the modernisation mission. These professional women perceived themselves as representatives of modern Turkish women (Arat 1997). The new identity of Turkish women represented a duality between the new, modern Western ideology and the traditional Islamic identity (Kadioglu 1998). This situation created 'emancipated but unliberated' women (Kandiyoti 1987: 3).

For feminist scholars (Arat 1997; Diner and Toktas 2010; Kandiyoti 1989) women's emancipation was the symbolic pawn through which Kemalist ideology articulated the modernity project and construction of nationalism. There were no social and political platforms or opportunities available to Turkish women to develop their feminist aspirations and movements during the Republican era. After gaining suffrage in 1934, women's modernisation was believed to have been, to a large degree, completed. Women were believed to have been granted all the rights they needed, thus a long period of feminist silence ensued until the 1980s (Diner and Toktas 2010). During this period, the Kemalist reforms aimed at the emancipation of women could not be contested and no feminist movement was founded to fight women's subordination. Feminist activism was only carried out by women's organisations such as the Turkish Mothers' Union, or the Turkish Association of Women University Graduates. Their activities amounted to ceremonies praising Kemalism (Tekeli 1990). Additionally, Turkey's political atmosphere in the 1950s was complicated with the transition to multi-party democracy and three military interventions (1969, 1971 and 1980) that took place. This left little ground for civilian affairs, consolidation of democracy and women's involvement in politics (Diner and Toktas 2010). For these reasons, the political spectrum of women's activism was very limited until the 1980s.

Post-1980 Feminist Movements: The Feminist Awakening in Turkey

The development of feminist scholarship in Turkey corresponds to the second wave of feminist activism in USA and Europe. The women's studies in Turkey appeared in the national agenda of Turkey when the WID issue appeared on the global agenda at the first international UN conference on Women in Mexico City in 1975 (Kandiyoti 2010). After the Mexico conference, the first women's studies centre was established at the Middle East Technical University in Ankara with United Nations Development Programme (UNDP) support. Since then, Turkey has participated in international conferences on women of the UN which took place in Copenhagen (1980), Nairobi (1985) and Beijing (1995) and signed the international documents regarding gender equality including the CEDAW in 1985 (Kandiyoti 2010).

In parallel with these events, the development of feminist activism in Turkey emerged during the 1970s when many educated, urban and mostly middle-class women (especially those studying at universities) were influenced by the political environment in Turkey. They were mainly involved in leftist (mainly Marxist) movements against exploitation and domination because, being suppressed as women, they felt sympathy for the fight against domination (Berktay 1995). On the other hand, a number of women took part in far-right movements, engaging with religious activism and extreme nationalism.[7] Women's presence in these political movements can be said to have started the women's movement in Turkey and vitalised the feminist consciousness, because they established a place for themselves in the political sphere (Arat 2000).

In the context of the 1980 military regime (1980–1983), all political parties except those few which were newly founded and strictly controlled by the military were closed down. Military rule was authoritarian and limited the civic rights of the people (Kasaba 2008). Many of the leaders, labour unions and political organisations were banned from politics. The de-politicisation of society included suppressing all kinds of political groups such as student movements, labour unions and political organisations—but not those created by women. Women's activities were considered as being less influential upon society and politics, and therefore were thought of as having no specific significance or value. Additionally, since women's rights were still considered part of Kemalist reforms, women were not viewed as a potential challenge to the state and were allowed to practise their political rights (Diner and Toktas 2010). These changes opened a space for women to launch feminist movements. Formerly, leftist women activists formed networks among themselves and began to voice their demands and to discuss women's oppression, control over their sexuality, domestic violence and the misrepresentation of women in media (Arat 2000; Diner and Toktas 2010). They challenged the gendered nature of state feminism, rejecting the identities and missions assigned to women in the Republican era. The political activism of women in the 1970s, the closure of the political arena after the 1980 coup, the impact of feminist movements in the USA and Europe, the rising awareness of educated women and Turkey's intensified links with the Western world led to the emergence of a feminist consciousness and feminist movements in Turkey and the rise of a new actor in Turkish politics: women (Arat 1989).

Over time, feminists have formed unique ideologies and were separated into different groups in the 1990s: socialist feminists, Kemalist feminists, Islamist feminists and Kurdish feminists (Arat 1993, 1994a). While not all such movements necessarily aimed at liberating other women, each attacked existing policies and laws, demanding a more feminist state. These movements correspond to 'third wave' feminism in that they were identity-oriented and had diversified, differentiated and fragmented demands in accordance with the ethnic and religious identities of the women (Arat 2010b; Diner and Toktas 2010).

The 1980s women's movements were valuable in the sense that they opened a space for women's mobilisation and contributed to creating a democratic society in search of equality and opportunity (Arat 1994a). Diverse feminists' struggles and the raising of awareness of women's needs and problems (such as abortion or domestic violence), along with collective feminist campaigns, liberated society and altered the political regime; this is despite the notable absence of women in parliament and political parties. The movements did not change the patriarchal nature of the society or bring about radical change, but the solidarity and networking among women implied the importance of acquiring power in civil society (Arat 1994a).

Recently, Turkey's EU accession procedure and negotiations, underway since 1999, strengthened relations between feminist groups and women's NGOs to reach towards an equal treatment principle between men and women, and urged the Turkish state to make amendments to fundamental laws (New Civil Code in 2001; Penal Code in 2004; and Constitutional amendments in 2010) to constitute laws in a more egalitarian way, respecting both men and women's dignity, equality and liberty. Some important changes regarding gender equality comprised the recognition of marital rape as a crime, acknowledgement of sexual harassment, particularly in the workplace, acknowledgement of sexual assault under custody, more severe sentences for honour killings and child marriages and the banning of virginity tests (Arat 2010a). In 2012, Turkey accepted gender-based anti-discrimination laws which criminalised any act of discrimination against women (that is, on the basis of their gender identity) that was related to women's employment and job opportunities, promotion and wage, and education and health facilities. Further constitutional amendments concerned affirmative action in women's access to decision-making and political representation, to employment and equal pay and equal access to education (Muftuler-Bac 2012). Although women's movements since the 1980s made several attempts to impact legislation, it was only through the EU accession process in Turkey that the government took an initiative in addressing the gender issues. In this regard, the era after 1999 could be seen as a turning point for women's rights in Turkey since the Republican times.

Despite these changes, the Global Gender Gap Index 2014 ranks Turkey at 125th place among 142 countries (Hausmann 2014). The Gender Inequality Index—a composite measure reflecting inequality in achievements between women and men in three dimensions (reproductive health, empowerment and the labour market), ranked Turkey at 69th place (UNDP 2014). These show that women's equal participation with men in the educational, health, economic and in the political spheres have not been adequately addressed. This can be attributed in great measure to the increased political will of religious conservatives (Acuner 2013).

The next section argues why women's position is still problematic in Turkey despite the progress in legislation, and draws attention to the recent neo-liberal and neo-conservative policies which reduced women's status in society and increased their vulnerability; it further engages with the discussions on neo-conservatism and neo-liberalism vis-à-vis women's rights and the poor conditions in Turkey (such as the increase in domestic violence and child marriages or the decrease in the participation of women in the labour market).

Gender Issues in Turkey

Many feminist researchers analysed the changing policies and legislations in Turkey since 1999 (Arat 2010a; Cosar and Yegenoglu 2011; Dedeoglu 2012; Kilic 2008), as well as the aftermath of constitutional and legal reforms on women's quality of life in Turkey (Bugra 2013; Muftuler-Bac 2012; Stivachtis and Georgakis 2011). Their research indicate that there has been little evidence regarding the improvement of women's conditions in reality. Women still continue to remain less educated; participate in the labour market less than men; do more care work; and leave political participation to the men. Thus, it could be argued that new laws and policies indeed do not aim to change the vulnerable position of women in society, as they focus on the strategic advancement of women above their practical interests, and treat women as if they all have the necessary resources or opportunities to benefit from the rights provided to them. Women are not supported by measures to transform the patriarchal norms and roles within society. Their inclusion is not on the same terms as men and different experiences of women in accessing their basic rights are not being taken into account. Therefore, new legislations are accessible to only a small fraction of women. However, it should be noted that experiences are influenced by the cultural, religious, social and political norms that often govern women's communities and affect their individual life chances in turn (such as women in different geographical location—Eastern or Western Turkey, women with different educational or economic opportunities, women of different ethnicities or able/disabled women), and any policies or laws should take these differences into account.

In addition to lack of gender sensitivity in formation legislations, feminist authors in Turkey (Arat 2010a; Kandiyoti 2011; Syed et al. 2009) stress that cultural and patriarchal mind-sets need to embrace change and reforms. Thus, they underline that the key factor in gender inequality constitutes patriarchal norms, how these are reproduced and transmitted to the institutions, and how gender discrimination is institutionalised at multiple levels from family to government institutions. Research on women's empowerment projects in Turkey (Landing 2011); women's participation in the labour force (Gunduz-Hosgor and Smits 2008; Ilkkaracan 2012; Sural 2007) and women in management (Aycan 2004; Sumer 2006) confirms that women mostly suffer from patriarchal attitudes and institutionalised sexism, which stands as a barrier in their way in everyday life, from family duties to those of the workplace. The gendered nature of family (Ataca 2009; Kagitcibasi 1986; Kandiyoti 1977), state and public sphere (Göle 1997), and religion in Turkey are categorised as the foremost reasons affecting women's desires and aspirations negatively by holding them back from public life.

The above two factors of gender insensitivity in legislation and patriarchal mind-sets are also closely connected to political developments and the party politics of JDP. There is a growing body of literature (Acar and Altunok 2013; Bugra 2013; Citak and Tur 2008; Cosar and Yegenoglu 2011; Dedeoglu 2013; Goksel 2013) that also looks into how the increasing religious and social conservatism[8] in Turkey in recent years, with the election and governance of JDP, has reduced women's status in society and increased their vulnerability despite boosting reforms on rights. These studies relate gender inequality to rising neo-conservatism[9] and neo-liberalism.[10]

The common argument here is that neo-liberalist approaches of the JDP place emphasis on self-regulation of social economic domains (such as increasing privatisation of state-owned enterprises and withdrawal of the state from the provision of welfare services), and the neo-conservatism party politics of JDP ascribes moral value to the private spheres, focuses on traditional values foremost and constitutes a conservative approach to womanhood through shaping a new perception of the familial sphere based on social norms and religion.

In particular, this neo-liberal conservative approach defines the familial sphere as the natural locus of women and has regulated the public and private domains in the last decade in Turkey by creating a political culture based on religiosity. This inevitably restricts women's freedom of regulation of their life (Acar and Altinok 2013), employment outside the house and integration in the public sphere (Ecevit 2013); makes it uneasy for women to challenge traditional gender roles (Dedeoglu 2013); and marginalises women's movements (Cosar and Yegenoglu 2011). Additionally, neo-conservatism affects women's choices of education and marriage. If social norms reinforce that women's role is in the home, then it is very unlikely that in a conservative society like Turkey, women will have a high level of education, even if they want to. It is also highly likely that existing gender bias against girls' education investment will increase. In the same vein, women will have less freedom to choose their partners and therefore, less bargaining power in the household (Goksel 2013).

Gender equality and conservatism debates in Turkey have also been of interest in public discussion. In one of his interviews in May 2007, the prominent Turkish sociologist Serif Mardin (2007) brought up the term 'neighbourhood pressure' to explain how increasing conservatism in Turkey started to impact on individuals' freedoms. With this term, Mardin has aimed to capture the enforcement of communal and local pressure on individuals to adopt conservative religious norms in their values. This opened a lively debate in public and it was carried over to academic debates and research. Toprak et al. (2009) conducted extensive field work in 12 Anatolian towns and two districts in Istanbul to empirically examine the extent to which neighbourhood pressure existed and whether it excluded people or created 'otherness' and discriminated in lifestyles, freedoms, and agency of individuals who do not want to conform with religious norms. The results also addressed the question of women and the issue of gender inequality in Turkey, and argued that the dominant interpretation of Islam with regard to gender creates isolation and exclusion for women. In Toprak et al.'s research (2009) many interviewed women describe the experience of being a woman in Turkey as difficult and restrictive. Her research also indicates that women are the most affected subjects of social pressure in Turkey, because Islamic conservatism offers women little space to manoeuvre their interests and functionings, and substantively impedes their freedoms.

There is a growing body of research focusing on different aspects and problems of gender equality in Turkey. From a feminist perspective, it is possible to see the continuation of patriarchy since the Republican era, rather than a transformation. Increasing conservatism (along with neo-liberalism) deprives women of their freedoms and rights to enjoy full political, private and public life. A social and economic structure in which people can equally benefit from opportunities and resources, and respect for individual freedoms and rights without any sort of (gender, political, religious) discrimination, does not exist in Turkey. There is also a methodological and epistemological gap in the sense that very limited research gives voice to women to show how these structures and policies affect them in reality, and almost none of the studies use a feminist theory/frame in explaining the gender inequalities. Neither the legislations nor the studies mentioned above account for the differences and different experiences that women may have because of the methods they are using. Therefore, with this research, I aim to fill this gap by accounting for the differences and different experiences that women may have, and by looking into multiple dimensions and spheres in the lives of women from Western Turkey (their family life, intimate relationships, schooling, professional life) from a feminist approach. This gives a more detailed picture of how gender inequalities take place in women's lives and how the above-mentioned factors affect their lives and freedoms.

Having contextualised the women's movements and fleshed out discussions on women and gender equality, the next part now offers a brief presentation of the provision of education in relation to gender and social/gender equality across three different periods covered by this book.

THE CONTEXT OF EDUCATION IN TURKEY

This section does not aspire to give a detailed context of changing education in Turkey over the historical periodisation covered by this research, but to provide contextual information about education provision, and women's employment across the generations. Here, the education system of Turkey is presented under three periods: the Republican period (1923–1950); the process of repeated recurring military coups and the multi-party era (1950–1980); and contemporary times (1980 to present), in which the educational inequalities are also presented.

The Founding Ideology and Education (Republican Period, 1923–1950)

With the fall of the Ottoman Empire in 1922 and the declaration of independence of the Republic in 1923, the first reforms in the education system began with the Law on the Unification of National Education, which attached all educational and scientific institutions to the MoNE on 3 March 1924 (Akyuz 2006). This reform was followed by the Westernisation of the education system. To this end, coeducation was introduced in 1924 in all levels of education, including higher education (Okcabol 2005). The duration of primary education was set as five years and became compulsory for every Turkish citizen and was free of charge; the divide between secular schools and religious schools was abolished; religious education was limited and subjected to central inspection; laicist and positivist education was adopted (Gumus 2008). On the common terrain, the educational institutions were mobilised to spread Kemalism, to create national-minded and educated generations regardless of their religion and ethnicity (Zurcher 1993). Considering that Turkey was under the one-party era rule of the RPP, the social and cultural politics were authoritarian, centralist and reformist. Yet the political environment of 1920 and 1930s' Europe, where emergence of the nation-state was on the rise, was not substantially different from Turkey (Okcabol 2005).

The primary aim in this period was rather to give primary education to villagers and increase the literacy (Gunlu 2008). The literacy rate was only about 9 % of the whole population (only 1,111,496 out of a population of 13,648,270) and only 4 % of the female population was literate as of 1927 (Unluhisarcikli 2008). Adult education in nation-building was not only limited to literacy but also aimed at promoting national culture; expanding citizenship education; educating people in the villages in art, physical education, agriculture, health education and useful courses of daily life; and training the workforce needed. For these purposes, Public Classrooms (1927), Evening Art and Trade Schools (1928), People's Houses (1932), and Courses for Men and Women in Villages (1938–1939) were established (Unluhisarcikli 2008).

Compulsory education was one of the strategies to increase literacy, yet as Table 3.1 shows below, there was little improvement in the enrolment and graduate ratio of primary schools. Female primary school graduation was also relatively low because girls would drop out of school before grad-

Table 3.1 Percentage of school enrolment and graduates for primary schools, 1929–1930 to 1949–1950

Enrolments and graduates	Male			Female		
Year	1929–1930	1939–1940	1949–1950	1929–1930	1939–1940	1949–1950
Enrolment ratio (aged 7–11)	51	51	80	26	25	50
Graduates ratio (population aged 12 and over)	15	26	50	6	11	23

Source: Shorter (1985: 434)

uating to support their families as domestic or agricultural workers or to get married; and very few parents would support girls' education for long periods of schooling (Shorter 1985).

A significant problem pertaining to education in those years constituted the lack of schools and teachers. At the time of the establishment of Turkey in 1923, there were only 4894 primary schools, 72 secondary schools, 11,000 teachers and 348,000 students (TUIK 2012). Even by 1936, only 5000 villages of 40,000 villages had schools and teachers. Therefore, the founding of the Republic necessitated formal and professional teacher training to meet the teacher demands at school. Initially, 'Village Institutes' were established in 1939 to meet the increasing teacher demand, particularly in the villages (Okcabol 2005). These schools constituted the first formal institutions of teacher training. They were fully state-funded and comprised of five years' duration after primary school. Half of the curriculum was made up of theoretical studies and the other half was practical work. The importance of village institutes was that young villagers were given an opportunity to become teachers, and upon graduating they were sent back to villages to teach at schools and educate the village community. They would be provided with a home and land to demonstrate land cultivation and trade to the villagers.

As shown in Table 3.2, the number of women teachers gradually increased over the years. The women teachers in these positions did not only include women who were trained at the Villages Institutes from 1939 and onwards, but also women who were graduates of secondary/high schools but received accelerated teacher training to meet the teacher needs, as well as some middle-or upper middle-class women who had

Table 3.2 Number of teachers between 1924 and 1950 at all levels of education (primary school, secondary school and high school)

	Number of teachers		
Year	Total number	Male	Female
1924/1925	16,071	12,246	3,825
1935/1936	19,151	13,140	6,011
1945/1946	36,711	25,828	10,883
1950/1951	46,841	33,256	13,585

Source: TUIK (2012: 59–60)

Table 3.3 Percentage of the rural population aged 15 and over working in agriculture (1935 Census)

Sector	Male	Female
Agriculture	79	65
Non-agricultural job (industry or white collar professions)	15	2
Not working or unknown	6	33

Source: Turkey Central Statistics Office (1937: 332–333)

a chance to study at university[11] (Gunlu 2008). Being a teacher was very prestigious for women of that time and women teachers constituted a very small percentage during the Republican years as compared to the majority of women's economic contribution. A genuine picture regarding women's position in the economy can be obtained from the results of a 1935 census (see Table 3.3).

Table 3.3 shows that large proportions of adult women in rural Turkey were engaged in agriculture as their main occupation. There were only a small number of women in the non-agricultural sector, which mainly included factory, industry and modern textile mills. A small portion of these 2 % of non-agricultural jobs also constituted white-collar education requiring professions such as teaching, banking, government services, magistrates, post and telegraph employees, public services and administrations and hospitals as nurses or doctors, which were largely available in the cities with the exception of primary school teaching (Shorter 1985).

The Multi-Party Democracy Era (1950–1980)

Turkey entered a multi-party era of democracy with the election of the DP in the 1949 elections. In the 1950s, a phase of economic liberalisation and capital-based development began, and Turkey opened up to the West. This liberalisation and Westernisation brought industrialisation and the use of machinery in agriculture. Consequently, Turkey experienced massive internal immigration from rural areas to urban areas for better work opportunities (as many lost their jobs due to the rise of machinery in agriculture), better life standards, education and health opportunities (Nohl 2008). This increasing urbanisation placed a high demand on the education system. Yet this demand for education exercised little impact on the literacy rate of women. By 1955, 26% of women were literate and this only increased to 33% in 1965 and 46.6% in 1980 (TUIK 2012). In terms of schooling, both for men and women, primary school gross enrolment rates increased to 58%, secondary school enrolment rate was 14% in 1960 and the tertiary gross enrolment rate increased to 3% in 1960 (TUIK 2012). As Table 3.4 shows, these figures showed little improvement even in 1980.

The low schooling and literacy rate is often explained by the low urbanisation rate (43.9%) in 1980 (Okcabol 2008). The majority of the population did not have access to high schools and universities, which were situated in urban districts. The low rates of higher education can be connected to the fervent political atmosphere of the 1970s, which banned many students from high schools and universities (Demirel 1995). Particularly the involvement of students in political acts, the polarisation among students and the armed clashes aggravated in teacher training institutions and some

Table 3.4 Percentage of Turkish population by literacy and sex, 12 years and over, 1980

Educational level	Male	Female
Illiterate	16.8	46.6
Primary school	52.8	36.9
Secondary school	8.7	4.5
High school	4.6	2.6
Vocational high school	3.4	1.9
Higher education	3.4	1.0

Source: TUIK (2012)

universities; teachers' unions faced political pressure; students were barred from entering universities or schools, based on their political beliefs; and students and teachers were killed (Okcabol 2005).

Similarly, industrialisation brought little effect on women's employment because upon moving to cities, women were still responsible for care work and home making. In addition, much of the industrialisation work required vocational education and the majority of women lagged behind in comparison to men (Ecevit 1990). For instance, in 1955, women made up 11.9% of the total female labour force and this increased to 16.1% in 1980. The percentage of the women's work force in the services sector rose from 7.6% in 1955 to 12.6% in 1980. Women's employment in the agricultural sector increased from 53.2% in 1955 to 53.4% in 1980 (Ecevit 1990).

Contemporary Times (from 1980 to Present)

With the end of the three-year period of military rule after the 1983 elections, an era began of economic liberalism, privatisation, globalisation, opening up to international markets, and an increase in the influence of Islam arising from Turkish-Islamic synthesis in political and social circles. Turkey experienced privatisation of state industries, increasing export and import, opening up to international markets, and an enhancement of its tourism industry (Nohl 2008). The aim was to replace a highly regulated, inward-looking economy with an export and market-oriented liberal economy in the longer term. With the environment of economic liberalisation, state-run privatisation of education also started, as there was not enough state funding available for education (Ercan 1999). Thus, development of private schools started. This further consolidated the link between education and social inequality in Turkey, which has always been strong (Inal 2008), as better quality education became accessible for those who were well off.

Spurred by the global campaign EFA[12], the Ministry of Education launched 'A Compulsory Education Program' in 1997 to extend primary school education from five years to eight years. This programme aimed to expand schooling opportunities for all children and to increase girls' schooling, especially in Eastern Turkey (Dulger 2004). This was also Turkey's largest poverty alleviation programme (Dulger 2004) as it introduced social policies to improve the conditions of the poor. The state

Table 3.5 Net schooling ratio by educational year and level of education

Educational year	Primary education			Secondary education			Higher education		
	Total	Male	Female	Total	Male	Female	Total	Male	Female
1997/1998	84.74	90.25	78.97	37.87	41.39	34.16	10.25	11.28	9.17
2002/2003	90.98	94.49	87.34	50.57	55.72	45.16	14.65	15.73	13.53
2007/2008	97.37	98.53	96.14	58.56	61.17	55.81	21.06	22.37	19.69
2014/2015	97.10	97.08	97.12	79.37	79.46	79.26	39.49	37.95	41.10

Source: MoNE Statistics (2015)

provided free education, free health services for the poor, free meals to students coming from low-income families and free transportation for students in rural areas to encourage schooling of girls and boys (Engin-Demir and Cobanoglu 2012). This programme was conducted in collaboration with the World Bank. It provided Turkey with $600 million between 1997 and 2007 to support infrastructural and financial arrangements (McClure 2014). As Table 3.5 shows, good progress was achieved from 1997 to 2015 in terms of the schooling ratio of particularly women, which has historically been low since Republican times.

To increase girls' enrolment continuously, many campaigns have been established, among which 'Hey Girls', 'Let's go to School' and 'Father, Send me to School' have been most influential (Gumus and Gumus 2013; Batuhan 2007). Lastly, in 2012, the compulsory education expanded from 8 to 12 years, yet the impact of this expansion on the education system and enrolment rates is yet to be explored.

In terms of women's employment, until 1980, there was a strong focus on heavy industry and therefore few employment opportunities for women. However, since 1980, Turkey has actively participated in the global economy, and trade and export competitiveness has been encouraged (Gunduz-Hosgor and Smits 2008). This has brought an increase in women's employment in manufacturing, a decrease in agriculture and an overall decrease in the percentage of employed women. Particularly, the participation rate of women aged between 20 and 49 in the labour market shows that there is a substantial decrease over the years. This rate further decreased to 30.5% as of 2014 (TUIK 2014b). Some scholars (Bugra 2013; Ilkkaracan 2012) argue that Turkish state policies take the traditional family ideology for granted and continue positioning women as prime domestic workers rather than encouraging their employment in the

Table 3.6 Number of teachers between 1980 and 2010 at all levels of education

	Number of teachers		
Year	Total	Male	Female
1980/1981	326,675	199,692	126,983
1990/1991	389,734	231,413	158,321
2000/2001	484,984	277,067	207,917
2011/2012	751,620	373,007	378,613
2012/2013	807,549	375,961	431,588

Source: TUIK (2012), KSGM (2012)

public domain and providing them with adequate childcare and domestic help. Gunduz Hosgor and Smits (2008) pinpoint that the low educational level of Turkish women pushes women to work in informal sectors with low wages. On the other hand, in terms of teaching professions, there has been continuing growth in the proportion of women (see Table 3.6).

Although the number of women teachers exceeded male teachers as of 2011, women remain a minority in management and constitute only 11.9% of educational administration positions (KSGM 2012). This demonstrates that there is still a long way to go towards attaining equality in managerial or leadership positions.

So far, I have briefly presented the educational context in Turkey, and women's position within the education sector since the Republican period. In the next section, I focus on the educational inequalities in Turkey with a particular focus on gender inequality, in order to better illustrate what stands in the way of girls' access to schools.

Educational Inequalities in Turkey

Women's education has been a significant issue in national education policy since Republican times because it stood as a symbol of transformation, distribution of modernity and creation of intellectual existence through which official ideology (Kemalism) could be diffused. On the other hand, the education of women also faced many barriers originating from a strong patriarchal culture and sexist policies in education. For the Ministry of Education in Turkey, gender inequality is mainly a problem concerning the gender gap between boys' and girls' attendance of school or girls' attainment. The concern is limited to building classrooms;

supplying learning materials and filling schools with students rather than encouraging girls' participation in learning; eliminating gender differences in class; addressing inequities; or creating more girl-friendly schools (McClure 2014; Cin and Walker 2016). Thus the gendered nature of education in Turkey persists, creating inequity problems in different ways. I address three areas of significant inequality: (1) inequality of girls' access to education; (2) problems with curriculum and education system; and (3) teachers' under-representation in managerial posts and gendered ways of teaching.

Girls' Access to Education

In Turkey, one of the biggest forms of gender inequality in education is noted in girls' access to schooling. Despite free primary education, state-funded access to primary school for children of low-income families, the provision of conditional cash assistance to poor families, the distribution of all school books for free and imprisonment penalties for fathers refusing to send their daughters to school, many girls are deprived from schooling.

Research on girls' schooling/dropout and the gender gap in school enrolment in Turkey points out girls' schooling is at greater risk particularly in the eastern part of Turkey (Gumus and Gumus 2013; Rankin and Aytac 2006; Sahin and Gulmez 2000; Smits and Gunduz-Hosgor 2006). Two frequent causes of this inequity are socio-cultural structures and poverty (poor economic conditions).

The traditional culture in conservative districts of Turkey and gender roles shape girls to stay at home, deal with household chores or marry at an early age in return for a dowry (Smits and Gunduz-Hosgor 2006; UNICEF 2003). Social norms regarding the honour of family (Rankin and Aytac 2006; Smits and Gunduz-Hosgor 2003) and the low value attributed to girls (Rankin and Aytac 2008) set a barrier in girls' access to education. In addition, family size and mothers' educational level and ability to speak Turkish (for Kurdish mothers) are the significant predictors of girls' school participation (Duman 2010; Sahin and Gulmez 2000; Smiths and Gunduz-Hosgor 2006).

Economic difficulties also work against girls' school participation. Particularly in Eastern Turkey, the agriculture sector is the main source of income and employment. Free education or financial support does not necessarily decrease direct costs for students and their families (Alat and Alat 2011). Families tend to increase family income by making their children work at home or perform agricultural labour. Even if parents want to invest in their children's education, they prioritise sons' education because the labour market returns are not gender-equal (Akkoyunlu-Wigley and Wigley 2008; Smits and Gunduz-Hosgor 2006; Tansel 2002). To achieve gender parity in educational participation, national and international donors (such as the World Bank funds from 1997 to 2007, and the EU funds since 1999) and schooling campaigns[13] are in operation with the aim of elevating provision and deconstructing the widespread practice of the non-schooling of girls. Much of these efforts have been directed towards building more schools, renovating classrooms and distributing monetary funds, which has brought some increase in girls' primary education and enrolment rates[14] (McClure 2014). However, it should be noted that these enrolment rates can be deceiving, as there is little tracking of whether girls continue schooling once they have been enrolled, and many girls in the East and South-Eastern Anatolia are likely to drop out (Cin and Walker 2016). Redressing such equality may lie in the sensitive handling of families' concerns, in transformation of traditional gender role attitudes, and in improving the status of women, such as promoting educated women as role models, decreasing illiteracy among women and increasing women's employment.

Problems with Curriculum and Education System

An important aspect of (gender) inequality in education arises from the gendered and anti-human rights curriculum. The Turkish educational system underwent certain amendments in November 2005 to comply with EU directives. The changes introduced mainly concerned pedagogy, building a constructivist, student-centred and computer-based approach to learning; very few of these changes, however, addressed gender- and identity-based discrimination, sexist implications and teachings in textbooks, or the diversity of the ethnicities in Turkey (Tan 2005). Research in curriculum studies (Esen 2007; Sayilan 2008) and human rights concepts in textbooks (Cayir 2011; Cayir and Bagli 2011; Cayir 2015) show that there is little opportunity for expression of individual identity, freedom of thought and critical thinking surrounding the broader concept of equality between boys and girls or among ethnicities other than Turkish. There are also sexist stereotypes depicting women as passive, emotional and dependent in textbooks, and the trends of praising war and death and creating prejudice against some social groups and minorities (such as non-Muslims,

Greeks and Armenians). Additionally, some researchers (Ceylan and Irzik 2004; Kaya 2009; Kirdar 2009; McClure 2011) point out discriminatory practices towards certain ethnicities, such as mandating Turkish as the official educational language in Kurdish-populated areas, where some students cannot speak Turkish, thereby ignoring Kurdish existence and identity. Their research calls for references to Kurdish identity in books to promote a peaceable environment and to create inclusiveness in society.

By and large, the governments in Turkey (whether it is Kemalist, nationalist or conservative) have always used textbook and curriculum in the construction of gender identities, subjectivities and social meanings which directly or indirectly support the reproduction of patriarchal power relations and the official ideologies of the state. So, researchers working on issues of equality in education in Turkey place an emphasis on empowerment of (Kurdish) students, equal inclusion of cultural differences, and devising an education structure to promote the culture of democracy and gender equality.

Teachers

The third dimension of gender asymmetry in equality and education focuses on the insufficient number of teachers in economically deprived regions and culturally conservative districts such as Eastern or Southeastern Anatolia, the under-representation of female teachers in decision-making, and gendered classroom practices.

Female teachers constitute more than half of the teacher population in Turkey (KSGM 2012). Despite the high number of female teachers, the number of women teachers in rural or less developed areas, where girls' schooling practices are irregular and low, is insufficient and keeps girls' schooling at a low level (KSGM 2012; Tan 2000). Although very few research in Turkey (Cin and Walker 2016) address the particular importance of female teachers in these areas and how it can contribute to improving girls' schooling experience, broader literature on gender and girls' schooling (Kirk 2006; Raynor and Unterhalter 2008; Stacki 2002) highlights that the lack of female teachers in such regions maintains gendered relations and power structures both inside and outside the school, and thus opens little space for gender equality. Therefore, the particular presence of female teachers in these areas could increase the rate of girls' schooling because female teachers would be considered as role models, and would more likely be sensitive to gendered views. Families would feel more secure sending their daughters to schools where they are taught by women.

Recently, a growing amount of research has focussed on the under-representation of women in managerial positions in education (Altinkurt and Yilmaz 2012; Inandi 2009; Sanal 2008; Sumer 2006). This research points out that the relatively small number of women in administration positions (e.g. school directors or the upper directors of national education) reproduces the gendered structure of family and society within schools and shapes students' perception of gender aligning with traditional roles. Research looking into the inequality of opportunities in these positions (Aktas 2007; Celikten 2005; Inandi 2009; Sanal 2008) argues that the invisibility of women in such posts is an outcome of patriarchal values favouring men as leaders; societal prejudices against women's capabilities as leadership figures; and the tiring nature of the job, given women's double burden. This problem can be related to an education system or an upbringing in which female students are taught to be passive individuals, enforcing the perception that they are unfit or lack the adequate traits to succeed in male-dominated professions (Celikten 2005).

Another debate concerning teachers and gender equality in Turkey focuses on gender-based learning environments. On the basis of research (Akhun et al. 2000; Tan 2000; Koca 2004) investigating gender roles in education and teachers' manners at school, male-biased manners are found to be preventing the full participation of girls in learning environments. These attitudes include favouring boys in science classes, neglecting female students or giving more opportunities to boys to express themselves. The ethnographic research of Özkazanç and Sayilan (2008) on students' experiences at schools shows that educational practices, from the process of establishing authority and discipline to educational discourse, are shaped by gender. Social control is prominent and ensured through presenting different socialisation patterns to girls and boys, so that girls are exposed to more control over their clothes and manners, and disobedience is not tolerated, whereas boys' aggressive behaviours are more readily tolerated by legitimising the discourse of 'hot bloodedness' (delikanlılık).[15] Such double-sided treatment creates sexist discourse and produce socialisation patterns of gender. On the other hand, limited research (Sari 2012) exploring the effects of the gender roles of women teachers on their teaching practices in Turkey shows that being a female teacher has its positive aspects in understanding students' needs and establishing better communication emerging from 'mothering'. However, on the other side of the coin, it also brings diminished authority in the class due to the constructed image of women in family and society as having no power and authority.

Analytically speaking, teachers could play an important role in creating and reproducing inequalities at school and in a classroom environment through teaching practices or discriminatory attitudes. At the same time, they are also the ones who could work towards gender equality and change inequitable social system and institutions.

With its current content and form, the Turkish education system reproduces a patriarchal ideology and aims to educate the individual to adhere to moral and traditional values and customs with many agnostic and prejudicial attitudes attached to religious and ethnic minorities. In addition, little research has been conducted on whether the education women received in the past as well as the present day has given them the opportunity to be who they want to be or pursue what they value doing in their lives. Particularly, no research has been carried out on how women teachers could play an important role in improving quality and equality in education, and be an important ally in working towards gender equality and girls and women's development. This research aims to fill in this gap in the literature by looking into their own educational and professional lives and experiences.

CONCLUSION

This chapter offered a brief political context, women's movement history and educational issues covering the lifetimes of the women teachers who participated in this study. Despite a slow progressive positive change since the Republican times, Turkey still needs substantial reforms, changes, and actions to establish gender justice at all levels (from civil society to education): the Kurdish question in the political platform, the neo-conservative understanding in approach to women's issues, and human capital perspective and lack of gender/ethnic-sensitive approach dominating in education appear as the primary obstacles in promoting social/gender justice in a diverse society.

Focusing on the lives of educated women, I aim to illuminate to what extent they have experienced gender justice in terms of achieving their valued capability sets in their everyday lives (e.g. childhood, educational lives and marriage). At the same time, I also seek to address to what extent the education these women have received has enabled them to do and to be what they value, and to what extent they have been able to distribute gender justice through education. The next chapter briefly presents lives of women explored in this study.

NOTES

1. The word *Kemalism* refers to the new nation-building state ideology. It is used to refer to the modern and progressive reforms and principles Ataturk introduced as the founding ideas of the Turkish Republic (Arat 1994b).
2. Ezan is the call to prayers in Islam.
3. See Kasaba (2008) for further information on 1970s leftist movements and political atmosphere in Turkey.
4. Kurds are a Muslim ethnic group in Turkey.
5. PKK is designated as Foreign Terrorist Organization by the US State Department, the UK Home Office and EU Common Foreign and Security Policy.
6. In the context of the Turkish constitution, secularism means the separation of religion and state. Turkey advocates that a secular nation should be free of religious interference and should keep equal distance from every religion. Through secularism, Turkey aims to avoid any dominant religion that could oppress other religions in a co-existing society. See Azak (2010) for debates on secularism and religion in Turkey.
7. See Çaha (2013) for women's movement both in right- and left-wing movements, including Kurdish women's movements.
8. See Dedeoglu (2012), Ilkkaracan (2012), Bugra (2013) and Arat (2010b), for how conservatism rose in Turkey, particularly during the last decade with the election of the JDP.
9. Brown (2006: 697) defines neo-conservatism in as the 'state, including law, with the task of setting the moral-religious compass for society, and indeed for the world.' Acar and Altunok (2013) and Bugra (2013) use the term neo-conservatism in the Turkish context for the religion-inspired and patriarchal value system that the JDP presents and promotes.
10. Neo-liberalism started in the early 1980s. Some research has already shown that neo-liberal policies from 1980 to today brought process of feminisation of poverty in Turkey (Gokovali 2013), and declining female participation in labour markets (Ilkkaracan 2012; Öneş et al. 2012) and participation of women in informal sectors with low wages (Ecevit 2003; Gunduz-Hosgor and Smits 2008).
11. There were only four universities during the Republican era, two in Istanbul and two in Ankara. Even at the university level, there were no schools of education but medicine, engineering and law schools (TUIK 2012).

12. EFA was initiated by UNESCO in 1990 to promote education as a human right and to improve the quality of education across the world.

13. These projects are carried out in collaboration with the Turkish government, NGOs and the UN, some of which include 'Let's go to school, girls', 'Raising women', 'Father, send me to school', and 'I have a daughter in Anatolia, she will be a teacher'. See the Education for All Global Monitoring Report 2008 for Turkey by Batuhan (2007) for further information.

14. The first phase of World Bank funding project extended from 1998 to 2002 and the World Bank loaned Turkey $300 million. The net enrolment ratio for eight-year basic education increased from 85.6% in 1997 to 96.6% in 2001. In rural areas, girls' enrolment in Grade 6 increased by 162% (World Bank 2002). This progress encouraged the World Bank to fund a second phase (2002–2007), again with a budget of $300 million. This helped to increase the net enrolment rate for pre-primary education from 11% in 2002 to 25% in 2007 (World Bank 2002 in McClure 2014: 484).

15. Delikanlılık is a term used to describe the period of puberty for boys and entails the aggressiveness and disobedience displayed by boys in this phase.

CHAPTER 4

The Women and Their Micro-Contexts

REPUBLICAN WOMEN (THE FIRST GENERATION OF WOMEN)

The three women, Arzu, Berrin and Canan constitute the first generation of participants. They were all born between 1925 and 1932 to Ottoman Turkish parents who lived through World War I (1914–1918) and the Liberation War (1919–1922), and spent their lives in poverty as a result of enduring so many years of war. Therefore, like the majority of society, these women were raised under difficult financial circumstances. They were subjected to persisting patriarchal beliefs and norms, as their rights and status within the society dated from the Ottoman Islamic cultural heritage. This meant they grew up experiencing poverty at a time of nation-building, and were involved in this process as adults when they became primary school teachers. These women believed themselves to have represented the modern facets of Kemalist ideology of the Republican era and each described herself as a 'Republican women'. Their narrations collectively represent a generation of women who sacrificed much for the Turkish nation-building project, who acted both as resistors and as conformists to social scripts, and who were dedicated (nationalist) teachers and cornerstones for change towards women's emancipation.

Their early years of teaching experience were marked by the achievements of spreading Kemalism, modernising nation, and raising up of nationalist and modern youth. Their subsequent careers, however, were

© The Editor(s) (if applicable) and The Author(s) 2017
F.M. Cin, *Gender Justice, Education and Equality*, Palgrave Studies in Gender and Education, DOI 10.1007/978-3-319-39104-5_4

also marked by the bitterness of 1970s political polarisation, military coups, attacks and political discrimination; all of which combined to prompt these women to retire at an early age in 1978, 1979 and 1980, respectively. Still, they expressed pride in being the first qualified (female) teachers of the newly founded Republic, and in taking part in the nation-building process as educators and leaders of the society. I outline the life of each of the three 'Republican women' below.

Arzu was born in 1925 to a farmer father and a housewife mother. She was the eldest of three girls. Her father died when she was aged nine, and her mother became a widow and felt obliged to remarry, to freely regain acceptance and a place in society. Arzu was then raised by her stepfather. After primary school, she was forced to take a two-year break because her stepfather was against her schooling and her family was too poor to meet her schooling expenses. With the help of her aunt, she got enrolled in the village institute in 1939 in order to become a teacher. She qualified as a primary school teacher in 1944. In 1944 she married her husband, who was a classmate and also a teacher, and they worked together in different villages of Western Turkey. After having worked for 35 years, she retired in 1979 at the age of 54. She has two children.

Berrin was born in 1932 to a farmer father and a housewife mother. There were five siblings, four girls and one boy. She describes her father as enlightened and Kemalist. She claims that her brother, as the only son, was privileged in the family, but her father supported the schooling and education of his daughters despite the challenges in the neighbourhood. After primary school (1939–1943), Berrin enrolled at the village institute in 1943 and qualified as a primary school teacher in 1948. She met her husband, who was a colleague in one of her first positions, and married in 1950. They worked together in various villages in Western Turkey. She retired in 1980 after completing her 32 years of service. She has two children.

Canan was born in 1928. Her father was a shoemaker and her mother was doing casual work as a cleaner at school to contribute to the family income. She has one brother and two sisters. Her brother was privileged due to being a boy, but her father was a Kemalist and progressive man who supported his daughters' education despite the neighbourhood pressure on the family not to send their daughters to school. After primary school (1935–1940), she attended a village institute and qualified as a primary school teacher in 1945. In 1947, she married her husband, who was a classmate and also a teacher. They taught in rural villages of Western Turkey. After 33 years of service, she retired in 1978. She has three children.

The life histories of these women have commonalities in that they started their lives with limited economic and social opportunities. They were enlightened modern and role model women figures of the new Republic. As primary school teachers, they forged a respectable life for themselves and society and were committed to community education and working for social transformation.

AMAZON WOMEN (THE SECOND GENERATION OF WOMEN)

The second generation of participants are Irem, Hatice, Meltem, Nesli, Oya and Sinem. They were born between 1954 and 1962, into an era of political instability which was followed by coups in 1961 and 1980. Materially, these women had relatively comfortable lives compared to the previous generation, and were raised in urban areas; yet patriarchal beliefs about women and local neighbourhood control dictating appropriate behaviour for boys and girls were persistent. Their educational lives, particularly the high school and university years, were situated in a time of widespread politicisation of students in the 1970s, an era of mass movements (particularly student movements). Since the establishment of Turkey and Republican times, these women constituted the first activist generation of Turkey. Each women has a story of how she became a part of this activist or resistance movement. Thus, this generation of women's struggle and agency in creating their own lives, revolting against hierarchy, patriarchy, and declaring their resistance, inspired me to name them 'Amazon women'.

These women were teachers of a range of subjects. Their early professional experiences took place at a time when new collective identities such as fundamentalists and Kurdish nationalists had emerged. Some of these women were sent to complete their 'hardship' posts in Eastern and South-eastern Anatolia. There, they faced attacks from Kurdish militants; oppression from the conservative community on account of their lifestyles; gender- and ethnic-based discrimination in Kurdish-populated regions; and infrastructural difficulties in villages. Others, meanwhile, completed their hardship posts in Western Turkey and Central Anatolia, where they usually suffered from the effects of conservative community structures and lack of infrastructure. Upon completion of their hardship posts, their subsequent careers were spent in Western Turkey. At the time of the interviews, except for Nesli, all were still working as teachers.

Irem was born in 1955 to a teacher father and a housewife mother. She has one brother. Her family supported her education. She was encouraged by her family to study education and she enrolled at a social sciences teaching department at a university in her hometown. During her university years (1974–1978), she engaged in demonstrations, political acts and strikes. She was detained many times by the police and exposed to police violence. After having studied four years, she qualified as a social science teacher in 1978. To complete her 'hardship' post, she was sent to Central Anatolia, Eastern Anatolia and the Black Sea regions, where she was under the pressure of a conservative neighbourhood to practise Islam and faced social exclusion in Kurdish villages. She is one of the two women who worked as a principal in this generation. She was a principal for a period of three years (1983–1986) in Eastern Anatolia. Irem is a feminist and an activist women. She is single and never married.

Hatice was born in 1954 to a father who was running a small family business and to a housewife mother. She has five brothers. Her parents were very supportive of her education. She studied Turkish language and education at a university in her hometown due to the unaffordable costs of sending a student to another city during those times. During her university years (1972–1978), she was a frontline activist, pioneering and organising many demonstrations. Therefore, she was detained and was banned from university for six months. She continued her education after she had appealed against the decision to ban her. When she qualified as a Turkish teacher in 1978, she was sent to various rural places in Central Anatolia, where she was excluded by the local people for being a western-educated women and having a modern outlook. She met her husband who was her colleague and a maths teacher at the same school, and they married in 1981. She is a feminist, an activist and an organiser of trade union events for teachers' demonstrations and protests, which aim to better the quality of life of teachers nationwide. She has two children.

Meltem was born in 1960 to a father who had a small business, and a housewife mother. She has one brother. Her parents supported her to further her studies. Meltem was the only women in this generation who, as a girl, resisted against gender-based restrictions in her natal family, such as complying with behaviour and dress code considered appropriate for girls.

She studied Turkish language and literature. Although she took a strong political stance during her high school (1976–1979) and university years (1979–1983), she stepped back from politics with the 1980 coup for fear of reprisal. When she graduated in 1983, she was sent to complete her hardship post in South-eastern Anatolia, to a Kurdish-populated town. Here she experienced discrimination and sexual harassment, and survived three armed attacks by Kurdish militants. Meltem is a feminist and politically active women. She is single and never married.

Nesli was born in 1955 to a father who was running a small business and a housewife mother. She has one brother and one sister. Her father had a deep respect and admiration for teachers and he allowed her to further her studies on the one condition that she would become a teacher. After completing primary school in 1967, she was accepted to teacher training college where she studied for six years and qualified as a primary school teacher in 1973. Then, she decided to go to university to specialise in art teaching. During her university years (1974–1978), she was actively engaged in political acts and demonstrations. Having completed her degree in 1978, she was sent to a Kurdish-populated town in South-eastern Anatolia for her hardship post where she was exposed to violence from her students, as well as gender- and ethnicity-based discrimination from society. She returned back to Western Turkey in 1982 and had an arranged marriage in 1983. She is married to a civil engineer. She is not a feminist, yet has feminist aspirations which she tried to convey to her students and her children. She is politically active. Although she was retired at the time of the interview, she was still joining in demonstrations for the employee rights of teachers. She has two children.

Oya was born in 1960 to a teacher father and a housewife mother. There were five siblings; four girls and one boy. Her parents were supportive of her education. She studied at a history teaching department in her hometown. During her university years, she joined in many political demonstrations and protests (1977–1982). She qualified as a history teacher in 1982, and was sent to small rural villages in the Western Turkey to complete her hardship post. While there she suffered from a lack of basic infrastructure, and from the conservative attitudes of people towards her, such as trying to set her up with the gentlemen of the villages. At the same time, she started her master's degree in the history teaching department in 1982 and graduated in 1985. In 1985 she married her classmate who is a lecturer at the history department. She is a feminist and also an activist, and regularly joins in demonstrations and strikes to improve the working conditions of teachers. She has two children.

Sinem was born in 1957 to a father who was running a small business and a housewife mother. She has one brother and a sister. Her family did not support her education initially, but when they realised how successful and enthusiastic she was, they supported her in becoming a teacher. She studied art teaching at a university in her hometown. During her university years (1975–1979), she was not keen on expressing her political stance explicitly by demonstrations and by involving herself in armed acts. Still, she joined in some demonstrations. When she graduated in 1979, she was sent to a village in Central Anatolia for her hardship post. She came back to the west in 1981 and married her boyfriend who she had met at the university. He is a maths teacher. Sinem is a feminist and tries to convey feminist understandings to her students. She had worked as a principal for a period of three years, with intervals in Western Turkey. She was working as a vice-principal at the time of the interview. She is also an activist and regularly takes part in strikes to improve conditions for teachers. She has two children.

These women's life histories offer commonalities in the way that they were influenced by the collective moments of the 1970s, during which they were politically active agents as university students. Their early career lives illustrate a picture of hard times, facing gender/ethnic discrimination for being a women and Turkish, and suffering from a lack of infrastructural developments. Their subsequent careers would appear to be more comfortable, but have also involved struggles to improve their working conditions and quality of life as teachers.

Postmodern Women (The Third Generation of Women)

The third generation were born between 1976 and 1985: Aycan, Banu, Meryem, Seda, Tuba and Fisun. Like previous generations, they were raised in an environment where neighbourhood control and pressure was persistent in the production of gender roles, and on restriction of their freedom and actions. Yet, on the other hand, they did not experience the poverty of the first generation of women, and compared to the previous generations, they were more able to take education for granted. At the same time, this generation was born into an era of rapid globalisation, communication, technology and media, so that they are the first generation to have been socialised in a Turkey that is internationally and globally open.[1] These women were not as politically active as the previous generation. They have not experienced coups and blood feuds, and were raised in an apolitical environment brought about after the 1980 military intervention. Unlike previous generations, being able to teach in public schools and finding a job as a teacher was much more challenging. Some of these women were also sent to eastern and south-eastern regions to complete their hardship posts, where, just like the Amazon women, they have faced gender and ethnic discrimination, as well as resistance from the Kurdish-populated villages, while simultaneously being exposed to religious pressure from a conservative sector of the society. Some were sent to villages of Western Turkey where the conservative fabric of society was restrictive of their freedoms and their life in general.

Unlike the Republican or Amazon women, the narratives of this generation, as young women teachers of Turkey, do not reflect a collective picture of nation-building or activism. Perhaps they are too young to look back and see collective patterns in their lives because their narratives are complex and individual with little holding them together in comparison to previous generations. Therefore, I was inspired to label these as 'Postmodern women'.

Aycan was born to a father who was self-employed and a housewife mother in 1979. She has one sister. She studied primary school teaching (1997–2002). Upon graduating in 2002, she was sent to a Kurdish-populated village in Eastern Anatolia to complete her compulsory service. While there, she was socially excluded from the community for being an educated Western Turkish women, faced gender-based discrimination from her principal and the locals, and was exposed to sexual harassment many times in addition to difficulties arising from insufficient infrastructural development. She came back to Western Turkey in 2008. She is an activist teacher who is a member of a trade union and regularly joins in strikes to better teachers' employee rights. She is also a feminist but not a feminist activist. She is single.

Banu was born in 1975 to a father who was running a small business and a housewife mother. She has one sister and a brother. Her parents were very supportive of her education. She studied physics education (1993–

1997) in a city far from her hometown. When she graduated in 1997, she had to take the centralised exam three times to get an adequate score to become a teacher. After three and a half years, she was appointed as a teacher and meanwhile worked as a substitute teacher in her hometown. In 2001–2008 she was sent to a Kurdish-populated village in Eastern Anatolia for her compulsory service as a primary school teacher (this was the only option available to her as there was no need for a physics teacher in a secondary school). There, like most of her peers, she was exposed to ethnic and gender discrimination and faced problems arising from deficient infrastructure. In 2008 she came back to Western Turkey and got married in the same year to a teacher like herself. However, a year later in 2009, she got divorced.

Meryem was born in 1985 to teacher parents. She has one brother. Her parents were very supportive of her education. She studied pre-school teaching (2004–2008) in a university far from her hometown. She graduated in 2008 and was sent to work in a very small village in the Western Turkey to complete her hardship post, where she suffered from sexual harassment and religious pressure. She worked there for two years and was sent to another village as part of her hardship post. At the time of the interview, she was still working in that village. She is single.

Seda was born to a father who was running a small business and a housewife mother in 1984. Her parents have always supported her education. In 2002, she started to study information technologies and computer education at university in a big city far away from home. In 2006 she graduated and was sent to work in a village in Western Turkey, where she experienced neighbourhood pressure because she was a single, educated, unveiled and economically independent women. A year after she started working, she began her master's degree for professional development. At the time of the interview, she was still doing her master's degree and working at a high school (as a computer teacher) in the same region to complete her hardship post.

Fisun was born to a doctor father and a teacher mother in 1984. Although she was born and raised in the Aegean Region, she had to spend two years of her life in Eastern Anatolia because of her father's hardship post as a doctor. Her parents supported her education. She studied science teaching (2002–2006) in another city close to her hometown. Upon graduating in 2006, she was sent to a Kurdish-populated town in Eastern Anatolia for her hardship post, where she faced gender and ethnic discrimination from the locals and her Kurdish colleagues as well as a lack of basic infrastructural development. When she came back to Western Turkey upon completing her hardship post in 2008, she married her boyfriend whom she had met at the university. In 2009, she started her master's degree for professional development and at the time of the interview she was still continuing her degree and working as a science teacher at primary school. She has no children.

Tuba was born in 1976 to a father who was running a small business and a housewife mother. She has two sisters. She had parents who supported her education. She studied physics education (1994–1999) in a distant city out of her hometown. Upon graduating, she had an arranged marriage in 2000. Meanwhile, she waited two and a half years to be appointed as a teacher. She was finally sent to Eastern Anatolia in 2002, to a town on the border of Iraq, as a primary school teacher (because this was the position available there). She worked there for two years and experienced gender-based discrimination for being an educated, Western Turkish women; she also came across some difficulties related to infrastructural issues. Having completed her hardship post in 2004, she returned to Western Turkey. At the time of the interview she was still working as a primary school teacher in a small Kurdish- and Roma-populated village in Western Turkey. She has two children.

These women's short life histories display the commonalities of having family support to further their education in any town or university, and having concerns for the future in not being able to find a job in the current socio-economic conditions of Turkey. These women also reported having experienced gender and ethnic discrimination from the locals, Kurdish people or colleagues, as well as facing difficulties related to limited or no infrastructure in their early professional lives. However, no uniform picture emerges from their narrations, but instead fragmented stories of their lives, concerns and experiences emerge, which I will illustrate in detail in Chaps. 5, 6 and 7.

DATA COLLECTION PROCESS

I conducted semi-structured life history interviews with women. Considering the comprehensive and detailed nature of a life history and the involvement of a small number of research participants in life history research (Goodson and Sikes 2001), I had 15 (three in the first group, six in the second group and six in the third group) women's narratives. The purpose of working with 15 women was to allow comparisons across generations of teachers. It was not intended to be exhaustive but rather to provide an understanding of at least some women teachers' lives in Turkey. Additionally, the complexities of the analytical process necessitated working with a small number of life histories. Working with too many life histories or a more crowded data set would erode details and nuanced differences.

All participants have worked in either primary (6–14 years) or secondary (14–18 years) level education. They all have completed their hardship posts. The underlying agenda in hardship posts is to ensure that there are enough teachers, doctors and police/soldiers for facilities of education, health and security in underdeveloped regions. This is because there is a huge cultural difference between the eastern and western parts of Turkey as a result of these parts being situated in between two cultures (Europe and the Middle East). Therefore, different traditions, cultural values and lifestyles can be traced from West to East. The western parts are modern and economically wealthy, whereas Eastern Turkey is economically less developed, more rural and more traditional.

Since Republican times, teachers working at state schools must complete a certain number of years of their initial teaching experiences in any part of Turkey classified as 'hardship posts'. Due to the lack of schools in Eastern Turkey and the inadequate number of teachers during this period, the Republican generation of women completed their compulsory services in the poor villages of Western Turkey for around 25 years. Today, there are still many provinces in Western Turkey counting as hardship posts. However, a great majority of hardship posts are in Eastern and Southeastern Anatolia towns or villages, as these provinces have historically been less developed because the state allocated funding for investment in Western Turkey. The separatist activities of Kurdish militants, economic decline, socio-economic deprivation, unemployment and geographical dispersion also mark these regions as hardship posts (Sahin and Gulmez 2000). Eastern Turkey has different (dominating) ethnic origin, culture and economic development than the other regions. The locals are mainly of Kurdish origin and speak mostly Kurdish among themselves and in households. Turkish is a second language only used in public institutions. Interviewing teachers who served in such areas sheds light on the contributions that teachers can make to society and the power they have to change lives through education. Their work for community, gender equality, students or society can be best illustrated and teased out through their work in hardship posts.

Ethical Considerations

At all times the ethical principles followed in this research respected the women's stories. The women's willingness to participate was secured in the following way: Each was informed about the process, assured of confidentiality, and asked whether she had a problem with the time and effort involved. They were sent a document of informed consent, which they read and signed. The women in this study were also free to withdraw at any point and could ask me to stop the recorder during our conversation. None of the participants elected to do so.

After completing my interviews, I began transcribing them. Interviews were conducted in Turkish. I thus translated the transcriptions into English. I was aware that the issue of translation across languages cannot be ignored in qualitative research, particularly in research studies like mine, where the data are collected in a language other than the language of research. This raises the concern of whether translation can still transmit the meaning of source data or ensure that translation is correct and free of bias. To avoid this dilemma, I conducted back translation to ensure agreement between the original text and its translation. As both the researcher and translator, I had the opportunity to closely engage with cross-cultural meanings, interpretations and meaning equivalence within the research process.

Data Analysis

I used deductive and inductive thematic analysis, as it is theoretically flexible to analyse qualitative data (Boyatzis 1998; Braun and Clarke 2006). This method identifies, analyses and reports themes in detail within data. First, I used inductive analysis, which means I coded the data without trying to fit it into my theoretical framework or analytical conceptions. The reason why I did it was not to restrain the data. I wanted to increase the scope and possibilities of themes that could emerge from the data (Braun and Clarke 2006). This process provided me with many themes (related to gender, inequality, freedoms and education such as sexual harassment, gendered division of labour, gender/ethnic discrimination, gendered attitudes towards learning, community education, girls' education importance of education and limited social relations). Then, I went through a deductive analysis of identifying themes that are developed based on the theory. This means the process of eliciting the themes emerged from the inductive analysis relating to my list of capabilities and considering how different themes can fit into my five-dimensional capability list (e.g. being exposed to sexual harassment would be related as failing to achieve physical capability). This process helped me to draw from overall data to a more detailed analysis of data driven by my theoretical and analytic interest (Braun and Clarke 2006). Then, for each individual theme, I wrote an analysis identifying the story the theme tells and thinking carefully about how it illuminated the overall research question and contributed to explaining the gender justice thread across the thesis. In doing so, I also conducted my thematic analysis within a feminist epistemological framework and sought to theorise the socio-cultural, economic and political context or structural conditions that enable the individual experiences. For instance, if a participant talked about sexual harassment, I also noted the conversion factors causing this, which may be resulting from conservatism or gender discrimination or as a form of social exclusion.

After this, I was engaged in writing an analytic narrative that could address the gender justice argument in my research question. For this process I chose extracts that could capture the essence of the themes I was aiming to demonstrate with a succinct and clear account. In doing so, I was engaging with a semantic level of analysis and asking myself, 'What are the implications of this theme?' or, 'What does this theme illustrate in terms of gender justice or capabilities?'

In organising my analysis, I followed the life-trajectory sequence of childhood years, schooling period, marriage/personal life and professional life. Under each of these categorisations, I placed my themes with the capability set they match. When I finished this process, I realised that some aspects of life-trajectories such as family, including marriage, limited women's opportunities and freedoms and reproduced gender inequalities; whereas schooling and professional career opened space for more opportunities, freedoms and display of agency. For instance, the early context of childhood, in which I focused on upbringing, is important for understanding how women face the first gender inequalities through inequality of opportunities at home. On the other hand, their schooling and education was important for its liberating influence on women's lives. Schools were places where gender relations and their fallible interpretations of how they see values were contested. This helped me to pin down my analysis to three broad contradictory categories: personal lives (private sphere), experiences of education and schooling and professional lives. To better illustrate and highlight the continuities and nuanced differences across the generations, I discussed three generations of women's narratives one by one. Each life course holds specific importance in women's lives and plays an important role in shaping them.

CONCLUSION

This chapter has briefly introduced and familiarised the reader with the women whose life histories are presented in the book, and contextualised their educational stories with their familial and professional backgrounds, and then discussed some methodological issues regarding ethics and data collection and analysis. The next chapters will focus analytically on women's lives, revealing their capability formation, gender inequalities they faced, as well as their initiatives for social change. It is important to note that no claim is made that the women in each generation speak for all women teachers of their eras or for all women who themselves are culturally, socially, regionally and ethnically diverse. Especially, these women's lives do not speak for women from eastern parts of Turkey. This is not to say that they have nothing to say beyond these lives. Their narratives paint diverse pictures through their personal, professional and historical contexts over three different generations. The life histories may serve to 'illuminate the complexities for these women of living at the intersections of history, context, culture, and region, all permeated by gendered continuities over generations' (Cin and Walker 2013: 395). Their answers are partial, historically situated and contextual, but nonetheless make a significant contribution to public reasoning about women's capabilities in a complex country.

NOTE

1. As such, this generation can also be appropriately labelled the first 'globalisation generation' of Turkey (Lukuslu 2005: 33).

CHAPTER 5

Exploring Gender Inequalities in Personal Spaces and Private Sphere

INTRODUCTION

The women's narrations in this chapter reveal how family dynamics allowed or restricted opportunities and freedoms in natal family and marriage, and what kind of inequalities or patterns of negotiations the women faced in their personal space. The chapter has two sections. The first section focuses on women's personal lives in their natal families, upbringing and family relations. The second section looks at women's marriages and, for the unmarried women, it investigates their perceptions and expectations of marriage. Drawing from the list of capabilities (physical, social, intellectual, economic, and political) developed for this particular study and Amartya Sen's work on agency, I look into women's lives in the private sphere to determine the extent to which women achieve their valued capability sets, what conversion factors play a role in these capabilities and their enactment of agency. My overall findings for this chapter illustrate that the women's inability to achieve their capability sets in the private sphere arises as an issue of gender injustice and inequality of opportunities compared to their male peers, who were not culturally deprived of the same opportunities and freedoms.

© The Editor(s) (if applicable) and The Author(s) 2017   89
F.M. Cin, *Gender Justice, Education and Equality*, Palgrave Studies
in Gender and Education, DOI 10.1007/978-3-319-39104-5_5

PERSONAL LIVES: BEING BORN FEMALE

This section discusses how gender was (re)produced and articulated within the natal families and expanded space of mahalle[1] (neighbourhood). It focuses on three themes that recurred in the accounts of the women: gendered roles and hierarchy within the household, neighbourhood pressure and expectations, and family attitudes towards girls' education. These themes illustrate what it means to grow up as a girl in Turkish context and shed light on the status of girls within their families and in society. They present subjective experience of how being a female influenced freedoms, opportunities, aspirations and preferences when growing up as girls.

Women's early lives within their families present an understanding of how the gender perceptions and gender norms established by their families started to 'haunt' their lives by setting limits to their freedoms and opportunities at an early age. In the chapters to follow, this will show that entrenched gendered structures and beliefs are hard to challenge and continue to affect women's capabilities and opportunities in different ways, intersecting both with private and public lives.

Gendered Roles and Hierarchy Within the Household

In all three generation of women's lives, household tasks were sex-related, which caused women to take on a great deal of gendered duties, and they had fewer freedoms than their brothers. A generational change was noted in that the role of mothers' decision-making within the household and girls' autonomy in making decisions about their lives increased by generation.

The three women of the Republican generation (Arzu, Berrin and Canan) were born between 1925 and 1932 into nuclear, traditional Turkish families in rural areas, as with the majority of the population.[2] Like the majority of women of their age, their lives were framed within the traditional gendered division of duties and the hierarchy within the household: Girls were expected to help mothers with domestic duties, such as cooking, washing and cleaning. The father was the head of the family, the main income earner, held authority and power over the family members, and made the household decisions, whereas mothers had little voice. There was a clear distinction between girls and boys: boys were valued and desired more, parents took decisions on behalf of girls, and the girls were not able to voice their aspirations. As Berrin notes:

Girls never had rights within the family; parents used to make decisions on their behalf (...) The son was a very important figure. There was a clear discrimination between us (the daughters) and my brother in our family. He used to have the privileges because he was the one who was going to maintain the continuity of the family. Therefore, he was desired more and my father paid more attention to him (...) We, as girls, were only responsible for looking after children and doing household chores (...) It was always my father who would say the last word. My mum was silent and passive. She would not talk much (Berrin, G1[3]).

This configuration in domestic life was a severe limitation both on women's intellectual capability of being able to voice their aspirations and to plan their own lives, which was usual for the majority of women of their era considering that poverty was widespread, and that the social make-up was rural, traditional and patriarchal (White 2003). Thus, for women, there was a pattern of adaptive preferences because of limited opportunities to make their choices, which, at the same time, posed a limitation on the social capability of being treated as a dignified being whose worth was equal to that of their brothers, because boys were prioritised over girls, thus leaving girls little space for their aspirations.

The situation did not change much for the Amazon women. Five of the six second generation of women (Sinem, Irem, Hatice, Oya and Nesli) were born between 1954 and 1962 into traditional families in urban cities. Like the majority of women of their age, these women also had to comply with a gendered division of labour within the household and were pushed to help their mothers with the housework. The gender hierarchy continued: boys were reported to be favoured as they would ensure continuity of lineage, and girls had fewer freedoms than their brothers:

When my mother gave a birth to a son, everyone was blessed with happiness (...) We did not experience the same joy when my sister was born. He had a privileged position at home. He did virtually no housework and had more freedoms than us, such as going out whenever he wanted, spending time with his friends outside the house until late at night (Sinem, G2).

My brother got more attention and privilege than we did (...) He did not have to do the house chores we did at home and he would usually help my father in our shop (...) He was freer than us and would not even have to ask for permission for anything such as going out, playing outside, and going to market (Nesli, G2).

Like the Republican generation, this gender pattern of household tasks and favouritism of boys over girls was a barrier to women's social capabilities of being treated equally without discrimination in the household and enjoying leisure time outside the house as well as the physical capability of being freely mobile. These restrictions indicate that they had lower value. Nevertheless, with the spread of modernisation and urbanisation in society, compared to the Republican generation, these women suggested that their mothers had more voice in decision-making at home, particularly in expressing their desire for their daughters to receive a good education or in changing the final decisions of fathers, which can be interpreted as progress for women in having some control over their lives.

However, one woman from the Amazon generation, Meltem, was not raised in a typical and conventional patriarchal family. She was not expected to shoulder any family responsibilities (even though her paternal grandparents would often intervene with regard to her clothes and attitudes):

> My parents were not restrictive toward me. They did not try to shape me like a traditional girl who helps her mother (…) There was never a difference in the way me and my brother were treated. We had equal opportunities and freedoms. There was a democratic environment in our family. When I had some physical changes in my body, my grandparents started to interfere with my way of talking, dressing, and behaving (…) However, my parents did not oppose or control the pressure coming from my grandparents (…) They remained silent about it as if they approved (Meltem, G2).

Thus, even though she was not brought up with traditional gender codes and enjoyed equal freedom and agency in making decisions regarding her life and the household, to some extent she was exposed to the interference of her grandparents, who were conventional in their opinions about how a girl should act, behave or dress. This could imply that while the majority of families of the 1950s and 1960s were traditional, some families were moving towards a more egalitarian structure.

The third, Postmodern generation, born between 1976 and 1985 in (peripheral) urban areas to nuclear families were also expected to take responsibility for the gendered tasks of housework, and help their mothers. It was made clear by all three women (Aycan, Meryem and Banu) who had brothers that boys continued to have more freedom than girls and did no housework, leaving it entirely to the female members of the household:

When I became an adolescent girl, the gender differences within the household became more visible. My brother continued his life as if nothing happened (…) He could go out whenever he wanted (…) he could visit his friends and I was under surveillance and was expected to help mum (Aycan, G3).

I and my sisters would do all the cleaning and household chores. We were not allowed to go out to play. I do not have a brother, so of course I cannot tell the difference, but I am pretty sure even if we had, this inequality would continue: we would still be doing housework and he would not have any responsibility in these tasks (Tuba, G3).

For the women, the conventional model of the household was one of inequality, leaving the majority of household responsibilities to them and depriving them of the social capability of playing outside with their peers and being treated on an equal basis with their brothers. Despite the continuation of gendered housework responsibilities and the favouritism of boys, mothers shared the decision-making mechanism with fathers equally, and, as girls, they had more agency in expressing their ideas, particularly regarding their education:

My parents were strict on us because we were three girls. However, it was never such that we could not express our ideas. When it comes to education, they valued our choice of school (Tuba, G3).

Things were not always top-down. For instance, at high school, my parents saw that I was a successful student and asked me which school I wanted to attend, and allowed me to go to a good boarding school in another city (…) So when it came to education, I would be involved in decision making (Seda, G3).

Thus, the women's narrations suggest they had enhanced but limited agency and were able to make some decisions about their lives, which signalled changes in an equality-seeking direction in the traditional family structure.

Across the generations, family was an important factor in the formation of gendered expectations regarding the roles, status and freedom of women. There was little change in the patriarchal structure of the family, even though some evidence of change could be seen in gender relations, with a gradual erosion of hierarchy within the household in that mothers and girls gained a greater voice in decision-making and agency. This gradual change across generations may be explained by increasing modernisation within the society, which also increases mothers' educational level. On the other hand, the inequalities experienced by women were caused by intra-household inequalities and traditional gendered norms, which created the structural and relational coercions that limited women's social and intellectual capability sets across the generations; whereas boys were not culturally deprived of any of these opportunities. By and large, these women's narrations suggest that to achieve justice, girls' capabilities require a structural change in traditional Turkish families. However, women's upbringing is shaped not only by the patriarchal family ideology but also by the gendered peripheral neighbourhood space.

Neighbourhood Pressure and Expectations

Neighbourhood expectations and pressures played a significant role in shaping the vision of what it means to be a girl and restricting the women's action and behaviours. The three women of the Republican generation were born and raised at a time when, simultaneously, the influence of rigid Islamic norms from the Ottoman times was still visible in society, and the ongoing modernisation and nation-building process were gradually granting rights to women. Therefore, Islam-based norms were still a substantial barrier to women's progress, particularly for women of this generation in rural areas, because in comparison to their peers in the urban areas they had fewer opportunities to receive an education, to hold jobs and to exist in the public sphere due to the slow introduction of modernisation to these districts (Ozbay 1990). Under the influence of customs driven by Islamic tradition, which controls female sexuality and requires the subjugation of authority to men (Toprak 1990), girls of that time were expected to act and behave in a way that would not break the moral codes or put the family at risk (Kandiyoti 1987). The women's life histories indicated that these norms penetrated to and were enacted in neighbourhood space as 'the extension of the interior space of the family to the residential street' (Mills 2007: 336). This imposed limits on the lives of these women (but not on their brothers) through the creation of expectations about appropriate girl behaviours (i.e. being submissive and obedient), and brought restrictions to their freedoms and opportunities in a wide array of issues, such as schooling, mobility, leisure, gender relations and physical well-being. A stark example of the intrusion of the neighbour-hood was illustrated in the interviews with respect to schooling. Being the first generation of women to go to school, they were harassed or seen as odd for colliding with social norms and expectations:

> My neighbourhood was a bit hostile and oppressive towards the ones who were not like them. When my sister and I were on our journey to school (this was the only time she could go out of the house), the young boys of our neighbourhood would bully us because our parents were sending their daughters to school (…) We did not tell my father anything about this bul-lying but when he saw it, we moved to somewhere else nearby the school (Canan, G1).

> There was a common belief that girls don't need to study. We were raised under this neighbourhood pressure. They kept telling us, 'Girls don't go out! Girls stay at home.' Let alone playing outside with friends, indeed, I could only go out when I had a brother or my father accompanying me. Otherwise, it would be seen as inappropriate and create bad rumours about the girl and the family (Berrin, G1).

These unequal attitudes (in particular with regard to their schooling) towards women constituted a limitation on their physical capability of being mobile and visible in public. Although primary education was compulsory for both women and men at that time, it could be seen that there was not a supportive cultural environment for girls' schooling and the Kemalist reformed achieved little in changing community perception regarding the girls' education. Not complying with socially scripted rules (as Canan and her sister did by going to school) even posed a limitation on their physical capability of being free from violence and harassment.

On the other hand, six of the Amazon women were raised (1950s–1970s) when the nation-building project was completed and the majority of women in urban areas started to enjoy the economic, political and social rights granted to them by the Kemalist state. Their visibility in the pub-lic sphere through being professionals was promoted, whereas the vast majority of women in rural areas were still unaware of or could not access these rights. However, in general throughout this period and beyond, the influence of Islamic norms was still visible: women still occupied a sub-ordinate place to males; they carried out their household activities in the private sphere; female leisure activities within the public sphere were not tolerated. Male superiority was maintained through honour and shame codes[4] (Kandiyoti 1987). Within this socio-cultural context, women in this generation were under neighbourhood and community control and had restrictions on their social and gender relations with little space for leisure and visibility in the social sphere, whereas their male peers were not subjected to such restrictions. These patterns of oppression became more visible and intensified after puberty as the participants made the transition from childhood to womanhood:

> After I had some notable physical changes in my body, I felt that my freedom was over. I stopped playing outside. Relations with male friends stayed within the borders of school. We would even act as if we did not know each other outside school (…) My brother never faced any of these restrictions (Oya, G2).

> Even walking with a male relative of mine would make me uncomfortable because any male next to you outside your family circle would be enough to stigmatise you as 'the girl hanging out with boys' (Nesli, G2).

> The world outside the house, the society, was restricting (…) People try to shape you according to the norms, such as what you wear, how you act, what job you do (…) I was a resilient girl and I did not want to sacrifice my freedoms even for the sake of being excluded. Even if they criticised and excluded me for what I wore at school or in our neighbourhood or how I acted or with whom I socialised, I did what I wanted to (Meltem, G2).

The remarks above illustrate that, like the older generation, the prevailing cultural values and social monitoring were effective in regulating their space outside the household and affecting their physical capability of mobility as well as the social capabilities of having play and leisure time and establishing meaningful relationships with the opposite sex without feeling shame, because, in a society underpinned by Islamic-oriented norms and values, social interaction between an unrelated girl and boy could lead to misinterpretations of love that would give the girl's family a bad reputation. This was so even for Meltem, whose family were less restrictive towards her. No matter how egalitarian the family might be, Meltem's case shows that male culture is more dominant outside the house. Her resistance to the socially scripted imposition shows that she valued some of her capabilities over others. This can be seen as her valuing her agency in being who she could be or doing what she wanted to do, despite being excluded from society.

The six women of the postmodern generation were raised in urban or peripheral urban areas during a time (1980s–1990s) when Turkey started to establish ties with the outer world; when newly introduced neo-liberal policies of the government started to introduce people to new lifestyles, branding, clothing and food chains and rapidly changing technology (Neyzi 2001). Still, the pattern that women in urban areas had greater access to education or gaining occupations than their counterparts in villages and rural districts continued (Kandiyoti 1987). However, the traditional patriarchal social structure of Turkey remained the same, and these women's narrations suggest that they were subjected to a similar kind of neighbourhood pressure as the Amazon women. With puberty, they all gave up playing on the streets with their friends; their interaction with their male friends outside the school was socially condemned in the neighbourhood space; their mobility was restricted from home to school or home to market; they had to dress, act and behave properly; and they were appreciated to the extent they adopted shy and submissive girl behaviours, whereas their brothers or male peers enjoyed a wide range of freedoms:

> With puberty, my socialising with friends was limited to daylight only. During this period, I also started smoking secretly and only when I was out with my friends. However, I could see that people around me were looking at me with reproachful eyes and they stigmatised me as a 'bad girl' for smoking. I started to pay attention to the way I got dressed, the way I behaved, and I stopped smoking in public. This restricted my freedom of movement and turned me into a girl they would want to see. Otherwise, I would be excluded from the community, and my parents would feel sad and embarrassed because of what they heard about me. But if I were a boy, this would not be a concern at all (Seda, G3).

> Even if I went out with my male cousin, I would feel uncomfortable. Unavoidably, you wonder whether you will be misunderstood, whether people will start rumours or whether someone who did not know he was my cousin would misinterpret my intimate jokes with him in another way. So, I had a very self- and society-controlled life and I still do (Meryem, G3).

Yet, not all women were submissive to neighbourhood pressure. By dressing in men's clothes, two women (Fisun and Aycan) confronted the deprivation in freedoms and capabilities and challenged this pressure coming from both family and society. This was indeed a 'performance of femininity', as Butler (1990) calls it. Dressing like or acting like a man, they tried to illustrate that they could have greater freedom and power. However, they re-enacted cultural codes of masculinity and reinforced normative gender perception that masculinity represents the authority and freedom:

> From high school to the last year of my university life, I was dressing like a man. I would wear loose and black pants or a t-shirt and a cap. I think this was a way of protesting against my parents and community when I realised the amount of freedom that men have in society (...) I would have constant arguments with my parents regarding what time I should come home, whom I should see, where I could go (...) And I was supposed to sacrifice my freedom because I am a girl (Fisun, G3).

> Sometimes, at nights, my father would send me to the market. I was only twelve and there would be some drunken guys in the neighbourhood molesting girls. I was afraid that they might harass or rape me. Therefore, I would wear a cap and walk like a boy so that they would not recognise me (...) Since those times, masculinity has become a part of my identity because it makes me feel safe (...) it places a distance between me and men (Aycan, G3).

As these two cases show, adopting masculine attire is done for different reasons. Fisun acted in a masculine way to confront her deficient social capability of socialising and mobility, which created a sense that she felt even stronger than if she had been free. Aycan, on the other hand, adopted it to protect her physical capability of being safe from harassment and violence. This emerges as a resistance stronger than that found in previous generations, which women showed for leading a society-controlled life and having fewer freedoms. Although this confrontation did not necessarily bring much change to their lives, still, it showed that there was room for showing resistance and challenging these norms. This could also be seen as a display of active agency to change some things in their lives. Despite the traditional gender role system both within the family and in the wider community, girls' education was positively perceived and supported by most families and the next section explores family attitudes towards women's education.

Family Attitudes Towards Girls' Education: Breaking the Glass-Ceiling to Access to Schooling and Education

The positive attitudes of families towards girls' education was a key to developing their capabilities. A common trend across the generations was that the majority of families supported their daughters' education. Considering the socio-cultural and economical make-up of the 1930s, particularly for the first generation, such support could be categorised as exceptional. According to the women interviewed, the reason why their families were supportive of their education was that they regarded it as a way of securing the girls' economic freedom and future so that they would not lead a poor quality of life. The difference could be seen in the shift across generations towards seeing girls' education from being an indulgence to a necessity.

During the Republican era, Kemalism and the new reforms emphasised the importance of women's education for modernisation. Emphasis was placed upon raising up educated mothers and wives, so that the quality of parental care would improve, and better generations could be raised (Arat 1994c). The ultimate goal was to grant women 'the knowledge and habits that would make the family more hygienic, better and happier' (Maarif Dergisi Rehberi 1933; cited in Arat 1994c). Thus, in the Republican generation (with the exception of Arzu's stepfather), Canan and Berrin's fathers were committed to the principles of Kemalism and gave full support to their daughters' education. They wanted them to benefit from free primary schooling at least, in order to gain literacy and participate in a process that would enhance their quality of life. Considering that in the years these women started schooling, literacy rates were low (see Chap. 3) and the schooling of girls was uncommon because of cultural prohibitions, Berrin and Canan were privileged to have progressive fathers who were literate and modern. On the other hand, some people in the neighbourhood who were more attached to the old Ottoman traditions and values condemned the schooling of girls:

> We had grown up under neighbourhood pressure which allowed almost no rights or choices to women and restricted them to the home. When my father allowed me to continue my education at the village institute after primary school, his friends and relatives found this a very radical decision. They condemned my father for offering me so many freedoms through allowing me to study, but my father was a Kemalist man committed to the principles

of the Republic. He wanted us to study as far as we could and make the most of the skills and knowledge they taught us at school (Canan, G1).

The people of the neighbourhood found it odd when my father sent all his four daughters to school. They even told him that educating girls was not a good idea. Thank God my father was an enlightened man who was committed to the modern principles of the newly founded Republic. He always wanted his daughters to be educated and not be illiterate. He wanted us at least to know how to read and write and have some basic knowledge about our country (Berrin, G1).

The interviews reflected the reality of the socio-cultural situation. Although access to primary schools was mandatory for all children, it should be noted that in 1935, only 14% of villages had schools (Ozbay 1985; cited in Rankin and Aytac 2006). The secondary and high school numbers were even more limited; educational services were concentrated in urban areas (especially in large cities), a situation which required most families to send their children to other cities. In such a context, fathers valued education as a means to develop their daughters' intellectual capability of gaining literacy and basic life skills, and of widening their horizons of learning about the country so that such knowledge and capabilities could help girls develop new capabilities leading to better life conditions.

Arzu's case was more representative of the situation of the girls of her time and reflected the cultural perception towards girls' schooling. Her stepfather was against the schooling of girls but instead was in favour of marrying her when she came of age. Therefore, Arzu had to resist her stepfather in order to study:

My stepfather was a very backward-minded man. I had to confront him to be able to go to school by seeking the support of my aunt, who helped me to register at an institute. When I insisted on going to the institute, he said to me, 'What is the point in girls' education? At the end of the day, you will be married, look after kids, and do housework' (...) I left home and moved to my aunt's house. I told him that I would never return home if he did not sign the required documents for the school. People started to create nasty rumours that I ran away. It hurt his masculinity and challenged his masculine position as a man. Finally, he signed the documents (Arzu, G1).

This perception included ideas that girls do not need any schooling, as they are needed at home for domestic labour and should get married once they have found an eligible husband (Tan 2007). Such attitudes probably constituted a barrier to most women's intellectual capability of being literate and educated at that time and Arzu was lucky to have a support from a relative who created an opportunity for her to receive schooling.

Four women of the Amazon generation (Oya, Hatice, Irem and Meltem) had the full support of their families, and were raised with the awareness that a girl needed to further her education to enter the employment market, to have a safe and proper job, to gain economic independence for a good quality of life (referring to physical and emotional well-being), and to be independent of men in the case of an abusive marriage, divorce or the husband's death:

> My father was well aware of the difficulty of being a woman in Turkey. He wanted me to study so that I could have a decent job and economic independence and enjoy a good quality of life. He did not want me to be dependent on my husband or brothers. He regarded economic freedom as insurance for women in case of divorce or death of the husband (Hatice, G2).

> My sisters and I were made aware that a girl must study. My mother used to tell us that boys can do any jobs but girls need to study to be able to gain a proper job so that they could have economic independence and they would not be dependent on their husbands (Oya, G2).

As indicated by the interviews, girls' education held an instrumental (rather than intrinsic) value for parents, as a means to secure their daughters' future physical capability of having good quality of life (emotionally and physically healthy lives), the economic capability of generating an income and the intellectual capability of being in charge of their lives. Unlike the Republican generation, education was not a luxury but seen as a necessity for girls to be able to secure their capabilities in the future. This shift in the perception of education as a necessity is closely related to the developing economic structure of the 1960s and 1970s in Turkey, which created a demand for education (Gunlu 2008).

On the other hand, in this generation, Nesli and Sinem's fathers did not see education for girls as a necessity. Both of their fathers said that there was no need for them to further their education, but rather that they should work in the family business and get married. Their mothers were in favour of their schooling and were influential in changing the fathers' opinion regarding their daughters' education. Both fathers complied with their pursuing an education as long as they became teachers, because this was perceived to be a highly respectable profession for women:

> My father had a deep respect for teachers. He gave me only one chance: I would either achieve the entrance exams of teacher training college or work in our family business (...) If I qualified for the college, I would be an exemplary case for my sister and my father would also send her to school (...) Both me and my sister became a teacher (Nesli, G2).

> Upon seeing my enthusiasm and success in arts, he supported me to become an art teacher. My mother was also influential in changing his mind (Sinem, G2).

Moving to the postmodern generation, during the 1990s, there was a tremendous change in the opening of the Turkish economy, and the transformation of public life with the development of young urban professionals (Navaro-Yashin 2002). These changes required the expansion of education to survive in a competitive capital market, particularly in urban spaces. Therefore, it was not surprising to find that all participants' parents in the postmodern generation were supportive of their daughters' education. Families valued education for their girls so that they could gain economic independence, lead decent lives free from financial constraint or (male) oppression and be in charge of their lives. Indeed, some families pronounced girls' education to be more important than that of boys and saw it as the only plausible way for a woman to be independent:

> My father always stressed that girls should study to be economically independent. Men can even sell lemons in the bazaar, but, for women, education is a must to earn a life. He also impressed upon me the understanding that, as a woman who has her own economic independence, I would better stand on my own feet and could have a voice in my life (Banu, G3).

> The possibility never existed that I would not study. Education was a must for me. They stressed that as a girl I should study, get a job, gain my economic

freedom, or else I would end up with occasional jobs without insurance and endure life struggles such as financial difficulty. They felt that if I did not have financial freedom, my freedoms would be limited (Fisun, G3).

My parents stressed the importance of education in my life more than my brother. As a girl, they felt that I should definitely study to secure a good quality of life with economic freedom (Meryem, G3).

As the interviews reveal, for families, education meant securing girls' physical capability of leading decent/healthy/good quality lives, the economic capability of generating an income and the intellectual capability of being in charge of their life plan, thus helping them develop their agency freedom to acquire their valued capabilities in the future. To secure these capabilities and agency, education was expressed as a necessity for girls and a key to the development of all other freedoms and opportunities.

To sum up, despite the patriarchal order both in the family and in the neighbourhood, the interviews pointed to a change in the perception of women's education across the generations, with it moving from an indulgence to a necessity. For the first generation, the unaffordable costs of post-primary education in the early Republican era, inadequate numbers of secondary schools, cultural prohibition, diminished value attached to girls and nationwide poverty created the perception of schooling as being something luxurious. Still, for some highly unusual parents, education was there to improve the life quality of girls. The aftermath of the nation-building project brought about some changing dynamics, such as urbanisation, the expansion of girls' schooling, the increase of women in professional work and public sphere and economic development. These changes meant that for majority of Amazon women and all postmodern women, education was associated with ample employment opportunities. It was also linked to enhancing girls' quality of life, economic, physical, intellectual capabilities and their agency freedom. This situation also points out some contradictions when considering that women, as highlighted in the previous sections, held less value and lower status than their brothers, but were afforded priority and received importance in relation to their education. This could be that parents believed education was the only asset that could give girls the necessary resources for them to live in better material conditions.

The findings of the interviews with these women point to two main arguments in relation to gender justice. First, in the Turkish context, the family is not a space for women to cultivate agency or achieve capability sets because little or no opportunity is afforded to them to speak out their aspirations; that is, women's social capabilities of being treated equally without discrimination and their intellectual capabilities concerning the taking of own decisions and shaping their own future were limited by a patriarchal family structure, which does not open them a space of agency freedom. It can be seen across the generations that there is continuity in how family (structure or upbringing) defines the construction of women, whereas men continue to claim more space to assert their rights as individuals. On the other hand, there is also an indication of changes taking place in the family: some cultural practices are fading away, such as the preference for sons, ignoring girls' voices, and the neglect of girls' schooling. These findings concur with those in other research in the Turkish family context (Aycicegi-Dinn and Kagitcibasi 2010; Kagitcibasi 1990; Kagitcibasi and Ataca 2005; Kandiyoti 1990). This change can be explained by increasing modernisation, which brings higher education levels for parents and steady economic growth, and, in turn, justifies increasing familial support for girls' education across the generations, despite the existing gender discrimination at home. Second, it could be argued that neighbourhood monitoring, cultural beliefs and practices restrict freedom and girls' space to manoeuvre their interests, closely monitor their movements, and socialise girls and boys into different worlds, based on inequality of the sexes. In different contexts and times across the generations, neighbourhood pressure was a dominant force producing and regulating gendered social norms, which were applied to women only. It was only girls who had to live up to the expectations of society to be able to live without suffering public humiliation. Therefore, all the women grew up with limited capacity to articulate their capabilities, and had to accept adaptive preferences because of coercive environments and multiple forms of gender inequality. On the other hand, nuanced changes could be seen in the neighbourhood space. With the younger generations, girls' schooling is no longer condemned, and the social visibility of girls is tolerated to the extent that it does not threaten the norms or family reputation. Nonetheless, the constant watching and fault-finding of the surrounding neighbourhood, coupled with gendered family structures, continued.

So certain challenges remain for Turkish society. Family structure and community define women's life options and continue to restrict them. Intra-family roles are basic cultural elements that are most resistant to change. So, a change is needed within the private sphere to bring about more egalitarian society where women are fully able to achieve their valued capability sets, have agency and choose from the range of identities they value. The more penetrating and prevalent such change is, the greater is the accomplishment towards an egalitarian and gender-just society. Having outlined and discussed women's lives in their natal families above, I continue this chapter with another realm of private life: marriage.

Marriage and Personal Spaces

This section examines women's intimate relationships with their husbands to find out about women's intra-family status, power relations in the decision context, and role differentiation between spouses as well as distribution of income, opportunities and freedoms. The nine married women (three Republican, four Amazon and two postmodern) reveal three common strands across the generations. First, there was generally unequal division of labour at home and the majority of women in dual-career households were under more time pressure and more greatly burdened by work than their husbands because social norms allocated them more responsibilities. This configuration, particularly in the second and third generations, did not open up enough space and time for the women to pursue their valued social, physical and intellectual capabilities. Second, none of the women had full control of their own income because they handed their salaries over to their spouses to pool incomes, which curtailed their financial agency. Third, despite these inequities, they all had an equal voice and agency in decision-making in the household.

All six unmarried women (two Amazon, four postmodern) claimed that the traditional Turkish marriage[5] was not egalitarian towards women. Therefore, they preferred not to marry, as it would restrict their freedoms. In this respect, they talked about how they enjoyed more freedom than married women and had more time and space to pursue their aspirations, even though this brought some sacrifices, such as being seen as a 'spinster' or 'odd', or not having children. Yet, none of these women were completely against the idea of marriage, and they would welcome a marriage based on complete equality.

Unequal Division of Labour Within the Household

In all three Republican women's marriages there was an unequal and gendered share of household chores. The household tasks were segregated by sex and each woman's narrations suggested that they undertook the majority of domestic work, such as childcare, cooking, cleaning and laundry, whereas their husbands were responsible for outdoor tasks, such as repairing things around the house, taking out the garbage or shopping for the coal for heating. Yet, there was some spousal support to women with regards to childcare when they were busy cooking and cleaning after long hours of work. None of the women discerned their married situation as an expression of an inequality in labour division. This perception may be because they had internalised the patriarchal arrangements in their natal families, and their education under the nation-building project culturally legitimised these tasks as the women's domain, curtailed their feminist aspirations and assigned their main role as homemakers and the professional work as being complementary (Kadioglu 1994). When asked if they had any support from their spouses, they gave the following responses:

> Well, not so much. When we had children, he just looked after the children when I was cooking in the kitchen. I would be doing the housework and he would be doing the outdoor labour (...) such as mending the broken stuff, buying coal for the school and the house. This was our division of the household (...) Even if he wanted to help with the house chores, he would cause more of a mess (Berrin, G1).

> My husband would spend his time after work with peasants, teaching them farming or reading newspaper articles to them. I would be at home cooking, spending time with the kids or working in our small garden in the backyard (Arzu, G1).

> He did not know how to cook or clean. He would be engaged in outdoor tasks such as paying bills, mending broken things (Canan, G1).

The women's narrations show that they felt less reliant on men with regard to household chores and generally saw them as incompetent and peripheral to the running of the household. Yet, it could also be seen that women were satisfied with their lot because the cultural expectations for the nation-building project motivated the women of this era to take their place in the social and economic life, working towards the goal of building a modern nation but masking the gendered division of labour. Thus, patriarchal gender relations continued to exist in the private sphere through emphasising the importance of motherhood and homemaking for social harmony (Arat 1994c; Durakbasa 1998).

In the Amazon generation, the picture is more mixed. Two (Sinem and Nesli) of the four married women enjoyed almost no equitable share of household work; they were responsible for the greatest proportion of family work from childcare to food shopping, whereas the other two women (Hatice and Oya) shared these responsibilities with their husbands because they had established the grounds of these expectations before marriage. For Sinem and Nesli, the unavailability of role-sharing in their marriages allowed them no personal space and gave them less control over their time to take up hobbies, to socialise and to focus on school work, whereas their spouses continued to enjoy their freedoms. This soon started to affect their emotional and mental well-being:

> I used to come home from work at the same time as my husband. He would sit in the corner, read his newspaper and wait for food to be served (...) After dinner, I would do cleaning, laundry and pay attention to the kids' homework. Then, I would stay up late to get prepared for the next day's class (...) I started to feel like a machine. More importantly, I realised that I was not an efficient and productive teacher (...) I started to become aggressive towards my children and husband (...) I decided to pay someone to take care of the housework once a week to solve this problem temporarily (...) Now we are both retired, but still not much has changed in our family. I still do the majority of the jobs. I never confronted him harshly on this matter as I do not want my marriage to be affected by this. I know it is not fair; it still affects my physical and emotional well-being, but I got used to it (Nesli,G2).

> On the night of our marriage, my husband gave me a list of what to do and what not to do. According to the list, I was supposed to take care of only domestic work and he was supposed to deal with any outdoor labour such as repairing broken stuff, paying bills (...) But, my conditions as a woman got harder over the years as I had two daughters, started working in the gallery we used to run, and had to care for my mum who was bedridden, in addition to my responsibilities at home and at school. In the end,

I was both psychologically and physically damaged and worn out due to the unequal share of workload I had as a woman working full-time (...) I was not talking to anyone, I was not enjoying life; I was not socialising (...) I was diagnosed with depression. My husband still showed no understanding for my situation. Then I thought that I did not need him because I was financially independent. It was when I told him that I wanted to divorce that he suddenly became helpful and supportive (...) A year later it was the same; he stopped helping me (...) and I felt too tired to challenge or change him again (...) I still undertake the majority of the work and I learned to live with this double burden. Being a woman is being on the losing side of a marriage because you have to put up with one more gender inequality in your life (Sinem, G2).

The double burden of these women in their marriages, combining career and family obligations and particularly the care work which extensively fell on women rather than men, made them vulnerable. This brought a limitation to their physical capability set of being emotionally and mentally healthy and their social capability of being able to socialise with friends, or have personal time and space for their interests. Nesli decided to hire someone as she did not want to jeopardise her marriage by initiating a dispute on this matter. Sinem, on the contrary, confronted her husband for a divorce because she knew that she was financially independent. However, in the long run, they ended up in the same vicious cycle. As the women's narrations suggest, the inequality of an uneven distribution of labour was still persistent at the time of the interviews, affecting their physical and emotional well-being.

On the other hand, Oya and Hatice shared household responsibilities with their spouses to a large extent because they stated their expectations of a marriage before they got married. This negotiation, at least, ensured that their physical or emotional well-being was not challenged by the double burden, and they could have some personal time and space. For instance as Oya states:

Women tend to compare the amount of work they do with other women rather than with their husbands. Therefore, they naturally accept this as fair. My friends tell me that I am lucky because my husband helps me. They are unaware that housework is also their husband's responsibility. I talked about all this with my husband before we got married and he agreed to my terms (...) Compared to my friends, I feel less worn out and I can create more personal time for myself. I engage in a lot of self-development courses, undertake different history education projects, and I go on excursions (Oya, G2).

Unlike the marriages of Sinem and Nesli, in these women's households, there were egalitarian intra-family relations, which made it possible for women to fulfil their valued intellectual and social capabilities sets as they had more time, space, and energy to cultivate their interests, personal/professional development and their relations with other people. In general, unlike the Republican generation, we can see that these women were aware that unequal role-sharing constituted an inequality. In this regard, they have a strong gender awareness of what a companiable marriage should be.

Moving to the next generation, two (Fisun and Tuba) of the six women were married, while Banu got divorced after ten months of marriage. These women were responsible for almost all the housework, including shopping, childcare, laundry and cooking, whereas their spouses had little or no responsibility for the household. They were not happy to be positioned as prime domestic workers in addition to long working hours at school. The double burden they had both as teachers and domestic labourers made them feel psychologically and physically vulnerable and also gave them no personal time and space:

> No one asks whether you want to cook, do the cleaning or do the dishes because you have to do all these things, you are expected to! So why is it that he only does household chores when he wants, but I have to do housework because I feel obliged to do it. I am doing everything at home from market shopping to ironing. In a marriage, both parties are supposed to take equal responsibility! In the first year of our marriage, I was confronting my husband about this, but nothing changed. After each dispute, I would feel angrier or more worn out, so I stopped challenging him. I feel like I am not a full teacher, not a full mother. I can never spend more time with my children. I never have free time to go out, or visit my friends. I never have time to start a Master's course, attend professional training courses, programmes or Comenius Projects (...) I do not even have a hobby. I feel both psychologically and physically unwell. I sometimes miss the times I was single (Tuba, G3).

I more or less knew that I would be the one who would bear most of the responsibilities in this marriage. I married him acknowledging that he would be working twelve hours a day, since he is a police officer, and therefore he would not share my burden; but I also work 8 hours at school. I come home at 6 pm. I cook, clean, and then get ready for tomorrow's class. Teaching is not a job you do at school [only]. It requires preparation for class, marking, reading homework. I had more freedoms and fewer responsibilities before I got married. Now I don't have time to go out to enjoy myself. I have been doing a Master's degree for the last 3 years because I don't even have time to write my thesis. This unfairness makes me psychologically worn out (Fisun, G3).

These women were able to enjoy greater freedom before they got married. With marriage, they went through a process of role expansion (adding new responsibilities such as the ones mentioned above), which was a challenge to their physical and emotional well-being. At the same time, it did not allow space for them to fulfil their social capability of enjoying a social life and their intellectual capability of being able to pursue self-/professional development and postgraduate education. Like the second generation of women, it is evident that these women also had gender awareness of conceptualising these tasks as a gender inequality. They confronted their spouses to express their marital dissatisfaction, which means they were able to display their agency to change their conditions and improve their lives.

Despite this domestic inequality, the women I interviewed who have adequate economic and social power were able to enjoy some equality in decision-making, which enhanced opportunities to develop their capabilities and agency. In the next section, I present the patterns of decision-making across the generations.

Equality in Decision-Making

The women's narrations across the generations show that they all shared equal position with their spouses in making decisions concerning household matters and in their mutual lives. This was mainly an outcome of sharing the 'breadwinning' role with their spouses. Thus, they all had the intellectual capability to state their opinions, and had enhanced agency freedom to have more control and negotiating power than most women in the household. This also meant that they were in control of decisions that might reduce their opportunities and curtail their capabilities. For instance, women's narrations in the first generation show that they all had bargaining power in stating their opinions and making decisions related to their families and households, such as on the children's education, making purchases or deciding on where to move. In some cases, they could be straightforward and stated their opinions in scathing terms. According to the women, this agency was related to their economic capability of generating their own income, and equally contributing to the subsistence of their households:

> We used to take our decisions together, but when we had different views, I did not hesitate to challenge him. For instance, one of the villages we were working in was really poor and deprived of basic education and health facilities. I saw an advertisement looking for a teacher couple to work at a school on a coal mine campus with better conditions. For the future of our children, I asked my husband to apply for that post. A month later, I found out that he never applied for it because he had heard false rumours about the working conditions there (...) I told him that I would apply and move there, taking my children with me. I also added that he was free to join us or stay in the village alone. He did not dare to say a word. I applied for the post and got accepted. We moved to the coal mines and he came with us too. I was confident and could challenge him because I had my own economic freedom. I don't think that I would do this if I was dependent on him (Arzu, G1).

As some research on educated women of this era would also show, Republican women who enjoyed equal status and earned salaries equivalent to their husbands were in a privileged position compared to the majority of their peers, who were unable to work outside the household and had no say in negotiations about family decisions (Acar and Ayata-Gunes 2000).

Likewise, all married women in the second and third generations also equally shared decision-making with their spouses in all matters concerning the household. Like the Republican women, their economic freedom and financial contribution to the household granted them an equal say in decision-making. Yet, unlike the Republican women, this equal share of decision-making also included asking their children about important issues, such as their education or making expensive new purchases. This might represent change in the sense that modern and egalitarian family relations were established where everyone participated in decision-making:

> I also earn money, and bring home as much as he brings, so naturally we take decisions together and compromise (...) but we don't exclude our children,

we also consult them and ask what they think about major decisions such as buying a car or about their education (Oya,G2).

We don't have equal sharing of house chores but at least we have equal say in decisions concerning the household, such as when to go on holiday, what to buy, or on our toddler's education. I think at least this should happen as I also earn at least as much as he does (Tuba, G3).

Women's narrations across the generations assert that their economic capability was a significant factor in enjoying the equal share in taking decisions relating to the family. This was a privileged position, as these women were educated professionals of their time and constituted a small group of women who could enjoy economic freedom, compared to the majority of Turkish women who were deprived of such economic power and a strong bargaining position at home. Much research on Turkish women's status at home argues educated and independent women working as professionals in urban Turkey have enjoyed an improved status both in society and in family life (Ataca and Sunar 1999; Gunduz-Hosgor and Smits 2007; Kagitcibasi 1986). On the other hand, in the more traditional families in which most women find themselves, women enjoy relatively fewer freedoms and participate less in decision-making than the women teachers I spoke to. This is because women's high intra-family position in Turkey is also dependent on a combination of education and women's economic freedom (Smits and Gunduz-Hosgor 2003; Kagitcibasi 1986). The highest status is associated with white-collar professions requiring education, such as teaching, law or medicine.

Given the importance of earning an income in order to hold an equal position in decision-making, in the next section I look into the extent to which women could enjoy their economic freedom and power, how income is shared within the household and whether income allocation creates unequal opportunities in women's lives.

The Hierarchy of Financial Responsibility

Across the generations all the married women handed their salaries over to their husbands in order to pool their income and considered it joint income. Except for Oya from the Amazon generation, the women did not consider this as a limitation to their economic capability of being able to control their own salaries. However, the women's narrations imply that there was a hierarchy of financial responsibility within the household, as it was their spouses who had the control over the management of money and who made the important decisions concerning how income was distributed for different areas of expenditure. Women had little or no control over their earnings. For instance, none of the Republican women reported having control over their income because they handed their salaries to their husbands for them to run the family budget, or sent some of it to their families. According to them, this was a way of pooling their income to create a joint budget rather than a constraint on their economic freedom:

> My husband has the control of the family budget. In the past, we used to send money to our parents, and the children had educational costs so it was easier if one of us arranged it (...) Still, every month I give my salary to him and he pays the bills and gives me some money for house shopping (Canan,G1).

Likewise, the married women of the second and third generations also had limited economic capability and reported the same practice of handing their income to their husbands to run the household budget.

Except for Oya, none of the women considered this as a limitation to their economic freedom, but rather as a way of creating a joint income; they ignored the fact that they had little or no control over money allocation for expenditures. Oya illustrated the problem of not having full control over her own income. She wanted to do English courses to be able to start a PhD. However, her husband prioritised himself because he also needed to gain a certain level of proficiency in English to enhance his career. She felt that she was neither able to spend her money freely nor pursue her aspirations of an academic career:

> We have a joint budget and my husband is in charge of it. I also earn money, but I cannot really spend it as I wish. I sacrifice my own needs and suggest that my husband goes on a language course because he needs it. On the other hand, I also need to learn English to start a PhD, but he does not make the same sacrifice for me. He does not say that we can cut on that expenditure and do a course together. He prioritises himself (Oya, G2).

The deficient economic capability of spending her income freely or having control over it limited Oya's intellectual capability of advancing her own professional and self-development because her husband tended to prioritise his interests above hers. This shows that women's agency and intra-household position does not depend only on whether they have an equal share of domestic work, decision-making or an economic contribution, but also on the extent to which they have control over that income.

The women's narrations across the generations indicate there was a 'male managed pool' (Vogler 2005) system, in which both spouses created a joint income and the man was held responsible for managing the household finances. However, seeing male partners as more responsible for managing income could hide the reality of women's maintenance of traditional gender roles (Vogler 1998). Some women also stated that they have little knowledge of how their spouses allocated the income. So, male partners tended to exercise more direct control over financial decision-making, which could bring unequal outcomes for women. As the few studies on educated professional Turkish women who have economic freedom and contribute to the household argue, women may not always enjoy their financial independence completely because of husbands' interventions (Bespinar 2010; Tekeli 1988). Women's narrations indicated that although they, as educated and professional women, considered a joint income and the managing thereof as a necessity of companionate marriage, they were unlikely to see that they lacked the agency freedom and economic capability to plan their own income until it started to create unequal opportunities for them.

Up to this section, I have presented the family dynamics in women's marriages. However, not all women were married and some chose not to get married at all. So, in the next section, I present the unmarried participants' perception of marriage, their expectations of marriage and their reasons for choosing not to marry.

Unmarried Women's Perception of Marriage

Here, I look into the attitudes of the two unmarried Amazon women and four unmarried postmodern women towards marriage. All six women's narrations suggested that they perceived the institution of family in Turkey as highly patriarchal and restrictive of women's freedoms. Therefore, they claimed that it had been a personal choice to remain unmarried rather than forming a marriage that would deprive them of their current physical, social and economic freedoms. They all stated that they had greater freedom and opportunity than their married peers but that they were not entirely closed to the idea of a marriage, which would be based on complete equality.

For two Amazon women (Meltem and Irem), who were in their early 50s at the time of the interview, this decision clearly involved some sacrifices, such as not having children or being seen as 'spinsters' in society. They regarded the traditional Turkish family structure as un-egalitarian towards women; as not opening autonomous spaces for development of both parties; or as an institution where responsibilities were not equally shared. Therefore, they felt that a traditional marriage would endanger their freedoms of enjoying leisure activities; pursuing their hobbies; and would make their physical conditions harder by assigning them a number of domestic responsibilities:

> I did not want to be one of those stereotypical Turkish women who work like a slave at home. I would like my husband to help me at home, support me in my career and respect my social life or hobbies. I have not come across such a man yet (Meltem, G2).

> I am a feminist and reject all cultural impositions of how a woman should act in a marriage such as that women should be competent in domestic work, and should spend more time at home than outside. If I ever find a feminist man, then I would marry (Irem, G2).

For them, a traditional marriage would limit their valued social capability sets (listed above) that they already had. Therefore, they preferred not to get married in order not to risk these freedoms. At the same time, they were not fully against idea of marriage based on full equality. The decision not to marry brought some sacrifices for these women. Meltem mentioned compensating for the non-fulfilment of her motherly instincts (not having children) with her profession, whereas Irem talked about how the society stigmatised unmarried woman as pathetic and defined them as 'spinsters':

> In our society, if you are unmarried, they see you as a 'spinster' or 'pathetic'. No one considers that it is a personal choice that you make. They don't respect this choice (Irem, G2).

Indeed, these women's narrations imply that there was post hoc justification and a trade-off in the decision to remain unmarried in order to have freer lives.

For the four unmarried women (Banu, Asli, Seda and Meryem) of the postmodern generation, being unmarried meant facing social monitoring of their acts and behaviours in their peripheral neighbourhood and being subjected to match-making, which in return restricted their social capabilities and freedoms. These women, who were in their late 20s and early 30s, expressed their concerns about leading a married life in which they might have to conform to socio-cultural norms and enact traditional gender roles. According to them, the Turkish marital family structure is demanding on women and brings a double burden which rests solely on women's shoulders, thus restricting their freedoms, and opportunities in the outer world and their career options and making them introverted individuals. Therefore, they did not want to give up their social freedoms of going out often or going on holiday with friends, or their economic freedom of spending their income freely, by getting married. On the other hand, some were not completely against the idea of marriage:

> My relatives and friends are trying to arrange blind dates. But I want to know my partner in person. I want to love. I also want to see if he is going to meet my expectations in marriage such as whether he will help me with housework, whether he will be okay with my social life, my going on holiday with my friends. I do not want to marry for the sake of marrying. I may marry in the future if it won't end these freedoms (Meryem, G3).

> I work 40 hours a week. My weekends are mine to go to the cinema, theatre, shopping or to write my Master's thesis. I see my friends' marriages and I do not want to be like them. Their social life diminished with marriage. They go out less and do more housework. They all have financial problems. Love and romantic involvement is important but one's freedom is equally important. Now, what I earn is mine and I can live comfortably. To be honest, I enjoy my freedoms now, maybe in future, I can marry (Seda, G3).

Banu, as a divorced woman, also believes that marriage should not restrict a woman's freedom while the man continues to live with full freedom. In her marriage she felt devalued and deprived of many freedoms, such as meeting friends, pursuing her interests and spending her money freely; and she was confined to a house with a man who did not respect her ideas and personal choices. She chose to divorce in order to prevent her marriage from doing further harm to her emotional and physical well-being. Yet, it should be noted that Banu was lucky in the sense that the decision of getting divorced was rather easy for her since she had economic freedom, and that for many women in Turkey, being financially dependent on their husbands or elder male members of family entraps them in a marriage that leads to negative outcomes, even including the murder of many women by their husbands:

> With marriage, I lost all my freedoms of going out, enjoying the weekends, relaxing. It started to wear me out at some point and I wanted to get divorced (...) Divorce was a relatively easy decision for me because I was not depending on him financially and I knew that I could be better off without him. In the future, maybe, if I believe it will be based on equality, I could try marriage again (Banu, G3).

Like the second generation, some women's decision of being unmarried involved challenges, such as being under social monitoring to make sure that they complied with the social norms of how a single woman should act, or being subjected to match-making or blind dates. This caused a loss in their social capabilities:

> I am a single women living alone. My neighbours know this and they constantly watch my house to check when I come home, when I leave, with whom I arrive home, and for how long I have been absent. This kind of disturbs me and restricts my life. They may misunderstand even if my uncle or father comes to my house if they don't know that they are my relatives (Seda, G3).

> In our culture we have a great solidarity when it comes to match-making. Some old ladies in my village approach me and ask if I would be interested in meeting their sons. I feel disturbed by these attitudes because they all know that I am the teacher of the village (...) They approach me for the sake of my profession. According to them, I can both work at home and at school, and then hand in my salary to my husband. An ideal slave model! (Meryem, G3).

As these unmarried women's narrations show, they believed that a traditional marriage in Turkey is unlikely to constitute a supportive or complementary component of an individual's basic capabilities. Therefore, they expressed their concerns of losing their freedoms and opportunities to enjoy their lives as they wish upon marriage, and prioritised romance, love, and mutual understanding and support. On the other hand, women also experienced the disadvantages of remaining single, which left some of their freedoms to the control of neighbourhood and social monitoring. We could see that they were open to the idea of marriage as long as it would be an egalitarian one respecting their valued capabilities. Thus, among the single women there was a negative perception towards marriage due to the concerns of an unequal share of household responsibilities, in which they would not be able to achieve their valued physical, social and economic capability sets. Therefore, they were reluctant to give up their freedoms for the sake of marriage even though they were aware of the disadvantages of being single.

The married women's narrations confirmed Koggel's (2003) thesis that women's freedom and agency are not always improved when they enter professional life, but one needs to look into the private sphere, such as family life, where their work is invisible, to see how their freedoms are restricted. These professional women's experiences suggest that a gendered, intra-household distribution of labour opens little space and time for them to pursue their self-interests, and affects their valued capabilities, such as social relations, personal and professional development or well-being outcomes; whereas men maintained their freedoms and were not exposed to the same social restrictions and expectations. Still, compared to the majority of women in Turkey who do not contribute economically to the household, the interviewed women's family relations across all the generations were more egalitarian. Research on middle-class urban professional women's lives shows them as enjoying relatively higher intra-family status and equality in their homes, and that marriage is not per se always exploitative, but opens some space to enjoy a measure of decision-making within the family and taking equal responsibility on household matters (Bespinar 2010; Gunduz-Hosgor and Smits 2008; Kagitcibasi 1986; Sumer 1998). For the unmarried teachers I interviewed, a family institution based on equality, respect and support that could nourish the opportunities and freedoms of both women and men as well as respect their agency, constituted significant assets for them to consider marriage. This stance could indeed be interpreted as a way of challenging cultural and gender norms in a marriage with younger generations of women.

Conclusion

Looking at these women's natal family lives, their intimate relations with their husbands and their views of marriage through a capability lens made it possible to uncover the intra-household inequalities and to evaluate the genuine opportunities available to women in changing socio-cultural and economical contexts. In relation to household inequalities, unequal care and domestic responsibilities confined women to the private sphere while men, through their participation in public spaces, had greater access to freedoms and opportunities outside the household. Much of the feminist literature argues that paid work and unpaid domestic/care work should be equally shared between men and women or societal institutions should allow couples to share all kinds of work equally without disadvantaging any party (Folbre 1994; Okin 1989; Robeyns 2010b). In reality, as shown in this study, much of the care work is done by women; this in turn indicates that the cultural context of households in Turkey demonstrates low gender egalitarianism (Fikret-Pasa et al. 2001) and that women are socialised into gender identities that make them internalise the wishes of their family members and their husbands. Many of the (intra-household, family and extended neighbourhood) inequalities pointed out in this study are products of gender, as a structure of power, as well as products of cultural and gender norms which act as social conversion factors in the achievement of capabilities. Looking from a capabilities perspective, these factors positioned women and their male peers unequally in relation to their access to valued physical (loss of physical and emotional well-being), social (not being able to pursue their interests and connect with other people), intellectual (undertaking professional development courses and postgraduate education) and to some extent economical capability sets (not being able to control how the pooled income is allocated). They also pushed women to pursue a limited range of possibilities and to tolerate inequities embedded in their society and families. Additionally, women's earned income is perceived as a contribution to household, whereas their house/care work is taken for granted. Sharing equal decision-making and breadwinning roles at home did not necessarily influence the volume of care and domestic work women did (Kabeer 2007); rather the dual burden of working outside the home and doing household work continued. Gendered division of labour in younger generations became more egalitarian, yet men could not go beyond 'helping out' their partners. Therefore, only marginal progress in relation to women's status within the household and their opportunities could be seen. By and large, the women's narrations show that the unjust nature of gendered division of labour at home cannot be kept out of gender inequality assessments, because in the private sphere the overall well-being of women is affected more than men's (Marphatia and Mouissie 2013; Robeyns 2010b). Gender justice will be achieved and gendered division of labour will be just only when the opportunity sets themselves between women and men are equal, as well as the constraints on choices (Robeyns 2007). The inequalities and conversion factors examined in women's personal lives and intimate relations are largely seen beyond any government's terrain. However, some work should be done on the regulation of public welfare policies that recognise, support and even compensate unpaid family care work and household work. Far more crucial is a change in gender norms devaluing women and privileging men in society and familial space. This is because patriarchy is first created within the family, later gender inequalities in the private sphere are transferred to and reproduced in the public sphere in a variety of institutions, such as in the labour market or in the education system (Okin 1989). Therefore, it is also important to look into women's lives in the public realm. The next chapter aims to evaluate women's educational lives in relation to gender justice.

NOTES

1. 'Mahalle' (neighbourhood) can also be categorised as the public sphere. In the Turkish context, Mills (2007: 335–336) explains 'mahalle' and its infusion to the private sphere as: 'the mahalle is the space of intimate daily life in the Turkish urban context, and narratives of and ways of life in the mahalle articulate competing notions of what it means to be a woman in Turkey (...) In Turkey, the traditional urban neighbourhood is a space, which extends the interior space of the family to the residential street; it is a space of belonging and collectivity'.
2. In 1935, only around 25% of the population were living in urban areas or big cities (TUIK 2013a).
3. G1, G2 and G3 stand for the first, second and third generation, respectively.
4. Honour and shame are defined as particular characteristics of Mediterranean and Middle Eastern societies. Peristiany (1966: ii) defines honour and shame as 'the constant preoccupation of individuals in small, exclusive societies where face-to-face personal, as opposed to anonymous, relations are of paramount importance and where the social personality of an actor is as important as his office'.
5. Kagitcibasi (1986), Kandiyoti (1988) describe Turkish family culture as a patriarchal household where power is in the hands of males and women are subordinated to men, reflecting patterns from both Middle Eastern and East Mediterranean culture.

CHAPTER 6

Education and Changing Lives

INTRODUCTION

These women's educational experiences can offer us ample material with which to explore the constraints impacted on their capabilities and agency, as well as to find out how schooling and education, as a foundational capacity according to Amartya Sen (1999) and Martha Nussbaum (2000), enabled the development of further capabilities and sufficient agency for the women to live lives that they have reason to value. Therefore, this section, through the women's voices, presents the ways education has been a transformative space in providing them with real opportunities to develop their capacities for choosing and enacting valued ways of being and doing. It also draws attention to how education can enact certain gender norms, which reproduce gender inequalities for women and put them in a disadvantaged position in comparison to men. The women's narrations are organised around two themes: The first part looks into the women's perception of education as an intellectual capability, and the second looks into how education processes (dis)empowered women in a number of ways.

The Women's Perception of Education

A persistent factor common to all three generations was that every woman believed education was important to expand and secure their range of physical, social, economic and intellectual capability sets and strengthen their agency, particularly in making strategic life choices.

© The Editor(s) (if applicable) and The Author(s) 2017   121
F.M. Cin, *Gender Justice, Education and Equality*, Palgrave Studies
in Gender and Education, DOI 10.1007/978-3-319-39104-5_6

The schooling experiences of the three women of the Republican generation took place between 1932 and 1948 at a time when the country had the lowest literacy rate. The schooling rate of girls was low and few women were able to benefit from the opportunity of entering primary school (although primary school was compulsory) under the control of patriarchal power. Access to education after primary school was even more difficult due to poverty, the inadequate number of secondary and high schools across the country and the unaffordable cost of schooling. Considering the given context, it was unusual that these three participants went to school and furthered their education at fully funded village institutes. For them, education was the only pathway towards having more freedom and getting a qualification to gain an occupational skill so that they could work, gain economic independence, and be freed from poverty as well as the influence of gendered and rigid family norms. At the same time, they had little hope of furthering their education after primary school due to poverty:

> I wanted to further my education so much, just to be able to get a job and look after my mother and sisters and release them from the oppression of my stepfather (…) and to look after them (Arzu, G1).

> Studying was important for me to gain a job and economic freedom so that I could live in better conditions (…) Seeing that even rich families' children could not study because there were not many secondary schools, let alone universities or colleges, it was only a dream for me until my father sent me to the village institute; it changed my entire life (…) I could have been married at an early age with many children, lived in poverty, and spent my entire life working on the farms to feed myself and my family (Berrin, G1).

> We could barely feed ourselves. I never thought I would be able to study and become a teacher. (…) Being able to further my education was important for me to change my life and get out of poverty (Canan, G1).

These women valued education as a means to expand their physical capabilities of being free from poverty and having adequate food and shelter. Further, it was a means of expanding their economic capabilities in order to be able to generate their own income, and to develop agency in order to be in control of their lives rather than forming adaptive preferences and living up to social expectations. What is noted in this analysis is education's role in alleviating poverty, including escaping from the network of relationships in which gender and poverty overlaps and shapes structures of inequality (Unterhalter 2012a). So, women stressed the importance of schools and education as a platform to break gendered relationships of poverty that limits their freedom and choice about their lives such as who they marry and at what age.

All six Amazon women's schooling experiences took place between 1961 and 1983 at a time when girls' schooling was gradually increasing with modernisation of the country. However, the literacy and schooling levels of women remained low.[1] Like the Republican generation, these women were among the small minority of women who were able to further their education to university and receive higher education. They valued the attainment of education as a means to acquire the freedom to develop the economic capability of generating an income, and the social capability of being treated on equal terms with their male peers. Education gave them the capability to have a voice and bargaining power in their future marriages, as well as developing the intellectual capability of practical reasoning in making life decisions. They believed education was important in granting them freedom and agency to choose a life that they valued:

> By the age of 7, I witnessed the gender hierarchy in my family; my mother was doing more house chores than anyone else, and this was being taken for granted by everyone (…) These small things made me understand what kind of a life was waiting for me (…) I became aware that I had to study to get a job, to emancipate myself from this world and to form my own family where I would not be working like a slave as my mum did (Sinem, G2).

> Studying was important for me to gain more freedoms. I knew that this could happen only by economic independence (…) Then I could work, earn my own income, decide whom to marry, form a more egalitarian family (…) I would lead my life without being in need of anyone in case of the death of my parents, or divorce (Oya, G2).

Unlike the Republican women, these women valued education more for economic independence rather than for being released from poverty, because gaining their independence was a pre-requisite for a number of capabilities they could develop. The women's narrations also pointed to gender becoming more important as sheer poverty recedes. In comparison to the previous generation, these women expressed their desire to be free from any gender oppression or gendered family life through the independence that education would grant them.

All six women of the postmodern generation received their education between 1984 and 2006. In their time, the schooling of girls, at least at the primary level, was high and there had been a considerable increase in the enrolment rates of girls in higher education. Cultural prohibition condemning girls' schooling still continued but was mainly limited to the conservative and/or economically deprived parts of the country, which generally constitute the Eastern and South-eastern parts of Turkey. These women stressed how education supported the attainment of economic independence, and agency in leading a life that they valued:

> Men can do any work, but, for women, education is a must to build a life and to gain economic independence. I knew from my primary school years that, as an educated woman, I would stand better on my feet, could have a voice in my life, and would not have to put up with an abusive marriage (Banu, G3).

> Education, without doubt, was a must for me. It is a security for a woman to gain a job, to earn her economic independence, to have a life of her own and to make choices; to release one's self from the pressure of the family or neighbourhood (Fisun, G3).

> I knew that if I became a teacher, I could be freer, spend my salary as I wished, live my life as I have always wanted, and marry whomever I want. I believe educated women are less likely to put up with the gendered and cultural expectations and have the potential to challenge the structures that put them down (Tuba, G3).

These women's narrations, like the Amazon women, suggest that the importance of education lies more in the economic independence of being free to make their own choices in life rather than escaping from poverty. Similarly, as poverty was not an immediate concern, they placed greater emphasis on gender issues depriving them of their freedoms and expressed the importance of economic independence as a necessary condition for releasing themselves from gender pressures of living up to social expectations.

In summary, common to the women's narrations is that each generation saw education contributing to an expansion of their freedoms and independence. Particularly economic independence was believed to bring greater freedom and opportunities regarding the formulating of their own preferences without any interference, and escaping from traditions.

The variance could be seen in the importance that generations attached to the different capabilities which they wished to achieve through education. The Republican women highly valued the physical capabilities of living a better life (such as having adequate food, shelter and being healthy) as they were brought up in poverty. With the younger generations, poverty was not so great a concern, whereas their aspiration to achieve a level of gender equality in their lives through education was prominent. They valued the social capability of being treated on equal terms, building more gender equitable families/relations and leading a life without any societal and gender restrictions. This variation suggests the link between education, gender and poverty that Unterhalter (2012a) has described: With poverty, the sexual division of labour at home is associated with the economic relations of survival, and therefore it becomes difficult for women to transform the gender relationships which are embedded in their lives. Even schooling as a means for rising above the poverty threshold does not guarantee that the individual will develop the ability to challenge gender inequalities, because inequalities also exist in schools (such as distribution and inequitable gender norms, misrecognition of certain groups, girls or minorities). This was the case particularly for the Republican generation of women, as I will explain in the next section. Thus, the poverty and enmeshed gender inequalities of Republican women's natal families did not necessarily lead the women to conceptualise gender equality as an important capability to aim for through education, unlike the younger generations.

Education Processes

Experiences of education processes that emerged from interviews included curriculum, extra-curricular activities provided by the school; pedagogical approaches to girls' learning; the socio-political setting of the schooling experience; and the school environment. Women highlighted different aspects of their education processes and experiences across different eras and education provision contexts; therefore, this section does not aspire to equally address each education process by generation, but rather to present the processes women have highlighted in their lives as an important factor of their schooling experiences.

In all three Republican women's educational experience, two dimensions of the education process appeared as a significant factor in expanding women's physical, social and intellectual capability sets and agency.

First, the curriculum and learning outcomes were meaningful for learners to meet their practical needs in the poor socio-economic conditions of the country. Second, gender relations opened up space for women to get recognition and attain equality under the socio-cultural context of patriarchy. Considering that these women's educational lives took place during the nation-building process, the education of boys and girls at primary schools was uniform and constituted co-education in the real sense that a gender-biased curriculum was followed at every level of education (Arat 1994b). Women, as students of the village institutes, had gender-segregated courses in addition to the academic classes such as maths, history and science which were offered to both girls and boys in the same classroom. According to the Minister of Education of the time, the reason for the gendered curriculum was to offer training for work that would be of 'concern to villages and housewives' and would include activities such as sewing, childcare, nursing, agricultural crafts, embroidery and home economics for girls (Yucel 1938, cited in Arat 1994c: 92). Boys, on the other hand, would study painting, handcrafts, calligraphy, military instruction, house construction and masonry. Therefore, upon becoming teachers, both men and women could teach the peasants the skills of their gender. Given that the society of the 1930s and 1940s was very poor and uneducated, these skills were considered as a springboard for peasants to enjoy modernisation and improve their quality of life.

This curriculum in the village institutes was highly gendered to the extent that it strengthened gender roles and promoted gendered socialisation by today's standards. However, for that time, it was quite empowering for women because they underwent a transformation in terms of gendered relationships and the development of their capabilities:

> As girls, we would learn a different skill every week, such as sewing, needlecraft, embroidery, cooking, childcare, nursing or home economics, whereas boys would be taught forging, or architectural design, carpentry and house construction (...) Life conditions in villages were tough in our time (...) They taught us all the necessary skills we might need there. Otherwise, we would not be able to overcome the infrastructure, housing, water or electricity problems we faced (Arzu, G1).

> At school, both girls and boys had different vocational specialisations. For instance, when boys were building the food hall during the summer time to practice the skills they learned, girls were doing the gardening or painting. We were working equally (...) If I had not learned those skills at school,

how would I bake my own bread in famine-stricken villages, or chop my own wood when my husband was away for compulsory military service? (Canan, G1).

The education offered to these women was empowering in the sense that it made them capable of managing many different skills that had relevance in their lives as it prepared them to work and live in the tough physical and economic conditions of the villages. At the same time, the schools contributed to the production of enmeshed gender norms concerning the kinds of activities women and men take up and thus shaped the socialisation of the women. Even in its gendered form, education distinguished them from other women like peasant women, as they were not being constrained in the same way because they had access to more opportunities than the uneducated women. For instance, the teaching of basic life skills such as bread-making or building houses and painting contributed to their physical capability sets of surviving and living in adequate shelter in the poor districts. For these women, education served to develop their social capability sets of sharing an equitable amount of labour with men (though gendered), thereby placing them on an equal footing with their male peers for the first time.

Not all courses were deeply gendered. These women also talked about an educational formation that involved mixed relations and activities with boys, as well as a common curriculum they followed in subjects such as literature, geography and science. All of this contributed in their view to their academic and intellectual knowledge, and shaped them as teachers:

> We were raised academically and intellectually well-equipped (…) The co-education structure of village institutes used to create qualified and confident Turkish women who can freely talk among men. Boys would always support women (…) We all received equal treatment from our teachers. We enjoyed literary works, world classics, and different kinds of world music. They took us on a thirty-three day tour of Turkey where we got to know more about our culture (Arzu, G1).

Curricular and extra-curricular activities also triggered the women's intellectual capability of developing self-confidence and self-respect, expanding their horizons in terms of different lifestyles, being able to read world classics, learning different cultures within Turkey, and having knowledge about the world.

Additionally, the co-educational practice and the availability of mixed gender relations constituted an important aspect of the education that the Republican women received. It was an opportunity for them to release themselves from the rigid moral and social oppression they experienced as girls in their natal families. They portrayed gender relations that were based on equality and there was a trust and brotherhood between girls and boys. Nonetheless, to some extent, their narrations also implied that there was a rigid monitoring of gender relations and of the extent to which they could mingle with each other: the entering/exiting of schools, the seating in classrooms and the dorms being separated by sex:

> Boys and girls were equal. We would work on the farm together, eat together, build our school buildings together. We would learn both traditional dances and modern dances such as the waltz. We were like brothers and sisters. These were important things to modernize the country and to eradicate backward thoughts regarding girls (…) of course, there were some rules at school, any kind of emotional relationship between a boy and a girl was banned. I even remember that a boy and a girl from the older classes were sent away from the school as they had mutual feelings for each other. So, even if you loved a boy, you would keep it secret, like I and my husband did (…) On the day we graduated, we announced our relationship and got engaged. Our teachers were happy because they supported marriage among students upon graduation so that we could be sent to the villages to work together as couple teachers (Arzu, G1).

> We were nine girls and 61 boys, but still our dorms would be separate. The girls' dorms were outside the school campus and they used to drive us fifteen minutes to school every day. We would only gather with guys during the classes (…) but girls would sit in front and boys in the back (…) but we would come back to school, work with boys to mend our own school, work on the farm with boys (Canan, G1).

Mixed gender relations and the fact of being only a few girls in a highly male-populated school was an important opportunity for them to develop their social capability of having the space to appear with boys without shame in a public setting like school. In this sense, the schooling experience transformed social inequalities by sparking a process of recognition that girls could be on the same terms with boys. Even with the restrictions on the extent to which girls could mingle with boys, for these women, there was a transformation of their gender relations which they could have never gone through if they had not studied. Therefore, they did not consider any of the control and regulations as restrictive, but rather valued being engaged in mixed relations and sharing social activities with boys.

For a generation who had lived through extreme poverty and illiteracy, education, albeit gendered, was designed to serve the existing conditions of the country at the time and provided many openings for women in developing their physical, social and intellectual capabilities. It prepared them to work as teachers in the public domain and thus further expanded their social capability set of being able to take responsibility for their own nation and community without a feeling of harassment. As the first formally educated women teachers of the country, this opened a potential space to develop collective agency to work for the modernisation of the country in the nation-building project. In contrast to other social institutions such as family, the neighbourhood and society in general, schools, as sites for equity and justice, emerged as the only places where they received a minimum level of justice, treated them in an egalitarian way and placed them on equal footing with boys. As Walker (2006) argues, education in these women's lives had a redistributive effect in reducing gender inequalities being perpetuated by the household and in family settings.

The Amazon women's educational experiences pointed out four different processes of education which influenced their capabilities. Extracurricular activities and being engaged at a social and intellectual level with teachers and other peers developed their capabilities. Contradictory to these two processes, rigid control on female bodies and the unsafe school environment outside the school and state repression during the 1970s diminished their capabilities.

With the closure of the village institutes in 1954 and the end of the nation-building period, from 1950 to 1980, a major socio-economic change took place in Turkey, which was also reflected in the educational context of these women. First of all, growing industrialisation and Westernisation increased the demand for education and diverted the gendered curriculum to girls' and boys' vocational high schools exclusively. However, receiving an education up until higher education and becoming a teacher were still achievements. Second, towards the end of the 1960s, the political atmosphere of Turkey diversified. Students' movements increased and many students, teachers, universities and teacher unions became highly politicised and caused polarisation of the left and right wing which lasted for a decade (1968–1980) (Nohl 2008). This affected the educational system directly as numerous acts of violence took place, mostly at high schools and universities. Students were denied entrance to their schools based on their political ideology, teachers and students were killed and schools and universities had to close because of certain incidents (Okcabol 2005).

Returning to the women's educational experiences, first of all, for Amazon women, schools were the only sites where more progressive gender relations were normalised. They talked about how gender relations and their sense of self-worth and confidence were encouraged at school through a wide variety of facilities both within and outside the school, such as in theatre plays, cinemas, school festivals and end-year ceremonies. These social events organised by the school were an opportunity for these women to enjoy gendered relations without worries of neighbourhood pressure, monitoring and feelings. They also afforded opportunities for the girls to discover their potential, talents and abilities. In particular, their female teachers played a progressive role in encouraging gender relations and in breaking down cultural stratification:

> In high school, I became outgoing with the influence of my teachers. Particularly our female teachers gave us the understanding that it is quite normal to go to a café with your male friends and enjoy your time. They motivated us to take part in different activities. I joined the debate club, danced folklore, and went to youth camps (...) My parents would approve and allow anything organized by the school (Oya, G2).

> With puberty, I was taken from playing outside in the neighbourhood to socialising at home and helping my mother (...) The only relations I could have with boys or opportunities I had to engage in mixed gender games, group works or activities, were within the school. In this sense, I think schools were one step ahead of society (Irem, G2).

As these remarks suggest, the school atmosphere, through various engagements and the support the girls received from their teachers, was highly important for the women to enhance their social capability set of speaking back, taking responsibility, being able to establish relations with the opposite gender and engage in social events, as well as their intellectual capability of developing self-confidence and recognising their own potential and inherent value (which were not entirely available to them in their families).

Second, four of the women (Meltem, Irem, Nesli and Sinem) talked about the regulation and disciplining of girls' bodies as well as imposing uniforms and behaviour rules. These women were subjected to scrutiny regarding their behaviours and dress codes at school (by their teachers), whereas no such restrictions were applied to boys. As Meltem puts it:

> There were certain things that I disliked about my school years. For instance, every morning we were allowed to walk to the classrooms in a single row. Teachers and the school principal would check our uniforms, skirt sizes, ties, and hairstyles (...) They would not intervene with boys. I have always thought this was for girls (...) Things did not change when I went to university because I was studying at a school of education. Our lecturers would expect us to dress like teachers, neatly and elegantly. The particular way in which I dressed, in tight jeans or leggings with short tops, would disturb some of them and they would reprimand me saying that I don't look like a student who is going to be a teacher in the future (Meltem, G2).

This points out that schools and teachers were the agents of keeping moral order, reflected the appropriate gendered norms and beliefs in the girls' lives and reproduced the patriarchal ideology. Such attitudes displayed only towards girls promoted certain societal values, such as that girls should be dressed in an acceptable manner that does not reveal any lavishness or sexuality, or that they should act in a way that displays obedience or submissiveness, suggesting that the female body should be under scrutiny. This can be seen as a limitation of the participants' social capability set of being treated without gender-based discrimination. These findings also reflect a similar result found in the research of Tan (2000) as well as Acar et al. (1999) in Turkish schools, whose studies showed that girls are exposed to more oppression and control concerning their manners and clothes at schools as compared to boys.

Third, the issue of unsafe environments surrounding the school came up in two of the six Amazon women's (Sinem and Nesli) accounts. Sinem talked about the verbal and physical assault she was exposed to at high school, while Nesli told the story of having razor blades thrown at her by the conservative young boys of the region when they were marched to the stadium for the celebration of national days (Republican Day, Children's Day and Youth Day). The purpose of this assault was to condemn the length of girls' dresses, which was the same for all performers:

You know each school prepares a dance to perform at the stadium. When we were walking from school to the stadium carrying the Turkish flag and singing songs with our performance clothes, the bigoted and narrow-minded young boys would throw razor pieces at our legs to hurt us. Thus, in their own way, they were trying to give us a moral lesson. This was very scary indeed for all of us (...) The school could do nothing about it because it was outside the school (Nesli, G2).

Outside our school there would be guys hanging out and harassing girls verbally. One of those guys once followed me until the shop where I was selling my carpet design models and he started to chase me in the street at the back of the shop until I was able to run safely into the shop. Other days, I asked my elder brother or mother to accompany me to school (Sinem, G2).

The women's narrations illustrate that unsafe school conditions constituted a limitation on the women's physical capability of being free of violence. It could be argued that having a safe environment in which to study was only limited within the school, and the conditions threatening the students' well-being out of school was often recognised as falling outside the responsibility of school administration or education policies.

A final point is that women's schooling experience fell into an era of immense politicisation of society and students. Schooling, coupled with the socio-political context of the time, opened up transformative space in which women engaged in critical and inquiring dialogue with others, developed their critical reflection on their own positions, developed political identities, became politicised and found themselves in new positions as political activists in the public sphere. The intellectual debates with teachers and their peers at school were particularly influential in their process of politicisation:

My high school and university years coincided with the 1970s political era. I remember even in high school debating about politics with my friends and in some classes with my teachers (...) We were talking about why there was political chaos (...) and the dominant political debates of the age. I was conscious about what was going on (...) When I was at university, I became a pioneering activist of my age (Hatice, G2).

In high school, we would talk politics with our female and male friends. Everyone was talking politics. Some of our teachers would scatter comments during the classes, some would try to impose their ideas, some would make comments in favour of anti-capitalism and sovereignty and some would condemn communist ideas. In a way you listen to these at school, talk about this and then when I went to university, I became irresistibly politicised as I engaged more with political groups (…) and organised many events (Irem, G2).

At high school, both our teachers and students would have ongoing debates regarding the political situation of the country. We could see the polarization and politicization among the teachers, which were very often reflected to us (…) Having been in this environment, as I started university I found myself irresistibly driven in these acts through preparing leaflets to invite people to join our side of the cause (Nesli, G2).

Gender and social relations at schools (including universities), teachers and the socio-political context of the eras were all influential in the process of women's identity transformation to developing powerful voices. This also developed their political capability set of developing political knowledge to speak up on their political ideas, and developing their political participation through protests and their agency in being part of collective movements to bring change. However, their legal rights of freedom of speech and taking part in political acts were curtailed in their university schools' years by the repressive and violent acts of governments to suppress the increasing student movements. To this end, although all the women had witnessed and experienced physical/verbal assaults, two of the six women (Irem and Hatice) were particularly affected by this. Hatice was denied access to university on the basis of her political ideology and endured a long trial process, and Irem was exposed to police violence and harassment in demonstrations and was under the police custody:

I usually took my place on the frontline, pioneering and organising many demonstrations at my school. I could not attend university for six months. I was on the blacklist of the university and the police did not allow me inside the campus because, according to them, I was an anarchist and a communist who was causing social disruption. I did not give up and brought my issue to court with a couple of my friends who were in the same situation. After a year of struggle, I won the case and continued my degree (Hatice, G2).

I organised unauthorised acts, but I was never in favour of armed action. However, as frontline activists in the demonstrations, we would be exposed to police violence. Even in custody, harassments and tortures would continue. But, this did not deter me from my cause to strive for a just and equal society (Irem, G2).

As is evident, state repression of the time not only curtailed the women's political freedoms of protest and physical well-being but also deprived them of having access to education. Despite the hollowing democracy that highly constraints their well-being and options, women displayed their agency to pursue what they value and possessed altruistic goals to challenge the system.

The postmodern women's educational lives were spent in an apolitical environment and at a time when women's education was widely spreading, although higher education was not very common. Their experiences revealed that three different forms of educational processes had been both empowering but also limiting of their freedoms. Extra-curricular activities at schools, which brought engagement in wider social relations, expanded the women's social and intellectual capabilities, whereas unsafe school surroundings and gendered perspectives towards girls constituted factors diminishing their intellectual, social and physical capability sets.

First, like the older generations, for all these women, schools were also the sites where more enabling gender relations were normalised and the socialisation of students was supported by extra-curricular activities. Women valued the opportunity of being able to engage freely in mixed gender relations at schools, which were morally undesirable in their neighbourhoods. Being able to engage in social activities was also an important factor in developing their own interests, recognising their potential and supporting their self-confidence and enhanced self-worth.

Second, like the Amazon women, two women out of the six (Seda and Aycan) talked about the unsafe school environment and the verbal harassment they experienced around school, which made them feel unsafe:

> There would be a group of boys roving in front of the school, waiting for girls to leave the school so that they could molest or mock them. They would verbally harass you, stare at you, and point at you. They could even follow you with the intent to attack you. I used to feel a bit unsafe outside the school because of these people (...) The teachers and the principal must definitely have seen this but I don't think any steps were taken to prevent it (Aycan, G3).

> In Turkey, I find the school environment very unhealthy. Many gangster-looking guys hang out outside the school and this was the same during the time I was studying. There would always be some boys wondering around and harassing girls or trying to hit on them. I would feel unsafe and was worried that they would stalk me (Seda, G3).

Unsafe school environments and gendered interactions around the school were not given attention, as they were likely seen as falling outside the remit of the school. Therefore, school management did not feel obliged to secure female students' physical capability of feeling secure and comfortable on their journey to and from school. This could imply that women's issues are not given serious enough consideration in education settings.

Finally, four women (Seda, Aycan, Meryem and Fisun) mentioned a gendered perspective towards girls and their learning at school. Undermining perceptions towards female students' ability and capacity to learn and academic ability in maths and science classes, as well as the promotion of male candidates for the students' school union, were discouraging factors of girls' academic achievement and motivation:

> One of my teachers was obviously discriminating. He did not appreciate girls' achievement. He was more interested in boys. It could have discouraged someone else but this behaviour of his spurred me on to study, because I needed to reply five correct answers to prove my success and worth as a student, whereas a boy would need only one (Seda, G3).

> We would hold an election at school for school presidency. There would be both female and male candidates. However, male candidates would be encouraged more and therefore a boy would be elected as a president, whereas a female student could only be his deputy. I wanted to become a president in my final year but was not really supported much by my teachers. I remember feeling very disappointed about it. It feels that there is a limit to what you can be or achieve as a girl (Aycan, G3).

It can be seen that gendered practices amplified discriminatory practices, which posed a limitation on women's social capability of being treated equally without discrimination and their intellectual capability of feeling self-confident. This also suggests that schools reproduced gendered assumptions and perceptions about girls' and boys' learning, thus influencing girls' identity by suggesting that certain courses are not culturally appropriate or that girls should remain in the background. There is, however, no systematic data or extensive research showing how social and cultural reproduction takes place at schools in Turkey. From the limited research in this topic in the Turkish context, some scholars (Cin and Walker 2016; Akhun et al. 2000; Tan 2000; Sayilan 2008) have argued that arrangement of learning process and education based on a gender-based model and the gendered manners of teachers discourages girls' participation in learning and makes them lacking in confidence. Likewise, a 2003 UNICEF report on gender review in education in Turkey touched upon the role of teachers in constructing a weak sense of gender identity, in that they accept cultural scripts about subordination and that most of the time teachers cannot recognise gender discrimination because of internalised gender roles.

Conclusion

The women's educational experiences showed that education opened up opportunities that they were culturally deprived of in their private spheres (e.g. the social capability of engaging in mixed gender relations and adopting a wide range of social activities that mattered to them). It contributed to their capacity to participate in a democratic life, develop authentic and expressive voices and construct a life they valued living. School was the only institution where they received some level of justice. So, education served as a transformative space in fulfilling women's aspirations, widening their opportunities to make life choices and giving them the necessary resources to secure their future well-being.

It also became apparent how the socio-political context was also a determinant in the educational experiences of all generations. The context that interferes with the education system and its practices determines which capabilities are more likely to be developed. For instance, we could see that the state ideology of building a nation offered a gendered education based on raising strong, Kemalist and nationalist women so that they could be active participants of the political revolution of the Republican era and act as representatives of a new modern Turkish woman. Such an education enabled the necessary conditions for women to achieve all their valued capabilities and to lead a life they value. The political context of the Amazon women triggered the capability expansion of their political ideas and women adopted activism as an essential part of their lives.

Additionally, schools were also gendered sites of power and created inequalities in relation to learning and teaching, that is the kind of work women could do, the subjects they could study. We could see how this inequality causes women to perform reserved, shy, obedient girl identities. This suggests gender inequality at school is much more associated with the informal spaces of schools such as families and also with labour market and institutions (which is the focus of the next chapter). Relations in these institutions shape the gender roles such as who does the care work and who becomes more prominent in decision-making. In this sense, schools are the back-garden of social realities and to an extent reflect gendered practices and cultural codes. Nonetheless, schools and education can also transform some of the gender inequalities of the private sphere; but they have a limited ability to do this with respect to social, cultural and political relations (Unterhalter 2012b). This is because education, particularly in Turkey, usually reflects the cultural hegemony of the ruling class and state and does not ensure gender equality. Whatever their agenda is (imposing conservative or nationalist education), developing a balanced perspective and education towards gender equality is never a priority. Therefore, prevailing masculine norms and pattern remain deeply rooted in education and offer women a marginal space to truly achieve who they want to be.

Generally, the women's educational lives opened up spaces and freedoms which would otherwise not have been possible. One of these freedoms was their ability to take up work and take their place as professional women in the public sphere. This is a significant aspect of this book in terms of highlighting how these educated women (empowered by education) are engaged in education to work for gender justice. So, the next section presents professional experiences of women.

NOTE

1. The literacy rates of women in 1955, 1965 and 1980 were respectively 26%, 33% and 46.6%. Women with a primary level of education constituted only 36.9% in 1980, although primary education was compulsory (TUIK 2012).

CHAPTER 7

Working for Social and Gender Justice

Introduction

This chapter is organised into three parts. The first part deals with the women's early careers, where all generations completed hardship posts in economically undeveloped, rural areas of Western Turkey or the mainly Kurdish populated villages of Eastern Turkey. I highlight the role of teachers as significant actors engaged in education to expand the capabilities of others. At the same time, I raise the challenges involved in their work, such as the cultural, economic, ethnic and political impediments to their own capabilities. Despite these limitations, which were differently configured in the different generations, this phase arose as a significant aspect of their career, as they reported satisfaction and joy in working for the good of society and other people, as actors with the power of changing things.

The second part focuses on the women's subsequent careers when they returned to Western Turkey or were sent to more prosperous areas upon completion of the hardship posts. Generally, the women experienced professional dissatisfaction, as they no longer found themselves in powerful positions to bring about substantial change. Rather, they were disappointed by the unequal power relations among female and male teachers, devaluation of teachers in society, the diminished value attached to their voice at school, the lack of opportunities to access higher positions, and the difficulties they faced as a result of their political public participation in teachers' strikes.

© The Editor(s) (if applicable) and The Author(s) 2017   139
F.M. Cin, *Gender Justice, Education and Equality*, Palgrave Studies
in Gender and Education, DOI 10.1007/978-3-319-39104-5_7

The third part briefly presents the women's overall reflections on their entire professional lives and their perception of their role as women teachers in society. Thus, this draws together the first and second parts, arguing that despite the differing contexts and challenges across the generations, each woman's perception of being a woman teacher is based on a challenge to gender inequality and a lack of opportunities for women in Turkey.

EARLY CAREER LIVES: WORKING FOR CHANGE

The women's early career lives were spent completing 'hardship posts'. All three generations of women placed particular emphasis on the early years of their professional lives because, in these regions, they reported having the power and agency to initiate change in people's lives as the most educated and notable people of the district. They specifically pointed out that their presence as women teachers at these schools was important in addressing the concern of (gender) equality, improving the life quality of the local women and enhancing girls' schooling experiences, which gave them professional satisfaction.

However, the experiences of all three generations of women in those regions included undeveloped infrastructure (such as poor housing, limited forms of transportation and lack of health services) and environmental settings (such as climate or the geographical location of the towns). For the second and third generation of women there was the additional challenge of the prevailing socio-cultural and political factors (such as Turkish and Kurdish ethnic conflict, conservative neighbourhoods and lack of safety due to the armed attacks of the Kurdish insurgencies). These difficulties were a significant barrier to helping other people, as well as limiting their own capabilities and agency. Under these hardships, a nuanced difference can be noted in how the first generation was involved both in community education (educating local women peasants) and children's schooling within the spirit of nation-building, whereas the younger generations did not reach out to the community but rather prioritised female students' schooling experiences, due to being excluded for being female, Turkish and coming from Western Turkey in Kurdish populated districts. The two younger generations experienced more social exclusion and were exposed to more gender discrimination, making them more vulnerable to assaults by men or to neighbourhood pressure, whereas the Republican woman did not mention such experiences because they worked alongside their husbands in villages, which was a secure way of existence for them. By and large, reflecting on their experiences, the women who spent their hardship posts in Eastern Turkey believed tough experiences in these regions prepared and developed them as teachers, which would have been difficult otherwise. On the other hand, women who completed these services in undeveloped villages of Western Turkey did not make much mention of professional satisfaction or added value to their careers resulting from their hardship posts.

All three Republican women started working in Western Turkey in the mid-1940s at a time when poverty, illiteracy and inadequate infrastructure were nationwide problems; Turkey was still trying to recover from the aftermath of the independence war. In this socio-economic context, poor working and living conditions were not exceptional, but they were seen and felt more in the rural villages. These difficulties included a lack of health/transportation/poor housing facilities, weak road infrastructure, unsanitary water and lack of access to electricity, all of which brought significant challenges to both these women's lives and peasants' lives. Despite these challenges, the women's professional lives reflect dedication, passion and enthusiasm in working for the country, because their education at the village institutes was aimed primarily at raising teachers who would play a leading role in developing the rural areas, increasing awareness of the modernisation of social relations and lifestyles, and spreading Kemalism and Turkish nationalism (Karaomerlioglu 1998). Women teachers held particular importance for this aim as they were expected to represent modern Turkish women and stood as leaders and role models for female peasants and girls in the villages. Therefore, in their narrations, there was a particular focus on their work in the community rather than the teaching facilities at school, because community education constituted a significant part of their roles which they carried out through a gendered division of labour with their spouses. Their husbands would read newspapers to male peasants and teach them modern agriculture, and the women would educate the female peasants, teaching them necessary skills and imparting knowledge in sewing, childcare, gardening, home economics and health issues. The female peasants would also often consult them about problems concerning health, pregnancy and contraception methods:

> My husband would read newspapers to peasants and they would have daily debates about politics, the economy or farming. I would visit the households, gather with women in my house and teach them needlecraft, how to sew dresses, how to do gardening. We would also have conversations

on their reproductive health, methods of contraception, breastfeeding and bringing up infants (Arzu, G1).

We (herself and her husband) would do our best to help peasants. I would organize different classes for the female peasants such as sewing or gardening, or we would gather in someone's house and talk about home economics (Canan, G1).

As many of the female local population had little or no education, the women's presence in the villages and close relations with female peasants played a significant role in educating and guiding the female population on a wide variety of issues, from reproductive health matters to home economics. Their presence contributed to the expansion of the female peasants' physical capability of being knowledgeable on issues concerning their health and well-being and their social capability sets of being connected to other women of the village, forming a network, and engaging in dialogue and friendship with other people. Such gatherings and networking under the leadership of women teachers represented an important opportunity for them to expand skills that mattered to them (such as home economics or learning ways of contraception) and to improve their quality of life.

In addition to community life, the significance of the women's presence could be seen at the school level, in improvements to the quality of students' schooling experiences. Due to the poverty of the 1940s and 1950s, many schools were physically in bad condition and had no desks, blackboards, doors or heating. As the first teachers at these schools, these women took it as their personal responsibility to improve the conditions through resourcefulness and passion. Improving the physical conditions of schools was only one aspect of their contribution. Many students lacked knowledge of basic hygiene due to poverty and uneducated parents. Particularly for girls, this situation was worse as they did not know how to take care of their menstrual cycle or to avoid fleas in their braided hair:

When I was sent to my first school to work, I was the only and first teacher of the village. They took me to the school building (…) There were no desks, chairs, or blackboards (…) I painted it myself, with the help of a few peasants. We mended its doors and windows. I asked for spare desks from nearby schools and bought the rest, including heating, with my first salary because the state did not have any money. The state was still paying the debts of the Ottoman Empire, while simultaneously trying to improve the infrastructure of the country and allocating some of their budget to the army in case the country had to enter the Second World War to protect its borders against Nazi invasion (...) So, it was my responsibility to improve the conditions and I also wanted to give the students a real schooling experience (...) I wanted them to have access to a healthy, warm school with the necessary sources (...) This was not enough, of course. There were also other problems. In most of the villages the students were dirty and lived in unhygienic conditions as their parents worked till late hours on the farms. Thus, to help them as a woman teacher, I felt it was my responsibility to teach students how to wash their uniforms, brush their hair, and apply basic hygiene rules such as tooth-brushing, face-cleaning, the cleaning of fleas and, for girls, taking care of their personal hygiene in menstruation (Berrin, G1).

As women teachers we would spend time with the girls, take care of their uniforms and clothes, teach them to patch the holes in their clothes as their mothers worked full-time on the farms and at home and did not have time for such things. We would teach them how to clean, to cut their nails, and to use toothbrushes and toothpaste. We would make sure they brought these things with them to school every day, with a face towel, to teach them basic hygiene rules (Arzu, G1).

Once again, the women's particular presence at the schools was different from that of the male teachers. They helped students (particularly girls) to expand their physical capability of being healthy (clean and neat) and having access to a proper, clean and warm school environment.

Their early professional experiences further revealed how, as teachers, they were sensitive to creating equal opportunities for every child in school. They worked in an equality-seeking directive in education, paying particular attention to economically and culturally disadvantaged groups (poor and Kurdish students) and developing their intellectual capability set of receiving adequate and equal education compared to others:

I always helped poor students more and paid special attention to them. I never discriminated between my students, but I have come across teachers doing so. When we were posted in other villages to work, I realised that small groups of Kurdish students could not read and write although they were in the third grade, because the teacher before me ignored them due to their ethnicity. I created a separate corner for those students in the class, and I sometimes asked them to stay a few more hours after school had finished and was personally involved in their literacy and education to compensate for the past three years (Canan, G1).

When I was working on the coal mines campus, there was a class system. There were mainly two groups of people: workers and engineers. There was a segregated socialisation between these people, which was even reflected in the school. They placed workers' children in one class and engineers' children into another. My husband and I opposed this and desegregated. This was an obvious discrimination and we formed mixed classes (Arzu, G1).

Although these women's narrations suggest that they were sensitive to the promotion of equality, they also revealed that it was their colleagues who were creating these inequalities. This shows that not all teachers of their time were equally considerate in providing equal opportunity.

In different ways the women appeared to have worked enthusiastically and with much dedication for the good of their students and the community. However, some difficulties were involved because of a lack of infrastructure. Although these difficulties were the same as those endured by men (although not always equally experienced by all men), in some cases women were more severely affected, for instance when they lost their infants or health due to lack of healthcare workers:

The physical difficulties were the same for everyone (...) the real difficulty lay in the lack of availability of cars or horse carts when we needed to go to the city, and a lack of medical staff in villages. Because of the lack of health care facilities, we lost our first child when she was three-and-a-half months old (...) We could not find any transportation to take her to the hospital in town (...) The death of my baby was completely devastating for me. I almost lost my sanity when I saw how she died in my arms as we were walking to the city centre to take her to the hospital. If I had been more experienced, I would have waited to be posted to a better village where I could have access to health facilities (Canan, G1).

I was seriously ill after my first birth; there was nothing, no medicine, no doctor to help me in the village. I had a difficult birth with the help of a midwife in unhygienic conditions at home. I couldn't get out of the bed for a long time and lost my reproductive health, thus could not have a child for five years (...) Even when I was confined to my bed after the birth for a couple of months and was unable to move, I invited my students to my home every day and taught my classes in the room so that they would not be left without a teacher (Arzu, G1).

The socio-economic conditions of the time caused women to lose their emotional and physical well-being. Despite these difficulties, the women did not refer to these as potential reasons for leaving their jobs. They felt a duty to improve the conditions of the peasants and children and to serve to the public good.

For their part, the Amazon women served their hardship posts between 1978 and 1990. These women's professional experiences took place at a time when there was an armed conflict between the Kurdish insurgencies of the PKK and the Turkish army in mainly Eastern and South-Eastern Anatolia. There was an intensive attack and raids of the Kurdish militants on the civilians, and especially teachers. In these regions, in addition to the Kurdish and Turkish conflict, there was strong gender stratification and conservatism, to such an extent that girls' schooling was culturally prohibited, early marriages were common, and being a girl meant having little or no value in the family (Rankin and Aytac 2008; Smits and Hosgor-Gunduz 2003). Additionally, there was little improvement in infrastructural development in Eastern, South-Eastern and Central Anatolia since Republican times. This is because industrialisation attempts took place in Western regions, so the infrastructure needed for regional development built up there earlier than in other regions (Gunduz-Hosgor and Smits 2008).

Under the above mentioned socio-economic and political conditions, Meltem, Irem and Nesli served in Eastern Anatolia; Hatice served in Central Anatolia; Oya served in villages of Western Turkey; Sinem served in both in Central Anatolia and in villages of Western Turkey. The narrations of Meltem, Irem, Nesli and Hatice reflected their enthusiasm in helping girls, but no work was mentioned for community education, due to the socio-cultural challenges excluding these women on the basis of their gender. On the other hand, two of the women (Oya and Sinem) worked in relatively more prosperous and more modern regions (Western Turkey and Central-West Turkey). They did not face as many socio-cultural and political challenges as their other peers.

Meltem, Irem, Nesli and Hatice talked about how their presence as women teachers, particularly in Eastern Turkey or in highly conservative districts of Central Turkey, exercised a positive impact on the expansion of girls' schooling opportunities. Their presence as female teachers brought greater enrolment of girls, promoted girls' academic performance, boosted their self-confidence and motivation to study, created more girl-friendly school environments and increased the exposure of girls to professional role models:

> I gained a girl from almost every household. I built good relations with some locals as they got to know me and witnessed my good intentions; they

felt safe about sending their daughters to my class (...) There were not many teachers at school so I was also teaching for primary schools. Therefore, I guaranteed them that those girls would only be my students. Their worries were alleviated with the idea that their daughters would be taught by a female teacher. That is a privilege of being a female teacher in these areas. A male teacher would not achieve the same (Hatice, G2).

In the years I worked as a principal in eastern Anatolia, many families were against the schooling of girls. They trusted me, and many families, even the most conservative families, sent their daughters to school. They knew that, as a woman principal, I would take care of them at school, would not allow any nasty rumours that could damage the family honour, and would keep them safe and secure from any possible harassment (...) I also founded a branch of the NGO *Association for the Support of Contemporary Living*, which was specifically aimed at encouraging girls' education through sponsoring their schooling and reaching out to the community to increase awareness of girls' education. Through funding their school expenses and giving them one-to-one attention, we tried to motivate girls to start schooling and to persuade their fathers (...) Even if we knew that some would drop out because of familial and neighbourhood pressure, we aimed to ensure that each girl at least got a basic education (Irem, G2).

These women's presence as teachers and their close relationships, based on trust, with some of the locals in the conservative regions addressed the problem of girls' schooling to an extent. They alleviated the fears of some families about sending their daughters to school. Knowing that their daughters would be taught by a female teacher, fathers felt more secure and positive about their schooling. This created an opportunity for girls to develop at least their intellectual capability set of getting adequate education to gain literacy and numeracy skills and discover other cultures in an environment where they were considered as equals, felt confident and could imagine a different life.

Nonetheless, these desirable outcomes were not easy to achieve, and women faced infrastructural underdevelopment such as houses with no electricity, toilets or water, heating; unavailability of transportation in harsh winters; and lack of healthcare workers. All of this deprived them of their physical capabilities of being healthy, having bodily integrity and being mobile. These conditions were the same for men working in those areas, but some challenges, such as lack of transportation and doctors, had more severe consequences for women, as in the instance of Hatice, who lost her newborn infant as she could not take her to hospital on time and therefore lost her emotional well-being:

> I lived in such a poor village in Central Anatolia that there were not even any doctors or regular transportation. I lost my six months old infant there because I could not take her to the hospital in time. It took me several months to recover from this loss and the emotional trauma (Hatice, G2).

In addition to the lack of infrastructure, these women also had to cope with conservatism and ethnic conflict (Kurdish vs Turkish). This influenced women teachers more than their male counterparts. Being women, these teachers were seen as easy targets both for harassment and threats. Their gender predisposed them to challenges that undermined their physical capability sets through being subjected to violence and harassment, and social capability sets through being discriminated against on the basis of ethnicity, religion and gender and not being treated with dignity and respect. However, the most striking experience belonged to Meltem, who luckily survived three terrorist attacks:

> When I was working in the East, I survived three terrorist attacks (…) The last attack I experienced was when I was staying in a teacher hotel. My colleagues and I were sitting outside in the garden of the house. It was night time. We had a chat for a while. Later on, I wanted to go back to my room since I was cold. I said good night to them. As I was going up the stairs, I heard shots and screams. I could not rush out because I understood that it was an armed attack. We called soldiers and an ambulance. When the soldiers came, we were allowed out. I saw the dead bodies of my colleagues in the garden. I suffered from a psychological destruction for a long time. Each time I closed my eyes I heard their screams and saw their bodies (…) Additionally, I was threatened by the male students in my class whose fathers were Kurdish militants because I was a woman and they assumed I could be frightened more easily (…) When I passed in front of coffee houses where only men would sit, they would all stare at me and disturb me or make me feel uncomfortable by their looks (…) in another case, I was harassed by local men who wanted to marry me as their second or third wife (…) Some would even follow me home (Meltem, G2).

> Being a woman in such a culturally conservative place was hard in every aspect of life, from the classroom to walking on the street (…) When I went to the supermarket to buy something, people were rude to me (…)

> At school I could see the issues of terror and gender discrimination in the attitudes of my male students and colleagues. Once I was physically attacked in class by one of my male students, who threw potatoes at me when I was doing a potato print activity. He, as a male student, was trying to challenge my authority because I was from Western Turkey and a woman, and did not share the same ideologies as him (…) Our Kurdish male colleagues would not talk to us. I remember them throwing chairs at me on my last day at school as I was leaving for the West (Nesli, G2).

The women's narrations point to a cultural conflict of two different sides (women teachers and the people living there) and reveal the cultural and political divide between them. It also explains why these women, unlike the Republican generation, were not able to work towards community education or help the other women in the communities to expand their capabilities. The cultural values of the time did not offer women much space to have public presence. The traditional values constituted powerful ambient forces inhibiting women's physical capability set of space, of safe mobility, of being free of harassment; as well as the social capability set of being able to lead a life free from religious pressure and neighbourhood monitoring. Therefore, women have developed at least their own strategies for protecting themselves since the state failed to do so:

> Armed attacks of militants used to take place between eight and nine pm. There would never be an attack after ten pm. If they climbed the mountain after eight to get their arms they would not go back to town because of the high and rugged mountains. People you saw in your daily life or chatted to in the grocery store could be a militant at night killing people. You would never know who is who. Therefore, we would lock ourselves in our homes after five pm, would not go out and often would avoid switching on the lights (Meltem, G2).

Despite these difficulties, the women's reflections on their experiences during their early career years showed that they gained a lot from those experiences in terms of professional development and personal satisfaction. All four women were of the same mind that the challenging life and working conditions in those districts prepared them as teachers and constituted an important role in their teacher development. The professional satisfaction they got from helping out girls and opening up new opportunities for them was greater than in their experiences in the West:

Now I talk about those events as if they were terrible years. Bu no, they were not! If I had not worked there, I would have missed a lot in this life. It made me stronger as a teacher. Now, I feel that I can teach and educate any student because I learned to how to work with students from different backgrounds, cultures and lives. They do not teach you this at university. Your experiences teach you (...) Now, when I look at my professional life in the west, I cannot get that much satisfaction (...) There I tasted the moral, personal and professional satisfaction of being engaged with girls, being a source of inspiration to them, helping them and seeing the consequences of my support in their achievement or confidence (Meltem, G2).

I never regretted going there because I had an opportunity to see the other side of Turkey, I learned to survive there as a woman teacher in most hostile and unsafe conditions, and I learned what it actually means to be a teacher (Nesli, G2).

Despite the cultural and infrastructural factors negatively influencing their freedom and well-being, the women's narrations show that their work of helping girls and expanding their intellectual and social capability sets gave them a feeling of achievement and professional development.

Moving to the postmodern generation, these women served their hardship posts between 2001 and 2011 in a socio-political and cultural context similar to that of the Amazon women. During their time of service, the armed attacks of the PKK still continued but posed little threat to civilians; yet there was still ongoing hostility and conflict between the Kurdish and the Turkish in the eastern regions. A conservative cultural atmosphere still prevailed, which devalued women and their status in society. Girls' schooling was still culturally prohibited. There was some improvement in terms of infrastructural development, yet a lack of healthcare workers, hospitals and transportation vehicles were still prevailing, to the extent that people's well-being was at risk.

Four of the six postmodern women (Aycan, Fisun, Banu and Tuba) completed their compulsory service in Eastern Turkey and two women (Seda and Meryem) completed their service in economically deprived villages of Western Turkey. Women who served in Western Turkey, Meryem and Seda, did not speak of any professional satisfaction or professional development gained through their hardship posts. This was because the life standards, as well as the economic, physical and infrastructural development in Western Turkey, are relatively developed compared to that of the East. Therefore, they had more comfortable lives. However, some districts of Western Turkey are still conservative and patriarchal. These women mentioned how these structures caused harassment and exclusion in public spheres, which restricted their freedom of movement, comportment and dress, through social monitoring. On the other hand, the other four women talked about how their presence as a woman teacher impacted positively on students'/girls' schooling. They helped by widening students' horizons through literary forms of art, developing their self-confidence and ability to aspire, and teaching Kurdish-speaking students to speak Turkish and express themselves properly in Turkish, so that they could benefit from legal rights and processes. They built role models and provided guidance to adolescent girls about their problems and personal hygiene:

> In my class students were not able to speak Turkish properly, and I had three students who did not know any Turkish at all. I did not know any Kurdish whatsoever. This caused many problems, such as not being able to communicate with students. Thus my primary aim became to teach them Turkish. Otherwise, there was no point in teaching them maths, science, or history. After five years, all my students were able to express themselves in Turkish, speak it properly and fluently. In return they taught me Kurdish in class and they felt very proud that I was learning their language too. At the end of the fifth year, I was not able to teach them the syllabus required by the Ministry of Education, but I taught them that they are valuable, deserve respect, are successful and have the full potential to achieve and gain self-confidence (...) Once they realized they were worthy of love and respect, their self-esteem increased (Aycan, G3).

> Just to get a few more girls to schools, I persuaded some fathers to send their daughters to school on a part-time basis so that they could at least learn to read and write (Banu, G3).

> When I started working, I saw the ignorance displayed towards girls (...). Some families decided to send their girls when they learned that I, a woman teacher, started working. I taught them what to do when they first had their menstrual cycle. I bought girls panties and gave my students some, because they did not even know they needed to wear them. I invited some girls to my home to have dinner with me, to watch movies together, to study. These little things that we teachers do take them into a different world and show them that they could have a different life if they further their education (...) and three of my girls continued to high school. This is something a woman teacher could do (Tuba, G3).

The women's narrations clearly depict a socio-cultural atmosphere which devalues women, their dignity, education, right to express themselves and right to plan their lives. The supremacy of male hegemony can be seen as a limiting factor for girls' practice of agency with regard to their various physical, social and intellectual capability sets. In this respect, women's presence in the villages was important to encourage families to send their daughters to schools or, as in Banu's case, to bargain over schooling time. In addition to cultural norms, it could be seen that there was little importance attached to this issue, as the laws protecting girls' right to education were not being implemented at all, thus encouraging fathers to keep their school away from school. On the other hand, language arose as an important issue limiting students' access to education when compared to their peers in other parts of the country, as the former students spent a number of years at school trying to master their Turkish skills. This situation causes students to fall behind in the syllabus and lower their achievement in central Turkish exams such as high school or university exams (Kirdar 2009), or to experience communication difficulties with teachers (Kaya 2009). By and large, these women's presence in these districts facilitated the access of girls to healthy environments for their physical, intellectual, emotional and personal development as teenagers and young adolescents, and compensated for some of the capabilities that they lacked in their social surroundings.

The women's struggles to improve the conditions of students, and particularly of girls, were also interrupted by socio-cultural (conservatism), political (Kurdish and Turkish conflict) and infrastructural challenges (such as frequent electricity cuts, no water access at home, lack of healthcare workers, unsanitary water, lack of transportation, internet, television or network coverage for mobile phones). This affected women's physical capability set of being mobile, having access to medical staff, fresh food and clean water, and being able to live in adequate shelter with electricity and water facilities; as well as their social capability set of being connected to their families and having leisure time through the internet. All these difficulties were similarly experienced by their male peers, and, unlike previous generations, none experienced the particular difficulties associated with loss of reproductive health or of their infants, because they did not have children then. However, the socio-cultural context and political ethnic conflict of those regions caused greater difficulty for women teachers than for male teachers. They were more exposed to sexual harassment, gender discrimination, physical violence and exclusion on the basis of their gender and ethnicity:

There were some respectful and friendly people too, but generally I was not very well treated. In addition to being Turkish, being a woman would make the situation hard for me because in their culture, women have no value. Even as a teacher, I had no value for people, but an imam would receive more respect than me (Banu, G3).

Local people preferred not to form close relations with us because we were Turkish, women, and could not speak Kurdish (...) As a women I felt exclusion and hostility more than men (...) because I was exposed to more harassment (...) For instance, once, as I was walking from school to home, a group of men in a tractor passed by and threw watermelon peels at my back and turned back and laughed at me (...) I was disturbed a lot by the young men of the village. Some of the men first threw rotten tomatoes at my windows. Later, they started knocking on my door and running away at night to scare me. In another situation, I was molested by one of the locals. He would follow me everywhere; spy on my house (...) Unfortunately, they would not send their daughters for fear that their family honour might be damaged if someone molests them. What about the harassment that women teachers were exposed to by the same men? (Aycan, G3)

As a woman, you cannot pass in front of kahvehane (Turkish village coffee houses) so frequently. You cannot pass so often from the centre of the village, especially in front of the markets and places that are populated by men. The local people of that region find it inappropriate for women to walk on the streets that men would walk. Women used to walk on the back streets. Back streets are not safe; they are full of militants. Even the cows were luckier than women. Believe me; you would not want to be a woman there (Tuba, G3).

It emerged that political and ideological biases and prejudices towards women, coupled with cultural values, did not offer women much space for having a public presence. The traditional values inhibited women's physical capability sets of space, of safe mobility and of being free of harassment. It similarly limited the social capabilities of being able to lead a life free from monitoring and of integrating into society as a respected individual. Despite these difficulties, women also commented on the value and satisfaction that they got from those experiences and hardships:

Now when I think of those days, I can say that I learned a lot. When I came to the West my responsibilities towards students decreased. In the East, I had a more intimate relationship with students and spent more time with them at school, because I knew that their parents were mostly uneducated and cared little about their children's welfare. Therefore, I felt greater responsibility for equipping them academically, educating them as much as possible, and compensating for what they lacked at home. It used to give me genuine professional satisfaction as students were eager to learn, to spend time with me. Here (in the West) I do not get the professional or spiritual satisfaction of helping, guiding, or making an impact on someone's life (Banu, G3).

My experiences there (in the East) were unpleasant and hard most of the time, but it greatly prepared me as a teacher. I went there very optimistic and with high expectations but I came across quite a different Turkey and atmosphere than I was raised in. Initially, I had difficulties, from classroom management to adopting the culture, but this taught me more than any professional development course could do. I learned how to manage students with different backgrounds and needs. I learned how to interact and communicate with students, as well as how to respond to different student behaviours. And, during my last few years there, I enjoyed teaching, my relations with my students, and our projects at school. Thanks to those experiences, I feel much more competent and successful as a teacher than my colleagues who have not been there. These were very valuable professional gains (Aycan, G3).

These women's narrations suggest that women's presence in hardship posts in the East was very significant in terms of encouraging girls' schooling, creating a friendly school environment for girls, developing their academic and personal abilities and thus expanding their opportunities and many of their physical, social and intellectual capability sets. However, the socio-cultural context's undeniable power, as well as the economic and infrastructural underdevelopment in women's physical and social deprivation, cannot be overlooked. According to them, these difficulties and hard experiences gave them professional satisfaction and made them better teachers.

In summary, across the generations, women's early professional life experiences were significant in reflecting how they were engaged with improving other people's, women's, girls' or students' lives, and showed concern and effort on the women's part to understand their students' emotions, wishes and desires. There is a notable difference between the Republican women and the younger generations. The Republican women worked directly with children and female peasants and therefore were at the forefront of the community to better conditions for everyone and to work for the nation. On the other hand, the younger generations were less engaged with the community due to cultural alienation, but more engaged in improving the girls' schooling opportunities and creating girl-friendly school environments. In this regard, they were able to display their agency of initiating change or being part of the change in girls' lives. Yet, as the women's narrations suggest, some infrastructural challenges were involved for all three generations of women, which impacted on their physical and social capability sets. Unlike the experiences of Republican women, socio-cultural and political challenges in the second and third generations brought harassment and violence to the lives of the women and made them uncomfortable in public, which was not the case for their male counterparts. However, these harder experiences brought more satisfaction and helped them develop better qualities as teachers. This was something mentioned only by the women who worked in the harder conditions of the East. The women working in the West faced considerably fewer challenges but, concomitantly, they did not make mention of personal and professional satisfaction of being engaged for the good, or of professional development gained through their experiences. So, it could be argued that there was a trade-off between working in harder conditions and gaining professional qualities.

In the next section, I investigate the women's subsequent professional lives—the professional experiences spent after their hardship posts when they were back in the Western Turkey—drawing attention to challenges these women face in their career and the experience of being a woman teacher in Turkey.

Subsequent Professional Lives

All women across the generations, regardless of where they completed their hardship posts, were less satisfied with their subsequent working experiences, as they were no longer in the position of improving lives or making visible contributions. They were disturbed by the power relations and hierarchy at school, their working conditions (low salaries, poor health services) and education policies/legislation of the state that devalued teachers. To this end, each woman problematised different aspects of education from their perspective. Therefore, in this section, I focus on these issues and look into two themes: working conditions of the teaching profession and underrepresentation in the workplace.

Working Conditions of the Teaching Profession in Turkey

This section looks into some of the women's dissatisfaction with the teaching conditions in Turkey. Across the generations, the decreasing status of teaching can be tracked as the women discussed the minimal value attached to teachers both at institutional level and society level. They also mentioned their low salaries and minimal professional satisfaction compared to that of their initial years of teaching.

The Republican women, after completing their hardship posts, were sent to big cities to work, where they had relatively comfortable lives in terms of infrastructural development, health and economic opportunities. However, this was followed by a radical change in their teaching experiences. Particularly during the last years of their profession, which coincided with the divisive political atmosphere and chaos of the 1970s, they were all unhappy about the prevailing attitudes held towards them by their colleagues and students. They talked about little importance being attached to the teaching profession, increasingly disrespectful attitudes held towards them by students, and the termination of financial support (such as housing) given to teachers:

> In the villages we were respected by the peasants, the local people (...) When we started to work in big cities during the last years of my professional life, I saw that respect had disappeared. With the political chaos of the era students started to act towards us disrespectfully (Arzu, G1).

> During the last years of my teaching, there was not a peaceful environment. Political conflicts created tension among teachers. I saw how teachers were killed and schools were closed down, and I decided to retire as I no longer enjoyed teaching. In addition to this, the government started to respect their teachers less. In the early years of my career, the state used to prioritise its teachers, provide housing in villages or not charging for water and electricity at schools (...) Within years this has changed (...) How can you expect the community to respect and value teachers if the state does not respect them? (Berrin, G1)

> Among our colleagues we were like brother and sisters. However, the 1970s political atmosphere and working atmosphere polarised teachers. They were politically divided, stopped talking to each other, and started to act rudely towards those who did not think like them (...) So, I felt it was time to retire (Canan, G1).

As suggested by the women's narrations, despite the improving physical conditions of work, the worsening working atmosphere due to the political environment,[1] and the decreasing status of teaching both at society and institutional level, pushed them to retire. They no longer got the same satisfaction from the teaching profession.

The women from the Amazon generation, like the Republican generation, all stated that the status of the teaching profession had decreased to a large extent in comparison with their initial years. This is despite the improvement of the physical conditions of work environments. The education system and the state's irresponsibility in improving employee rights and the salaries of teachers were cited as reasons for this decreased status:

> The decrease in education quality also brings decrease in status of teachers. Education system is diverted to prepare students for centralized high school and university exams rather than teaching them to aspire towards knowledge and research. This mentality affects the society's perception towards teachers and they are not seen as the ones who are educating a nation but preparing students to exams (Meltem, G2).

> I believe that teaching has lost its value over the years. Teachers are not respected as much as they used to be in the past. This started to bother me and that's why I decided to retire. Compared to previous years, I saw how the purchasing power of teachers decreased. For instance, my father-in-law was a teacher, and with one teaching salary he was able to send all his five children to university. Now you cannot do it. In addition to this, the state does not promote any social and cultural rights, or opportunities for teachers. It does not offer them any privileges (Nesli, G2).

On the other hand, these women were not silent about the conditions of teachers. In the spirit of activism they had as students in the 1970s, they were all committed to improve the living standards, employee benefits, and health services and welfare of teachers. For this reason, they participated actively in demonstrations, strikes and boycotts and were put on trial for taking part in such activities. They were accused of acting for and forming organisations against the state as civil servants.[2] They stood trial, faced with possible penalties including relief from duty, a two-year prison sentence or a fine. However, none faced sentences. Their sentences were either replaced with fines or subjected to general amnesty:

I have joined in many strikes or boycotts to ask for better salaries, health facilities and welfare rights for teachers. It was a social demand. Teachers' living conditions and employee rights were not good and I still cannot say that teachers get what they deserve. At the end of each activity I took part in, I was taken to court for taking part in organised movements against the state (…) If we do not create a social demand and form solidarity to act collectively, we cannot ask for change (Sinem, G2).

Throughout my teaching years, I was a member of a teachers' union and I have participated in more than 20 strikes. I was put on trial as a result, for acting against the state. I never received any fine. But what I want to emphasize is that activist struggle should be collective to create a voice. I am not a lame and timid person who would remain silent and expect other people to act. If there is going to be an action, then it should not be personal (Nesli, G2).

I never hesitated to join any strike organized by the teacher union. I still do not. These days, some young teachers are hesitant to join because the teachers' unions are no longer as efficient as they used to be. They are scared of losing their jobs or being put on trial. I understand their concerns but then they should not complain. You cannot improve teachers' rights and salaries unless you voice your demand (…) I am not scared to be put on trial (Hatice, G2).

The women's narrations suggest that they were not insensitive to injustices and were not passive in public and social life. They used their collective agency to bring change and create awareness regarding the disinterest towards teachers by the state, and voiced their demands in relation to a general decrease in the financial support given to teachers, a loss of understanding of the needs of teachers (such as financial, social, cultural and educational), and the failure to improve their salaries and welfare.

The Postmodern women, as teachers at the beginning of their careers, were not able to make the same type of comparisons. However, compared to their student years and how they perceived teachers in those years, they expressed their dissatisfaction at the lack of importance, employee rights and insufficient salaries given to teachers, as well as with the increasing difficulty of becoming a teacher in public schools due to the required high scores in central exams. They particularly emphasised that the central exam practice for selecting teachers made them feel as if they were privileged to be working as civil servants, despite low salaries. Except for Aycan, all the teachers were hesitant to join in strikes, for fear of standing trial, which could possibly end their careers:

> Our salaries are low and we do not get any benefits (…) Last month, there was a strike again to protest this; I wanted to go but I did not dare. I was scared to be taken to court and face the possibility of being fired (…) but an elderly teacher joined the strike and did not come to school. I admired her. I wished I could do the same (Meryem, G3).

> I waited for two years to become a teacher. There are many teachers out there who are waiting to become teachers in the public sector because the private sector is an exploitation of the workforce for even lower salaries. I know that our salaries are not very satisfactory but I wouldn't dare to go out and join strikes. When you do such a thing, it is immediately followed by an accusation and you are taken to trial, and I do not want to lose my job (Tuba, G3).

> Teachers are not valued in this country, and they get underpaid (…) I do my best to fight against this. I am a member of a teachers' union and I join all the strikes supported by them, because I believe collective action could bring change to our lives (Aycan, G3).

It is obvious that worsening teaching conditions, the difficulty of becoming a public school teacher despite the low salaries and no benefits, and even worse conditions of teachers in the private sector were an impediment to women's agency as they expressed fear of losing their positions. This is because, although their conditions were equally unsatisfactory, it was the best option for these teachers when compared to their options in the private sector.

In summary, there is consensus across the generations that teaching is no longer the prestigious job it used to be in the Republican women's era. The main reason for this is the minimal importance given to teachers by the state and, with the privatisation and liberalisation of the education sector, much less is being offered to teachers in terms of opportunities. To challenge this, all teachers of the Amazon women and one teacher from the postmodern generation displayed their agency through joining in strikes to better conditions. The Republican women's avoidance of such acts can be explained by their Kemalist and nation-building ideology that taught them never to criticise the state, whereas for the most postmodern it involved fear of losing their existing opportunities. This can be argued to reveal the movements that Turkish society has progressed through since its establishment: from constructing the nation, to challenging the state, to accommodation of norms, conflicts and inequalities.

The women's dissatisfaction regarding teachers' working conditions was not limited only to the lack of state input, but also expressed towards the gender-based discrimination they face at schools. This discrimination deprived the women of equal participation and opportunities for promotion, placing them as a secondary class of teachers in the system. Below, I present the women's positions at schools.

Women's Lack of Voice at School and Underrepresentation in Management Positions

The women teachers were systematically excluded from voicing their ideas and denied opportunities to participate in decision-making and to climb the career ladder to upper management positions, purely on the basis of being a woman. This impacted on women's social and intellectual capabilities and agency. A common pattern seen across the three generations is that these women, both in the workplace and in their access to higher positions, faced sexist and discriminatory attitudes from their male colleagues. However, the difference emerges in how each generation of women conceptualised this inequality.

During the time Republican women worked as teachers (between 1945 and 1980), teaching was a highly respected job both for men and women. However, all management tasks were handled by the men and, therefore, all the interviewees conceptualised management as the men's endeavour. When talking about the absence of women in managerial positions and their lack of voice in decision-making meetings, they did not perceive it as a matter of gender inequality but rather as a natural order that they were happy with. This may be because, as their narrations below reveal, there were no women principals in their times, or because these women were a part of the nation-building process of the time. As in every nation-building project, they were motivated to work for the nation without questioning their position in the process. This would also mean that, as women, they had little aspiration to such positions:

There were no women principals in our time. I have never worked with a woman principal. I never had a desire to be one either. All upper management positions would be those of men. I was never bothered with that. It is only recently that I see that there are some female principals. Even when I retired in 1978, I don't remember seeing one (Arzu, G1).

In our time, it was difficult to be a woman principal if you were married with children. Indeed, there was no such thing as a woman principal. I even remember that in teachers' meetings it would always be the male teachers who would take active roles, make suggestions and initiate the discussions. Women teachers would remain silent because they would be thinking of what to cook or how to prioritise house chores at home (Berrin, G1).

Such quotations illustrate how the patriarchal order of society favoured man as the leaders and assigned traditional roles and familial responsibilities to women. This in turn restricted these women's perceptions and choices of career path in their professional lives. Women, as transmitters of culture, internalised inequalities with respect to the gender role, such that they did not see them in terms of gender inequality. Therefore, women's ability to articulate their capabilities was limited to the extent that they had access to the possibility of change and what they saw around them (Unterhalter 2012c). This, coupled with the lack of equal opportunities to climb the career ladder and to voice their ideas freely in meetings, inhibited their intellectual capability set of developing their aspirations of being able to advance in their professional career.

The Amazon women's professional lives started in the late 1970s and early 1980s and, at the time of the interview, except for Nesli who retired in 2008, all teachers were still working. Among the six participants, Sinem and Irem had worked as head teachers, which is unrepresentative considering that only 11.9% of women teachers in Turkey hold administration positions (KSGM 2012). All these women expressed their dissatisfaction with the undervaluation of female principals'/teachers' ideas at the schools in which they worked, or/and the underrepresentation of women in management positions/decision-making mechanisms. For those who had worked as a principal, they faced challenges and humiliation from their male peers as women principals. Unlike the previous generation, these women problematised issues of gender discrimination as an inequality in their careers.

All six women talked in different ways about how they were exposed to gender discrimination in the workplace, from being seen as unprofessional because of the care and nurturing image associated with female teachers, through to gender jokes and harassment. For these women, this constituted a feeling of humiliation, thus imposing a limitation on their social capability set of being able to participate in the workplace on the same terms with their male peers:

> Male teachers have a tendency to label female teachers for being emotional, motherly, and instinctive. In one of the discipline cases at school, a female student was caught giving a love letter to her male teacher. I expressed to my colleagues that this was quite normal behaviour for teenage girls; they might have a crush on their male teachers. Yet my male colleagues found this an unacceptable behaviour and criticised me for approaching the case with motherly and protective instincts (Sinem, G2).

> I am not very happy with the attitudes with which men approach women teachers at work. Their sexist joking about women bodies, or undermining speech towards our ideas regarding education and students, causes me to feel humiliation (Meltem, G2).

The women also talked about the insufficient number of women in managerial positions such as head teacher and assistant head teacher, and the negative attitudes of male teachers towards female leadership. At the same time, those who had not worked as principals also expressed their reluctance to hold a managerial position for the reasons of familial responsibilities, the demanding workload of the position, and seeing themselves as unfit for the post:

> What I see is that women principals generally experience difficulties in maintaining authority over male teachers (...) Male teachers usually challenge their authority and ignore them. What do we expect? The situation is the same at home. Most of the time women cannot force themselves be listened to at home (Meltem, G2).

> I believe that the number of women principals should increase, because it is the only way that dominating gender dynamics could be changed; but, if you ask me, I personally never felt interested in taking up such a position, because it is not really my cup of tea. Being a principal requires you to stay

at work for long hours. As a woman teacher, you are constantly being challenged by male teachers (Oya, G2).

The women's narrations suggest that although they problematised the lack of women managers, they were not really interested in diverting their career in that direction. The observations by Meltem and Oya regarding female head teachers were also supported by the experiences of Sinem and Irem, who had worked as principals. Sinem and Irem represented a minority of women teachers who were able to reach the position of headship. Irem's story of breaking through the glass ceiling was that she was working in Eastern Anatolia where there was a shortage of teachers then, and her application for the position was immediately processed. Yet, she talked about being found odd as a woman principal:

> I worked for three years as a principal in Eastern Anatolia. When I was introducing myself to the Directorate of Education or was making phone calls as the principal of the school, I could see the astonishment on their faces or could discern a few seconds of silence on the phone as it would take some time for those people to register that I am a woman and a principal at the same time (Irem, G2).

For Sinem, the post was competitive, as she was in the West and therefore it was only with her third application that she was accepted (and only temporarily) to work for six months. It later on turned into a permanent position. She highlighted the structural and institutional factors affecting women's access to higher positions or dissuading women from becoming principals. According to Sinem, the hiring of principals is a decision that has little transparency. She argued that gender, coupled with nepotism/favouritism and the highly politicised nature of managerial positions in Turkey, leaves little space for women to pursue a career in the upper levels of management. She considers herself lucky to have found such an opportunity given the barriers mentioned above. However, even if women made their way to such positions, Sinem said that there are further problems awaiting women principals. Based on her experiences, she talked about the sexist attitudes she experienced as a well-groomed woman who would dress elegantly, wear make-up and nail polish. In this way, she was seen as a principal with little or no power due to her femininity. Whenever she visited the educational management unit of the district for seminars or meetings, her management strategies and ideas were devalued by her male peers:

When they see a well-groomed lady like me with full make-up, in nice suits, high heels and with red nail polish, they expect a feminine submissiveness from me. They give little respect to my ideas. It is as if a successful leader should be a man or should look like a man (...) There is also a lot of politics going on. Each government favours the people who share the same ideology (...) In my case, it is so evident in the way I dress – my nail polish, my make-up – that I am not a religious person. Those sitting in the Directorate of Education in the city are conservative people who support the government and they know that I am not one of them, so they constantly cause problems for me (...) Today, I would have been in a different position if I were one of them and a man, of course (Sinem, G2).

This generation of women's narrations suggest that gender stereotypes about female teachers (such as doing the mothering or lacking the traits of effective administration), the politicised nature of leadership, and culturally male-dominated institutions, constituted the coercive structures that formed a ceiling hindering women's participation and voice in school meetings and their promotion to administrative positions. These factors constituted major limitations on women's social capability of being treated equally without any gender discrimination, being valued and respected for their ideas, being able to climb the career ladder and being able to enjoy a professional life based on equality.

The postmodern women started their career lives in the 2000s and they were still teaching at the time of the interview. They all talked about the practices that afforded minimal value and voice to female teachers; the negative attitudes towards female principals; and the inadequate numbers of women in decision-making positions. They defined this as gender inequality and discrimination:

I do not want to generalise, but my principal thinks that women talk a lot of nonsense. I can sense that he pretends to be listening to us, but does not value our ideas and suggestions. Men still transfer the traditional woman figure to school and do not regard us as teachers or as their peers (Seda, G3).

I find being a woman teacher in Turkey particularly stressful because the managers are men. This influences my communication with my principal. I approach him in a professional way but I feel that he does not respect me (...) Male colleagues are more relaxed when they are talking in meetings or in one-to-one interactions. However, with us (female teachers) they are always sceptical of our ideas (Banu, G3).

Although women constitute the majority at school, in meetings male teachers are more dominant, they are given more voice, and their ideas are respected more (Fisun, G3).

At the time of the interviews none of the participants held a managerial position, and this was because they were too young or did not have a sufficient number of years of professional experience to be qualified for such positions. Among all the women, Aycan was the only one who aspired to become a school inspector. The other five women had no intention of becoming head teachers for reasons of familial obligations, workload, having negative self-perceptions and lacking self-confidence in their management skills. This negative perception and lack of confidence also led three women (Fisun, Tuba and Meryem), like the Republican generation, to have internalised the idea that leadership falls within the male domain of work, which could possibly be explained by being raised in a patriarchal society with clear-cut gender roles:

> I don't think I have the appropriate management skills to become a principal. I think male teachers are better at maintaining authority and order; they have more power (Fisun, G3).

> I would not want to take on such a responsibility. It requires a lot of work and commitment. If you are married and have children like me, it is not a very appealing post. I have to go home, pay attention to the kids, cook. For a man it is much more appropriate since they do not feel obliged to do house chores (Tuba, G3).

Aycan, the only woman of her generation who wanted a more responsible post, emphasised that the chances were slim for her because career development for women teachers was rarely prioritised and decision-making was seen as falling within the male domain and tradition:

> I want to become an inspector. I am ready to follow any courses in this field. I am also aware that it will not be easy for me. Society and the system favour men for this position. Nothing is easy for us as women (Aycan, G3).

Like the older generations, the women's narrations suggested that they were usually ignored or disrespected because of the general cultural perception attached to female teachers as incompetent and unfit, which caused significant barriers to their social capability of having a space to voice to their ideas, having equal opportunity in accessing certain positions and being able to enjoy a fulfilling professional life.

To sum up, the second and third generation of women have gender awareness in articulating the unequal opportunities or discriminatory practices against them. The male favouritism discourages many women from taking up managerial posts as, in the case of this study, the majority of interviewed women showed no interest in administration posts due to the exhausting nature of the position, family obligations, and bias against women and their management skills (Celikten 2005; Smulyan 2000). Although there is no law that discriminates against women accessing the same opportunities as men in the workplace, there is a persistent perception that in Turkish culture women are seen as unfit to develop a professional career. Turkish society still seeks out men to be in charge of administrative positions or to be dominant in the workplace. This suggests that gender/patriarchal structures in households are reproduced in the professional space, playing the same restrictive role affecting women's agency to take part in decisions. In this sense, women are almost colluding with the culture and the larger system.

Having discussed the women's subsequent professional lives, I conclude the chapter by presenting their reflections on their entire teaching careers and their ideas on the roles of women teachers.

Reflections and Ideas on Roles as Women Teachers

This section briefly presents the idea the women held concerning the roles of female teachers in Turkey, drawing from their reflections on their entire professional careers. For the postmodern women who are in the early years of their career, it focuses on how they envisioned the role of a woman teacher in their lives as young teachers. My findings suggest that, regardless of the cultural, social and political contexts in which they taught, each woman in all three generations, without any differences, saw women teachers having the potential to change the lives of others, but particularly girls compared to their male peers. This is because, as women, they are more aware of the limitations that gender and a dominating male hegemony can bring to women's lives. Therefore, they could address gender inequality issues more directly than the male teachers and work to create a more gender just society both inside and outside the school. To illustrate this I present one quotation from each generation below:

Change starts with women teachers. I saw this in the villages in which I worked (…) and as I said in this interview, I saw how my presence at schools and villages brought modernisation, improvement to the lives of women (…) There is still male hegemony in society (…) Women cannot be free as long as they live under this hegemony, but what women teachers can do is to challenge this hegemony to make women freer and to modernise society (Arzu, G1).

Unlike male teachers, women teachers go into a struggle of 'being' in society. They fight to get a place in the public sphere. They strive hard to be accepted, not just as a woman, but as both a woman and a teacher. Since men do not face such a journey, they do not understand the value of existing as a teacher (…) I know what struggle means as a woman. As a woman teacher, it is my foremost duty to give my female students the consciousness that they can change their lives through education (Oya, G2).

As a woman and a teacher, things have not been easy for me in this life. I learned to accept that, as a woman, I would always be in a disadvantaged position in relation to the world and face double standards. As a teacher, I waited long to be appointed to a public school to work (…) I sometimes nag about my life, husband, working conditions, or school, but at the end of the day I am always aware that this was a long, successful journey for me as a woman. As a woman teacher, I feel responsible for inspiring my students, motivating them to further their education, and expanding their horizons. A male teacher does not do this. But as a woman teacher, I look into the eyes of my female students and I feel morally obliged to do something for them, because if I don't there is no one around to help them (…) I think that it is the woman teachers who challenge the male hegemony, because we all know the path of being a girl, woman, wife, and mother (Tuba, G3).

As women of different generations say, being a woman teacher means displaying an agency of creating change, working for gender equality in society and challenging male hegemony. As women, they believe they have more agency than male teachers as a result of being on the relatively disadvantaged side of Turkish culture. Therefore, they could better sympathise with the difficulties that girls or women face in this life.

CONCLUSION

The women's professional experiences show that education can have redistributive and interpersonal effects (Sen 1999). As teachers, the women of this research used the benefits of education to help other women and girls to expand their capability sets, to improve the quality of life of girls and to promote girls' emotional, social, personal and academic development. Thus, they used education both to distribute quality to other lives and to enact their other regarding agency and imperfect obligation of making changes in individuals' lives. As their narrations emphasised, this was something that could be achieved only by women teachers because they could be closer to girls/women and they could identify with the gender inequalities that these girls experienced. In this respect, these women teachers' work and presence in schools and villages showed the potential contribution that they can make to address gender issues and to eliminate gender inequalities in education in the Turkish context. Therefore, these findings highlight the central role of education in promoting gender justice in the life of girls and women. However, their professional experiences also suggest that their agency and their physical and social capabilities were limited by the gender discrimination in the workplace and the ban on civil servants' participation in strikes. These factors influenced the extent to which women teachers could work for gender justice. If women teachers are to be the ones who can bring and deliver change, gender justice and social transformation, there should be more opportunities and support and better working conditions for them.

In the next chapter, the conclusion, I analytically discuss the results of this research across the three generations, pointing out what the findings suggest for gender justice in women's lives and for gender equality in education in Turkey. I also make some policy suggestions that could improve women's lives.

NOTES

1. As nation builders of the country, these women felt no belonging to either side of the political divide, because they believed that neither represented Kemalist thinking.
2. By the 1982 constitution, civil servants were banned from joining in any strikes against the state. Therefore, these teachers were taken to court with the accusation of opposing the state.

CHAPTER 8

Conclusion: A Capabilities-Based Human Development Approach to Gender Justice and Education in Turkey

INTRODUCTION

This book presents an original research project situated in feminist and education literature, drawing the links between education, women's lives and gender literatures. It uses Nussbaum's and Sen's capability approach to cover women's and teachers' lives from a human development perspective in the Turkish context. Capabilities are operationalised as an evaluation of gender justice to analyse three different generations of women teachers' lives, offering an historical and changing account of their lives; and an historical sequence is followed in order to present progress (or lack of progress), continuity and changes in terms of the opportunities and freedoms in their lives. Capabilities in this research allow us to understand what freedoms are available to women, why and how they have reason to value these freedoms in creating a good life with well-being and agency, and the continuities and changes in the freedoms women teachers in Turkey have reason to value. Drawing on the narratives of women, Table 8.1 aims at comparing the valued capabilities of the three generations of women regardless of whether or not they possessed the capabilities.

© The Editor(s) (if applicable) and The Author(s) 2017   169
F.M. Cin, *Gender Justice, Education and Equality*, Palgrave Studies
in Gender and Education, DOI 10.1007/978-3-319-39104-5_8

Table 8.1   Women's valued capabilities across generations

Capabilities	Republican women	Amazon women	Postmodern women
Physical capability	To live in houses with water and electricity; to have access to transportation and health care facilities; to be freely mobile, to have reproductive health; to have emotional well-being; not to live in poverty, and to have access to adequate food and shelter	To live in houses with water and electricity; to have access to transportation and health care facilities; to be freely mobile, to have emotional and physical well-being; to be free from physical/verbal violence, harassment and assault; to feel safe and secure	To live in houses with water and electricity; to have access to transportation and health care facilities, to be freely mobile, to have emotional and physical well-being, to be free from physical violence, harassment and assaults; to feel safe and secure
Social capability	To engage freely in mixed gender relations; to play and have leisure time; to be treated with dignity and non-discrimination on equal basis with their brothers; to be free from family and neighbourhood expectations and pressure	To be treated with full dignity and non-discrimination at home and in the workplace; not to experience any gender or ethnic (national origin) discrimination in social interaction; to engage freely in various social interactions; to be free from family and neighbourhood pressure; to have leisure time and play; to have equal opportunities with men in access to career opportunities; to have an equitable share of responsibility within the household; to pursue their interests and take up hobbies; to have personal time and space	To be treated with full dignity and non-discrimination at home and in the workplace; not to experience any gender or ethnic (national origin) discrimination in social interaction; to engage freely in various social interactions; to be free from family and neighbourhood pressure; to have leisure time and play; to have equal opportunities with men in access to career opportunities; to have an equitable share of responsibility within the household; to pursue their interests and take up hobbies; to have personal time and space

Table 8.1 (continued)

Capabilities	Republican women	Amazon women	Postmodern women
Intellectual capability	To have access to free public education; to develop practical reasoning; to enjoy different literary forms of art; to develop self-confidence	To have access to public education; to be able to use the senses, to imagine, think and reason; to advance their careers; to develop self-confidence; to join self/professional development courses	To have access to public education; to be able to use the senses, to imagine, think and reason; to advance their careers; to develop self-confidence; to join professional self/development courses; to start/continue postgraduate degrees
Economic capability	To be able to generate income; to be economically independent	To be able to generate income; to be economically independent; to be in charge of their income	To be able to generate income; to be economically independent
Political capability	To be able to say what they believe without fear and oppression; not to be discriminated against for their political stance	To be able to say what they believe without fear and oppression; not to be discriminated against for their political stance, to be free from state repression, to join in demonstrations and strikes	To be able to say what they believe without fear and oppression; not to be discriminated against for their political stance, to join in demonstrations and strikes

THE CONCEPTUALISATION OF GENDER JUSTICE IN TURKEY: WHAT DOES THIS RESEARCH SAY ABOUT GENDER JUSTICE AND EQUALITY IN TURKEY?

These women's lives illustrate how gender justice in Turkey is an issue of a patriarchal mindset and institutions, rather than a lack of legislation and legal provisions. As highlighted in Chaps. 2 and 3, gender justice in Turkey has been understood from a human rights perspective. Granting equal rights is regarded as an achievement and measure of gender equality. These women's lives confirmed the claims of many scholars that the focus on legalistic solutions improves women's lives only to a limited degree, because many countries grant these rights only rhetorically (Robeyns 2006; Tikly and Barrett 2011; Unterhalter 2003b). Once rights are granted, governments do not look at how women actually benefit from these rights or at the factors that limit women's access to rights. Women's situation in Turkey is not an exception. Taking a capabilities perspective, I have shown that, for these women at least, guaranteeing them a fair share of jobs, positions in management, employment opportunities, social security, work conditions, participation in public life and involvement in the party and in politics—as the current Turkish government has done—has had limits in terms of gender justice. This is because legislation only addresses 'correcting inequitable outcomes of social arrangements without disturbing the underlying framework that generates them' (Fraser 1997: 23), leaving the existing gender ideology and patriarchal nature of institutions untouched. Therefore, as seen in this study, these women continued to be discriminated against at work on the basis of their gender and faced inequality of opportunities with regard to their access to managerial positions. In social life, particularly during hardship posts in Eastern Turkey, they were exposed to violence, discrimination, harassment and exclusion on the basis of their gender identity. They worked in poor infrastructural environments with no safety and health services, which put their well-being at risk, and they were not welcomed in some conservative contexts because they were women.

These women's failure across the generations to achieve their valued capabilities, despite legislation, reveals the falsehood of the assumption that women and men have equal resources or commodities to use for exercising their rights and achieving their valuable capabilities. For instance, in these women's cases, female and male teachers had equal rights to access managerial positions and to appeal if they suspected gender discrimination. Similarly, education was compulsory both for girls and boys, but as women's narratives indicated, many girls in eastern provinces did not go to school despite legislation criminalising fathers for not sending their daughters to schools. From a rights perspective, these steps could be seen as sufficient and significant in achieving gender equality. In reality, however, women constituted a small number of the people employed in such positions and their narrations showed that legislation concerning the schooling of girls was ineffective. There were no transformative acts and programmes that corrected this inequitable outcome or restructured the gender codes that generate unequal access to such positions for women and to schools for girls. In other words, acts or programmes are needed that encourage women to apply for managerial positions, because we cannot expect that a legal framework which treats women as independent actors will increase women's participation in these posts (or increase girls' schooling rate) if they have been historically and culturally deprived of occupying such positions.

If the state sees the granting of equal rights as boosting development, then it must surely be 'a process of expanding real freedoms that people enjoy' (Sen 1999: 3). Such an understanding of freedom should be in the form of supporting individual capabilities women have reason to value and promoting equal opportunities for both men and women. To this end, this research presented a deep analysis of the lives of the women interviewed to highlight cultural, political, environmental and contextual conversion factors that impede women's access to their valued capabilities and to their full agency. For instance, the interviews suggested that the women worked under poor environmental and infrastructural conditions and were exposed to violence and harassment in conservative districts on the basis of their gender identity. In this situation, women in the first generation valued their capability of having reproductive health due to a lack of healthcare workers. On the other hand, women in the younger generation revealed valued capabilities as being free from male harassment. Ensuring that there are, at minimum, healthcare workers and fully equipped healthcare centres in the villages women are sent to could solve this problem. Whereas regarding solutions to problems of sexual harassment, laws criminalising the harassment of women in the public sphere are helpful. However, they have little value in reality if women are scared to take any legal action against these assaults, if they feel suppressed and threatened and are scared that they would attract further hostile attention. What may be needed for female teachers in such regions is to take measures ensuring their personal safety against such assaults so that women can fully enjoy their physical and psychological well-being.

Therefore, a capabilities lens on these women's lives suggests that women in Turkey need more opportunities, commodities and resources than men to achieve their valued capability sets to enjoy the same quality of life. What is needed even more than the equalisation of rights or the transformation of institutions is the capability improvement on the basis of human diversity, and a reciprocal relationship between social policy formulations, capabilities and agency (Sen 1999).

The Dual Potentials of Education: Education as a Catalyst for Empowerment or a Tool for Moral and Cultural Hegemony?

As argued before, education can both reproduce and interrupt inequalities. The lives of the women in this book uphold the link between education and women's empowerment and agency (Alkire 2002; DeJaeghere and Lee 2011; Kabeer 1999; Murphy-Graham 2012) and show how education played a critical role in expanding the capabilities and opportunities of women to live meaningful lives, providing an avenue for the cultivation of mind and processes of recognition, capacity building and action (Nussbaum 2003a). Through education, they developed the capacity to make strategic life choices, enjoyed the agency to be in charge of their lives, had self-determination and confidence and accessed employment opportunities. In this sense, education was a transitional and transformative space showing them the existence of other life options, different opportunities and alternative lives they could have. It could be seen how these women made their way out of poverty, cultural prohibitions or family/societal expectations that would have dictated their lives, forced them into marriage at an early age or into an abusive marriage that they could not leave. They discovered their potential and talents to decide what they could do and be; they gained social skills to connect with other people, earned economic independence and freedom to choose their husbands, had bargaining power in their relationships with their husbands, had the courage to leave an abusive marriage and developed agency to expand other women/girls' capabilities and impact on their lives.

At the same time, the lives analysed in this book show that the inequalities and gendered practices at home or in the community/society further played out in schools, limiting the women's physical, social and intellectual set of capabilities. Although education seemed to offer the women a more gender-just life, it is important to note that, simultaneously, education was a tool of the reproduction of moral and cultural hegemony, allowing space and freedom to women only to the extent that these did not disrupt the gender order. From a capabilities perspective, we could see how women's educational lives are influenced by structures (such as gendered attitudes towards girls' learning, the gendered codes regarding girls' behaviour and dress, curriculum, inegalitarian gender relations and unsafe school environment) in ways that do not promote gender equality or do not support women in terms of equal opportunities for pursuing what they have reason to be and to do as students. These practices exclude girls from participation and learning processes at schools; discourage them from achieving their aspirations; and suppress their desires and motivation, creating submissive and obedient identities.

Further implications of how schools disempowered students or girls were evident in women's professional lives, such as Turkish instruction in schools in Kurdish areas, where many students have limited Turkish knowledge and some students do not have any knowledge of Turkish at all. This situation impeded students' academic development and excluded them from participation, both in accessing the curriculum and attaining learning. As some studies show (Kaya 2009; Kirdar 2009) this also lowers the achievement of students or decreases their chances of furthering their education. The Turkish state is completely against the Kurdish people receiving education in their mother language in public schools, on the basis that it threatens the territorial integrity and unitary character of the country. However, the state neither provides any other solutions to solve these problems, nor supports Kurdish students through preparatory Turkish courses. A different curriculum could bring these students to the same level as their Turkish peers by hiring Kurdish-speaking teachers in these regions. Considering that the Turkish education system follows a rights-based model on the basis of making education mandatory and free for every individual, without taking into account the diversity within Turkey, it underestimates the problems that disadvantaged parts of society (such as girls in the East, or Kurdish students) or some religious groups face in the education system. A capabilities framework, as in this study, provides an entry to debate and action to take diversity in the society into account, as well as the functionings and capabilities that groups or individuals have reason to value and achieve.

Women Teachers as Agents of Change

The work and the presence of women teachers are significant for promoting gender justice and social change (Kirk 2004, 2006, 2008; Stacki 2002). This book points out that being engaged in education, their work as teachers contributed to enacting ethical/imperfect obligation of working for social good and helping other women and girls whose lives were much more constrained by gender inequalities. They were able to form close relationships with girls, expanding their physical, social and intellectual capabilities and opportunities and increasing their school participation. This shows that women felt ethically bound to promote greater gender equality as a matter of respect for human rights and acted as moral agents.

As listed in the introduction chapter, there are many campaigns to increase girls' enrolment rates, particularly in Eastern Anatolia; yet these focus only on the economic aspects of the problem through funding girls and their families and improving school conditions. Distribution of more resources to these families and girls addresses only one part of the problem and can do little to include girls and to promote equity as long as the concerns, attitudes or values of the families in the East regarding the education of girls are ignored. No actions have been taken regarding the prevalent mindsets and the cultural structures that impede girls' schooling in these regions, nor a focus on genuine solutions that could persuade fathers to send their daughters to schools. Turkey adopts a human capital and rights perspective towards the education of girls. Particularly, the state's approach to promoting the education of girls as a necessity, as a tool for creating healthier families, raising good, educated mothers and wives and contributing to the economic system, as the human capital envisages, is an indication that women are not seen as the directors of their own lives, but as instrumental players in the lives of others (as reproducers, caregivers). Such a perspective brings disadvantages, does not respect their human dignity and displays ignorance about human lives, particularly in the Turkish case, where there is a strong and persistent inequality affecting girls' schooling. On the other hand, women's work in these districts showed having a female teacher at schools and in the school environment alleviated the concerns of fathers who were sensitive about their daughters' honour, making them feel more secure about sending their daughters to schools. Furthermore, for families who insisted on keeping girls at home to look after sick, elderly people or infants, the negotiations with women teachers created an incentive to reach a consensus. The women teachers were gender-sensitive and fought for gender equality; at the same time, they were sensitive to the cultural values of the region and tried to create an atmosphere of co-education and to contribute towards the establishment of a culture of democracy and gender equality at schools, in which women have an equal say with men and, in turn, create and secure capabilities for everyone in the society. This study points to a need for understanding how some local and cultural norms and values increase girls' inclusion in education. However, many education campaigns and projects have so far ignored this aspect.

Overall, this book underlines the necessity and importance of capabilities-based gender justice as supplementary to the rights-based approach. The lenses of the capabilities approach are shown to help us to explore differences: the different forms of gender inequalities that women face and the different forms of capabilities that they value in their lives in order to establish a more women-friendly society. In particular, the multi-generational perspective adds another dimension in the sense that it is possible to comment on what has changed in the lives of women and teachers in Turkey and to track the extent to which norms, institutions and culture developed in a way that limited or expanded the freedoms of women.

OVERLAPPING CAPABILITIES AMONG WOMEN AROUND THE WORLD

Although this study focuses on women in Turkey to illuminate education, development and gender issues in a broader arena of gender justice, the experiences of women described in this book have much in common with those of women globally.

For this study, inspired by Nussbaum's work and list of capabilities, I have produced my own list of capabilities to use as a framework of development and evaluation and adapted it to the specific Turkish context. I have empirically applied my list to women's lives. The list that I used for this research underlined some context-specific capabilities, such as the values of being free from political violence and oppression and neighbourhood pressure. However, individually and collectively, women are deprived of their full participation in society and of opportunities; they are frequently treated as subordinate groups in society; they face discrimination, exclusion and isolation and are marginalised to various extents economically, socially and politically around the world. The lack of choices and opportunities women in this study experience and the human capabilities emphasised in this list can also appear in other contexts that share the same political or cultural divides with Turkey.

The list also shows considerable overlap with Robeyns (2003a) or Alkire and Black (1997) particularly in relation to the physical capabilities of life, physical and mental health and intellectual capability of right to education and knowledge. As Qizilbash (2002) argues, although all the lists produced so far deepen our understanding of quality of life, context and strategic reasons are important in determining the content of the list. Even though the capability sets generated here are context-specific, they can be applied to women's lives in all kinds of contexts which are at various stages of development. For instance, the lack of social capabilities of unbelonging, social exclusion or difficulties in access to schooling experienced by women in this research and the list are similarly experienced in Iraq after the collapse of the government, and in Afghanistan where tribal customs and religious extremism had a deleterious effect on women's political, social and physical capabilities, such as displacement, financial hardship, social disintegration or an increase in child marriages and a decrease in school attendance (Muscati 2012). Similarly, the experiences of women in Sub-Saharan and South-east Africa, where the lack of access to quality healthcare, unsafe abortions, maternal deaths and disabilities (Kashyap 2012), and early marriages and teenage pregnancies exclude girls from education or work and create deep poverty, which not only affects their physical capabilities but also leads to a lack of social capabilities, such as the loss of social belonging and association or vulnerability (Odhiambo 2012). As the limited political freedoms outlined in the list, women activists in China and in the Arab Spring report on the problems of finding themselves facing harassment or criminal prosecution for demanding women's rights (Hom 2012); again, women in China often face employment-related discrimination and experience persistent wage gaps despite legal framework guaranteeing equal pay and equal work (Prasso 2012). In the same vein, girls in Palestine or Afghanistan are often enforced to follow religious and traditional practices such as veiling or adapting certain dress code that thwart their freedoms and dictate their decisions, curtailing their options, from whom they can marry to how much schooling they can get. In contrast, the practice of a ban on full-face veils in Europe, in particular in France, curtails women's right to autonomy and the right to make a decision in accordance with one's beliefs and values (Sunderland 2012). The outlawing of abortion in Latin America causes women to terminate their pregnancies in unsanitary conditions that threaten their life and health. As seen, the capabilities generated in this list are, whilst context-specific for Turkey, at the same time expand well beyond the context of the experiences of women in Turkey. Women all around the world, be they in Europe, the Middle East or Africa experience practices, norms, lack of laws and legislations that undervalue women's dignity, equality and power. These inequalities are usually pushed to the margins of public policy and civil society and can be addressed by the political will of governments or intergovernmental agencies to promote women's opportunities and their collaboration and civic engagement with rights groups and experts. These actions and initiatives should be directed towards expanding the choices, opportunities and autonomy of women for development. Although the reorientation of economic, social and political structures can enhance human development, it is unfortunate that, in developing countries, the majority of women have limited resources and opportunities to develop their capabilities and some groups of women (those who are marginalised at the intersection of race, ethnicity and religion) continue to be structurally excluded from using and developing their capability sets (Saleeby 2014). For women's capability development and enhancement that does not erode agency, we need thoughtful consideration and enlightened policies that strategise gender equality.

IMPLICATIONS FOR POLICY AND PRACTICE

Drawing on the conclusions in this book, policy-makers and schools need to reflect upon and make further changes to address diversity and the valued capabilities of women/girls both inside and outside the school, to create a more women-friendly society and school environment. In this respect, the use of the capability approach lens in regulating the legislation, social policies and educational campaigns, redesigning the curriculum, teaching and learning, addressing girls' voices, exploring their valued capabilities and assessing their educational well-being can guide the formation of road maps and solutions for gender justice. This is necessary for the development of women and the country. In terms of educational implications, the findings suggest that first, the removal of gendered beliefs in pedagogy and sexist practices from schools are essential to facilitate the empowerment of women and achieve more gender equality. Second, societal structures/conditions are critically important for the safe and harassment-free schooling experiences of girls. These two points require the quality input of teacher/head teacher education and training, so they may act on issues related to girls' exclusion from learning experiences and schooling, and ensure that the necessary capability inputs are provided to enable girls to enjoy non-discriminatory education (Tikly and Barrett 2011). Third, there is a need to reconsider some aspects of the education system, such as the practice of instruction exclusively in the Turkish language, to include everyone in the learning process and education system. So, education policy in Turkey should no longer be seen as only a problem of the gender gap between boys' and girls' school attendance, or as only an issue of girls' schooling and bureaucratic politics for the Ministry of Education; rather, it should address the gendered aspects of teaching practices, curriculum and the education system in general, as indicated by many educational researchers (Esen 2007; Çayır 2015; Akhun, et al. 2000; Sayilan 2008). It should also go beyond these and should take the school surroundings and environment into consideration as a cause for gender inequality in girls' schooling. In other words, the informational basis for (gender) just education policy (Sen 1999) needs to be expanded beyond numbers, human capital and rights.

In terms of women teachers' lives, I suggest four principles that need to be addressed for the improvement of teachers' conditions and equality in society. First, educational policies could prioritise women's entry to decision-making/management posts. To this end, quotas for women's participation in such posts could be introduced in order to improve the representation of women in managerial bodies and to create equal opportunities for women. Also, women's posts to leadership in rural contexts where girls schooling is problematic can be prioritised. It should be noted that women's access to decision-making can influence the change of patriarchal legislations and can form a positive perception in society regarding women's roles. Second, improvements to the infrastructure and living conditions of women teachers in hardship posts are needed to provide equal opportunities to enjoy a healthy professional life for all teachers across Turkey. Teachers cannot be expected to work for change when they cannot even meet their basic physical capability sets. Nor can they work for transformation when they cannot practise their right to participate in demonstrations and strikes in order to voice their professional dissatisfaction about working conditions, civil liberties and employment benefits. Indeed, the repression of this capability is an important violation of the political freedoms and rights of teachers, which needs to be addressed both constitutionally and in practice. It is an issue of gender justice, as the already suppressed voices of women remain silent and any room for their political participation is denied. If teachers are believed to be capable of bringing about social justice, then the restriction of such freedoms by the state is a contradiction, for it forces them to remain silent about the injustices in society. Third, gender-aware teacher training for women/teachers who are to serve in Eastern Turkey, as well as throughout the entire country, is needed, emphasising sensitivity to girls' education and support for their schooling. Experiences of women who have served there could also be useful to share the potential difficulties future women teachers may come across and formulate solutions to eradicate these difficulties. Alternatively, creating local networks of women teachers may be useful for them to support each other. This is very important for teacher education in a highly unequal society like Turkey. Although women's professional experiences show that teacher education institutions in Turkey at different eras were engaged in raising teachers working for social transformation and reducing inequalities, teachers lacked 'public-good professional capabilities' (such as informed vision or social and collective struggle to empower communities and promote human rights) that should be considered when educating professionals who can go on to work for a more equitable, just society (Walker and McLean 2013). For instance, except for Republican women, the accounts of the younger generation of women show little informed vision, which means they had little understanding of how their profession is shaped by the historical, socio-economic, political contexts and how the structures in Eastern Turkey shape women's and girl's lives. They were barely aware of the conditions waiting for them in different parts of society and went to serve their hardship posts without understanding the challenges that awaited them. So, teacher-training institutions should not only equip teachers pedagogically or provide ways of teaching and learning, but also enhance professional capabilities oriented towards the public good. They should equip teaching graduates with the necessary skills, knowledge and values to contribute to the common good and make society more just and equitable. In other words, teacher education should adopt public-good professionalism grounded in capability theory. Finally, the recruitment of both women and Kurdish speaking teachers in these regions should be adopted, to connect with the community and to establish relations based on mutual trust and understanding. Women are potential critical actors in the education process, key agents of structural and societal transformation built on principles of gender equality. They can 'contribute to a more just and equitable social order that includes transformation as a goal of educational reform' (Stacki 2002: 12).

CONCLUSION

This book has sought to flesh out the restrictions and inequalities in women's lives. In so doing, it has highlighted cultural, political, environmental and contextual conversion factors within a human development paradigm. Of course, it is important to note that this research project can never hope to be exhaustive or provide a definitive account for all women's lives in Turkey and the rest of the world. The way women interact with or face gender inequalities every day may go beyond these lives on behalf of those who are less empowered and capable of practising their rights than these women teachers. However, the valued capabilities discussed in this book and research are important in guiding us towards designing policies or social and political arrangements, because it is clear that social policies do not effectively address the concerns of gender equality, due to the gap between legal equality and the reality of women's lives. Therefore, the use of the capabilities lens can respond to these needs by encouraging policy-makers to initiate and implement more gender-sensitive policies which focus on giving more opportunities and allocating more resources to women for building capabilities needed for equality. So, while this book contributes to an improved understanding of freedoms, capabilities and opportunities for gender equality, the ideas explored within it could certainly be further explored through a capabilities-based quantitative survey and the development of gender equality indicators, for which my five capabilities and the valued functionings might provide a starting point.

Appendix A: Interviews Undertaken with Women Teachers

The timing and the number of interviews undertaken with women teachers are set out in the table below. Semi-structured interviews were conducted which allowed flexibility to expand, shift or elaborate on women's answers in an interactional manner. Full anonymity was guaranteed to the interviewees. First of all, pre-interviews were conducted with the participants to get to know my participants on a personal level, to establish rapport, and to explain my research and the reasons for undertaking such research. Then, an interview date was scheduled for the research and a follow-up interview was carried out with women for this book. These follow-up ones aimed to give women an opportunity and space to reflect upon their experiences. Some of the follow-up interviews were conducted via Skype or phone for practical reasons.

Table A.1 Interview schedule

Name of the participant	Number of interviews	Type of interview	Date of interview
Arzu (G1)	3	Pre-interview	27 April, 2010
		Interview	27 May 2010
		Follow-up interview	5 October 2015
Berrin (G1)	3	Pre-interview	3 June 2010
		Interview	16 June 2010
		Follow-up interview	9 December 2015

(*continued*)

© The Editor(s) (if applicable) and The Author(s) 2017
F.M. Cin, *Gender Justice, Education and Equality*, Palgrave Studies in Gender and Education, DOI 10.1007/978-3-319-39104-5

Table A.1   (continued)

Name of the participant	Number of interviews	Type of interview	Date of interview
Canan (G1)	3	Pre-Interview Interview Follow-up interview	19 June 2010 21 June 2010 11 December 2015
Nesli (G2)	3	Pre-Interview Interview Follow-up interview	8 May 2010 5 June 2010 5 September 2015
Meryem (G2)	4	Pre-Interview Interview (2) Follow-up interview	15 April 2010 10–13 May 2010 12 September 2015
Hatice (G2)	3	Pre-Interview Interview Follow-up interview	1 June 2010 30 June 2010 22 February 2016
Irem (G2)	3	Pre-Interview Interview Follow-up interview	1 July 2010 12 July 2010 3 November 2015
Oya (G2)	3	Pre-Interview Interview Follow-up interview	15 July 2010 1 August 2010 4 November 2015
Asli (G3)	3	Pre-Interview Interview Follow-up interview	23 May 2010 28 May 2010 15 September 2015
Banu (G3)	4	Pre-Interview Interview (2) Follow-up interview	20 July 2010 25–27 July 2010 10 December 2015
Fusun (G3)	3	Pre-Interview Interview Follow-up interview	17 September 2010 19 September 2010 20 September 2015
Seda (G3)	3	Pre-Interview Interview Follow-up interview	30 August 2010 12 September 2010 5 January 2016
Meltem (G3)	3	Pre-Interview Interview Follow-up interview	12 August 2010 14 August 2010 23 February 2016
Tuba (G3)	4	Pre-Interview Interview (2) Follow-up interview	18 August 2010 2–3 September 2010 7 January 2016

Appendix B: Profile of Women

F.M. Cin, *Gender Justice, Education and Equality*, Palgrave Studies
in Gender and Education, DOI 10.1007/978-3-319-39104-5

185

Table B.1 Profile of women

Name of the participants	Year of birth	Field of teaching	Level of teaching	Hardship post experiences	Other professional experiences
Arzu(G1[a])	1925	Primary school teacher	7–12 year old (primary school)	1945 to 1968 in rural villages of the Aegean region	1968 to 1979 in urban areas of the Aegean region
Berrin (G1)	1932	Primary school teacher	7–12 year old (primary school)	1948 to 1971 in rural villages of central Anatolia	1971 to 1980 in urban areas of the Aegean region
Canan (G1)	1928	Primary school teacher	7–12 year old (primary School)	1947 to 1970 in rural villages of the Aegean and Mediterranean regions	1970 to 1978 in urban areas of the Aegean region
Irem (G2[b])	1955	Social Science teacher	12–15 year old (secondary school)	1978 to today, 1978 to 1980 in central Anatolia, 1980 to 1986 in eastern Anatolia, 1986 to 1992 in rural areas of the Black Sea region	1992 to today in a large city in the Aegean region
Hatice(G2)	1954	Turkish teacher	12–15 year old (secondary school)	1978 to 1985 in various rural areas in central Anatolia	1985 to today in the Aegean region
Meltem (G2)	1960	Turkish Language and Literature Teacher	15–18 year old (high school)	1983 to 1986 in south-eastern Anatolia	1986 to today in the Aegean region
Nesli (G2)	1955	Art Teacher	7–18 year old (primary, secondary, high school)	1978 to 1982 in south-eastern Anatolia	1982 to today in a large city in the Aegean region
Oya (G2)	1960	History Teacher	15–18 year old (high school)	1982 to 1990 in rural villages of the Aegean region	1990 to today in a large city in the Aegean region

Sinem (G2)	1957	Art Teacher	7–18 year old (primary, secondary, high school)	1979 to 1981 in rural villages of central Anatolia, 2005 to today in a rural village of the Aegean region	1981 to 2005 in a large city in the Aegean region
Aycan (G3c)	1979	Primary school teacher	7–12 year old (primary school)	2002 to 2008 in eastern Anatolia	2008 to today in a rural area in the Aegean region
Banu (G3)	1975	Primary school teacher	7–12 year old (primary school)	2001 to 2008 in eastern Anatolia	2008 to today in a rural area in the Aegean region
Meryem (G3)	1985	Kindergarten teacher	6 year old (pre-school education)	2008 to today in rural villages of the Aegean region	Still doing her compulsory service
Seda (G3)	1984	Information Technologies and Computer teacher	10–18 year old (primary, secondary and high school)	2006 to today in rural villages of Marmara region	Still doing her compulsory service
Fisun (G3)	1984	Science teacher	12–15 year old (secondary school)	2006 to 2008 in eastern Anatolia	2008 to today in a rural area of a large city in the Aegean region
Tuba (G3)	1976	Primary school teacher	7–12 year old (primary school)	2002 to 2004 in south-eastern Anatolia	2004 to today in a rural area of a large city in the Aegean region

aG1 stands for Generation 1, which represents the Republican Women generation
bG2 stands for Generation 2, which represents the Amazon Women generation
cG3 stands for Generation 3, which represents the Postmodern generation

BIBLIOGRAPHY

Acar, F., & Altunok, G. (2013). The 'politics of intimate' at the intersection of neo-liberalism and neo-conservatism in contemporary Turkey. *Women's Studies International Forum, 41*, 14–23.

Acar, F., & Ayata-Gunes, A. (2000). *Gender and identity construction: Women of the Central Asia, the Caucasus and Turkey*. Leiden: Brill.

Acar, F., Ayata, A., & Varol, D. (1999). *Cinsiyete Dayali Ayrimcilik: Turkiye'de Egitim Sektoru Ornegi (Gender Discrimination: The Example of Turkey's Education Sector)*. Ankara: KSSGM.

Acker, S. (1994). *Gendered education: Sociological reflections on women, teaching, and feminism*. Buckingham: Open University Press.

Acker, S. (1995). Carry on caring: The work of female teachers. *British Journal of Education, 16*(1), 21–36.

Acuner, S. (2013). Gender and development in Turkey. *Turkish Policy Quarterly, 11*, 71–78.

Ahmad, F. (2008). Politics and political parties in Republican Turkey. In R. Kasaba (Ed.), *Cambridge history of Turkey: Volume 4 Turkey in modern world* (pp. 226–265). Cambridge: Cambridge University Press.

Ahmed, L. (1982). Feminism and feminist movements in the Middle East: A preliminary exploration: Turkey, Egypt, Algeria, People's Democratic Republic of Yemen. *Women's Studies International Forum, 5*, 153–168.

Aikman, S. (2011). Educational and indigenous justice in Africa. *International Journal of Educational Development, 31*, 15–22.

Aikman, S., & Rao, N. (2012). Gender equality and girls' education: Investigating frameworks, disjunctures and meanings of quality education. *Theory and Research in Education, 10*(3), 211–228.

© The Editor(s) (if applicable) and The Author(s) 2017
F.M. Cin, *Gender Justice, Education and Equality*, Palgrave Studies in Gender and Education, DOI 10.1007/978-3-319-39104-5

Aikman, S., & Unterhalter, E. (2013). Gender equality, capabilities and the terrain of quality in education. In L. Tikly & A. Barrett (Eds.), *Education quality and social justice in the global South: Challenges for policy, practice and research* (pp. 25–39). Abingdon: Routledge.

Aikman, S., Halai, A., & Rubagiza, J. (2011). Conceptualising gender equality in research on education quality. *Comparative Education, 47*(1), 45–60.

Akhun, I., Bircan, I., Bulbul, S., & Senemoglu, N. (2000). *Kiz Cocuklarinin Mesleki Egitime ve Istihdama Yonelimleri (Orientation of Girls to Vocational Training and Employment.* Ankara: KSSGM.

Akkoyunlu-Wigley, A., & Wigley, S. (2008). Basic education and capability development in Turkey. In A. Nonhl, A. Akkoyunlu-Wigley, & S. Wigley (Eds.), *Education in Turkey* (pp. 271–297). Munster: Waxmann.

Aktas, N. (2007). *Problems faced by female school administrators.* Unpublished master thesis, Ankara University (in Turkish).

Akyuz, Y. (2006). *Turk Egitim Tarihi (Turkish Education History).* Ankara: Pegem Yayincilik.

Alat, Z., & Alat, K. (2011). A qualitative study of parental resistance to girls' schooling. *Educational Sciences: Theory & Practice, 11*, 1369–1373.

Alkire, S. (2002). *Valuing freedom's: Sen's capability approach and poverty reduction.* New York: Oxford University Press.

Alkire, S., & Black, R. (1997). A practical reasoning theory of development ethics: Furthering the capabilities approach. *Journal of International Development, 9*(2), 263–279.

Altinay, A. G., & Arat, Y. (2009). *Violence against women in Turkey: Nationwide survey.* Istanbul: Punto Publishing.

Altinkurt, Y., & Yilmaz, K. (2012). Being a female school administrator in Turkey: Views of teachers and administrators. *Energy Education Science and Technology Part B-Social and Educational Studies, 4*(4), 2227–2238.

Ames, P. (2005). When access is not enough: Educational exclusion of rural girls in Peru. In S. Aikman & E. Unterhalter (Eds.), *Beyond access: Transforming policy and practice for gender equality in education* (pp. 149–165). Bournemouth: Oxfam.

Arat, Y. (1989). *The patriarchal paradox: Women politicians in Turkey.* London: Associated University Press.

Arat, Y. (1993). Women's studies in Turkey: From Kemalism to feminism. *New Perspectives on Turkey, 9*, 119–135.

Arat, Y. (1994a). Toward a democratic society: Women's movement in Turkey in the 1980s. *Women's Studies International Forum, 17*, 241–248.

Arat, Z. (1994b). Kemalism and Turkish women. *Women and Politics, 14*, 57–80.

Arat, Z. (1994c). Liberation or indoctrination: Women's education in Turkey. *Review of Social, Economic and Administrative Studies, 8*, 83–105.

Arat, Y. (1997). Project of modernity and women in Turkey. In S. Bozdogan & R. Kasaba (Eds.), *Rethinking modernity and national identity in Turkey* (pp. 388–418). Seattle: University of Washington Press.

Arat, Y. (1999). Democracy and women in Turkey: In defence of liberalism. *Social Politics, 6,* 370–387.

Arat, Y. (2000). From emancipation to liberation: The changing role of women in Turkey's public realm. *Journal of International Affairs, 54,* 107–123.

Arat, Y. (2008). Contestation and collaboration: Women's struggles for empowerment in Turkey. In R. Kasaba (Ed.), *Cambridge history of Turkey: Volume 4 Turkey in modern world* (pp. 388–418). Cambridge: Cambridge University Press.

Arat, Y. (2010a). Women's rights and Islam in Turkish politics: The civil code amendment. *The Middle East Journal, 64,* 235–251.

Arat, Y. (2010b). Religion, politics and gender equality in Turkey: Implications of a democratic paradox. *Third World Quarterly, 31,* 869–884.

Arends-Kuenning, M., & Amin, S. (2001). Women's capabilities and the right to education in Bangladesh. *International Journal of Politics, Culture and Society, 15,* 125–142.

Arnot, M. (2002). *Reproducing gender essays on educational theory and feminist politics.* London: Routledge.

Arnot, M. (2006). Gender equality, pedagogy and citizenship affirmative and transformative approaches in the UK. *Theory and Research in Education, 4,* 131–150.

Ataca, B. (2009). Turkish family structure and functioning. In S. Bekman & A. Aksu-Koc (Eds.), *Perspectives on human development, family, and culture* (pp. 108–125). Cambridge: Cambridge University Press.

Ataca, B., & Sunar, D. (1999). Continuity and change in Turkish urban family life. *Pyschology and Developing Societies, 11*(1), 77–90.

Aycan, Z. (2004). Key success factors for women in management in Turkey. *Applied Phycology: An International Review, 53,* 453–477.

Aycicegi-Dinn, A., & Kagitcibasi, C. (2010). The value of children for parents in the minds of emerging adults. *Cross-Cultural Research, 44*(2), 174–205.

Azak, U. (2010). *Islam and secularism in Turkey: Kemalism, religion and the nation state.* London: IB Tauris.

Bacak, B. (2010). Discrimination between men and women in the working life in Turkey and regulations about positive discrimination. *The Social Sciences, 5,* 164–171.

Batuhan, A. (2007). Turkey country case study. *Country profile commissioned for the EFA global monitoring report 2008, education for all by 2015: Will we make it, 222.*

Benhabib, S. (1996). *Democracy and difference.* Princeton: Princeton University Press.

Benhabib, S. (2002). *The claims of culture: Equality and diversity in the global era.* Princeton: Princeton University Press.

Berktay, F. (1995). Has anything changed in the outlook of the Turkish left on women? In S. Tekeli (Ed.), *Women in modern Turkish society: A reader* (pp. 250–262). London: Zed Books.

Bespinar, F. (2010). Questioning agency and empowerment: Women's work-related strategies and social class in urban Turkey. *Women's Studies International Forum, 33*(6), 523–532.

Biggeri, M., Libanora, R., Mariani, S., & Menchini, L. (2006). Children conceptualizing their capabilities: Results of the survey during the first children's world congress on child labour. *Journal of Human Development, 7,* 59–83.

Boyatzis, R. (1998). *Transforming qualitative information: Thematic analysis and code development.* California: Sage Publications.

Bozalek, V., & Boughey, C. (2012). (Mis)framing higher education in South Africa. *Social Policy & Administration, 46*(2), 688–703.

Bozarslan, H. (2008). Kurds and the Turkish state. In R. Kasaba (Ed.), *Cambridge history of Turkey: Volume 4 Turkey in modern world* (pp. 333–356). Cambridge: Cambridge University Press.

Braun, V., & Clarke, V. (2006). Using thematic analysis in psychology. *Qualitative Research in Psychology, 3,* 77–101.

Brown, W. (2006). American nightmare: Neoliberalism, neo-conservatism, and de-democratization. *Political Theory, 34,* 690–714.

Bugra, A. (2013). Revisiting the Wollstonecraft Dilemma in the context of conservative liberalism: The case of female employment in Turkey. *Social Politics, 1,* 1–19.

Butler, J. (1990). *Gender trouble: Feminism and the subversion of identity.* New York: Routledge.

Çaha, O. (2013). *Women and civil society in Turkey: Women's movements in a Muslim society.* Farnham: Ashgate.

Cayir, K. (2011). Turkey's new citizenship and democracy education course: Search for democratic citizenship in a difference-blind polity? *Journal of Social Science Education, 10*(4), 22–30.

Çayır, K. (2015). Citizenship, nationality and minorities in Turkey's textbooks: From politics of non-recognition to 'difference multiculturalism'. *Comparative Education, 51*(4), 519–536.

Cayir, K., & Bagli, M. (2011). 'No-one respects them anyway': Secondary school students' perceptions of human rights in Turkey. *Intercultural Education, 22*(1), 1–14.

Celikten, M. (2005). A perspective on women principals in Turkey. *International Journal of Leadership in Education, 8,* 207–221.

Ceylan, T., & Irzik, G. (2004). *Human rights issues in textbooks: The Turkish case.* Istanbul: The History Foundation of Turkey.

Chatterjee, P. (1993). *The nation and its fragments: Colonial and post-colonial histories*. Princeton: Princeton University Press.

Chaudhury, N., & Parajuli, D. (2010). Conditional cash transfers and female schooling: The impact of the female school stipend programme on public school enrolments in Punjab, Pakistan. *Applied Economics, 42*(28), 3565–3583.

Cin, F. M., & Walker, M. (2013). Context and history: Using a capabilities-based social justice perspective to explore three generations of western Turkish female teachers' lives. International Journal of Educational Development, 33(4), 394–404.

Cin, F. M., & Walker, M. (2016). Re-considering girls' education in Turkey from a capabilities and feminist perspective. *International Journal of Educational Development, 49*, 134–143.

Citak, Z., & Tur, O. (2008). Women between tradition and change: The justice and development party experience in Turkey. *Middle Eastern Studies, 44*, 455–469.

Cosar, S., & Yegenoglu, S. (2011). New grounds for Pzatriarchy in Turkey? Gender policy in the age of AKP. *South European Society and Politics, 16*, 555–573.

Crocker, D. A. (2008). *Ethics of global development: Agency, capability, and deliberative democracy*. Cambridge: Cambridge University Press.

Dedeoglu, S. (2012). Equality, protection or discrimination: Gender equality policies in Turkey. *Social Politics, 19*, 269–290.

Dedeoglu, S. (2013). Veiled Europeanisation of welfare state in Turkey: Gender and social policy in the 2000s. *Women's Studies International Forum, 41*, 7–13.

DeJaeghere, J. (2012). Public debate and dialogue from a capabilities approach: Can it foster gender justice in education? *Journal of Human Development and Capabilities, 13*, 353–371.

Dejaeghere, J., & Lee, S. K. (2011). What matters for marginalized girls and boys in Bangladesh: A capabilities approach for understanding educational well-being and empowerment. *Research in Comparative and International Education, 6*(1), 27–42.

DeJaeghere, J., & Wiger, N. (2013). Gender discourses in an NGO education project: Openings for transformation toward gender equality in Bangladesh. *International Journal of Educational Development, 66*(3), 557–565.

DeJaeghere, J., Wu, X., & Vu, L. (2015). Ethnicity and education in China and Vietnam: Discursive formations of inequality. *Compare: A Journal of Comparative and International Education, 45*(1), 118–140.

Demirel, O. (1995). *Ogretmen Meslegine Yonelen Egitim Fakultesi Ogrencilerinin Sosyo-Ekonomik, Psikolojik Ozellikleri (The Socio-economic Conditions and Psychological Proporties of Students studying at Education Faculty)*. Unpublished Phd thesis, Istanbul University, Istanbul.

Diner, C., & Toktas, S. (2010). Waves of feminism in Turkey: Kemalist, Islamist and Kurdish women's movements in an era of globalization. *Journal of Balkan and Near Eastern Studies, 12,* 41–57.

Drydyk, J. (2013). Empowerment, agency, and power. *Journal of Global Ethics, 9*(3), 249–262.

Dulger, I. (2004). Case study on Turkey rapid coverage for compulsory education program. In *conference on scaling up poverty reduction, Shanghai, China.* Retrieved from http://siteresources.worldbank.org/INTTURKEY/Resources/Compulsory_Education.pdf

Duman, A. (2010). Female education inequality in Turkey: Factors affecting girls' schooling decisions. *International Journal of Education Economics and Development, 1,* 243–258.

Durakbasa, A. (1998). Kemalism as identity politics in Turkey. In Z. Arat (Ed.), *Deconstructing images of the 'Turkish woman'* (pp. 139–157). New York: St. Martin's Press.

Dyer, C. (2010). Education and social (in)justice for mobile groups: Re-framing rights and educational inclusion for Indian pastoralist children. *Educational Review, 62,* 301–313.

Ecevit, Y. (1990). An analysis of the concentration of women wage workers in Turkish manufacturing industries. In F. Ozbay (Ed.), *Women, family and social change in Turkey* (pp. 120–137). Bangkok: UNESCO.

Ecevit, Y. (2003). Women's labor and social security. *In: Acar, F. (eds.) Bridging the gender gap in Turkey: A mile stone towards faster socio-economic development and poverty reduction.* World Bank (Poverty Reduction and Economic Management Unit Europe and Central Asia Region), pp. 73–106.

Ecevit, Y. (2013). Gendering social policy and welfare state in Turkey. *Women's Studies International Forum, 41,* 1–6.

Eisenberg, A. (2006). Education and the politics of difference: Iris Young and the politics of education. *Educational Philosophy and Theory, 38*(1), 7–23.

Engin-Demir, C., & Cobanoglu, R. (2012). Kizlarin Okullulasmasinin önündeki engeller ve çözüm önerileri: alan arastirmasi. In: *Milli Egitim Bakanlığı ERG (Egitim Reformu Girisimi). 2011. Egitim Izleme Raporu 2011.* Sabancı Universitesi, Ankara.

Englund, T. (2000). Rethingking democracy and education: Towards an education of deliberative citizens. *Journal of Curriculum Studies, 32*(2), 305–313.

Enslin, P. (2006). Democracy, social justice and education: Feminist strategies in a globalising world. *Educational Philosophy and Theory, 38*(1), 57–67.

Enslin, P., Pendlebury, S., & Tjiattas, M. (2001). Deliberative democracy, diversity and the challenges of citizenship education. *Journal of Philosophy of Education, 35*(1), 115–130.

Ercan, F. (1999). 1980'lerde Egitim sistemini Yeniden Yapilanmasi: Kuresellesme ve Neo-Liberal Egitim Politikalari (Education System in 1980s: Globalization and Neo-Liberal Education Policies). In: Gok, F. (eds) *75. yilda Egitim* (pp. 23–38). Istanbul: Tarih Vakfi Yayinlari.

Esen, Y. (2007). Sexism in school textbooks prepared under education reform in Turkey. *Journal for Critical Education Policy Studies, 5*(2), 1–20.

Fennel, S., & Arnot, M. (2008). *Gender education and equality in a global context: Conceptual frameworks and policy perspectives.* Abingdon: Routledge.

Fikret-Pasa, S., Kabasakal, H., & Bodur, M. (2001). Society, organization, and leadership in Turkey. *Applied Psychology: An International Review, 50,* 559–589.

Filmer, D., & Schady, N. (2008). Getting girls into school: Evidence from a scholarship program in Cambodia. *Economic Development and Cultural Change, 56*(3), 581–617.

Folbre, N. (1994). *Who pays for the kids? Gender and the structures of constraint.* London: Routledge.

Fraser, N. (1989). *Unruly practices: Power, discourse and gender in contemporary social theory.* Minneapolis: University of Minnesota Press.

Fraser, N. (1993). Beyond the master/subject model: Reflection on Carole Pateman's sexual contract. *Social Text, 37,* 173–181.

Fraser, N. (1997). *Justice interruptus: Critical reflections on the "postsocialist" condition.* London: Routledge.

Fraser, N. (2003). *Redistribution or recognition?:A political-philosophical exchange.* London: Verso.

Fraser, N. (2007). Feminist politics in the age of recognition: A two-dimensional approach to gender justice. *Studies in Social Justice, 1,* 23–35.

Fraser, N. (2013). *Fortunes of feminism: From state-managed capitalism to neoliberal crisis.* London: Verso.

Freedom House. (2015). *Freedom in the World 2014: Turkey.* Available online at: https://freedomhouse.org/report/freedom-world/2015/turkey. Accessed 15 Jan 2016.

Gewirtz, S. (2006). Towards a contextualized analysis of social justice in education. *Educational Philosophy and Theory, 38*(1), 69–81.

Goetz, A. (2007). Gender justice, citizenship and entitlements: Core concepts, central debates and new directions for research. In M. Mukhopadhyay & N. Singh (Eds.), *Gender justice, citizenship and development* (pp. 15–57). New Delhi: Zubaan.

Gokovali, U. (2013). Everyone's own poverty: Gendering poverty alleviation policies in Turkey. *Women's Studies International Forum, 43,* 65–75.

Goksel, I. (2013). Female labor force participation in Turkey: The role of conservatism. *Women's Studies International Forum, 41,* 45–54.

Göle, N. (1997). The quest for the Islamic self within the context of modernity. In S. Bozdogan & R. Kasaba (Eds.), *Rethinking modernity and national identity in Turkey* (pp. 81–94). Seattle: University of Washington Press.

Goodson, I., & Sikes, P. (2001). *Life history research in educational settings: Learning from lives*. Buckingham: Open University Press.

Griffiths, M. (2006). The feminization of teaching and the practice of teaching: Threat or opportunity? *Educational Theory, 56*, 387–405.

Gumus, A. (2008). Turkish primary education: Structures and problems. In A. Nohl, A. Akkoyunlu-Wigley, & S. Wigley (Eds.), *Education in Turkey* (pp. 49–82). Munster: Waxmann.

Gumus, S., & Gumus, E. (2013). Achieving gender parity in primary school education in Turkey via the campaign called "Haydi Kızlar Okula" (Girls, let's go to school). *Education and Science, 38*, 17–26.

Gunduz-Hosgor, A., & Smits, J. (2007). The status of rural women in Turkey: What is the role of regional differences. In V. Moghadam (Ed.), *From patriarchy to empowerment: Women's participation, movements, and rights in the Middle East, North Africa, and South Asia* (pp. 180–202). Syracuse: Syracuse University press.

Gunduz-Hosgor, A., & Smits, J. (2008). Variation in labor market participation of married women in Turkey. *Women's Studies International Forum, 31*, 104–117.

Gunlu, R. (2008). Vocational education and labour market integration in Turkey: Requirements for vocational training and development. In A. Nohl, A. Akkoyunlu-Wigley, & S. Wigley (Eds.), *Education in Turkey* (pp. 107–130). Munster: Waxmann.

Gunter, M. (2008). *The Kurds ascending the evolving solution to the Kurdish problem in Iraq and Turkey*. New York: Palgrave Macmillan.

Gutman, A. (1987). *Democratic education*. Princeton: Princeton University Press.

Gutman, A., & Thompson, D. (1996). *Democracy and disagreement*. Cambridge: Harvard University Press.

Hausmann, R. (2014). *Gender Gap Report 2014*. World Economic Forum.

Hom, S. (2012). Claiming women's rights in China. In M. Worden (Ed.), *The unfinished revolution: Voices from the global fight for women's rights* (pp. 269–278). New York: Policy Press.

Hurriyet, (2013, October 22). Sex as a police punishment. Retrieved from http://www.hurriyetdailynews.com/sex-as-a-police-punishment.aspx?pageID=500&eid=258

Ibrahim, S. S. (2006). From individual to collective capabilities: The capability approach as a conceptual framework for self-help. *Journal of Human Development, 7*(3), 397–416.

Ilkkaracan, I. (2012). Why so few women in the labor market in Turkey? *Feminist Economics, 18*, 1–37.

Inal, K. (2008). *Egitim ve Ideoloji (Education and Ideology)*. Istanbul: Kalkedon.

Inandi, Y. (2009). The barriers to career advancement of female teachers in Turkey and their levels of burnout. *Social Behavior and Personality, 37*(8), 1143–1152.

Jansen, H. A., Üner, S., Kardam, F., Tezcan, S., Ergöçmen, B. A., & Koç, Y. (2009). National research on domestic violence against women in Turkey. *Summary report*. Ankara: *Institute public sector Gmbh, Hacettepe University Institute of Population Studies, BNB consulting Ltd Co.*

Kabeer, N. (1999). Resources, agency, achievements: Reflections on the measurement of women's empowerment. *Development and Change, 30*, 435–464.

Kabeer, N. (2007). *Marriage, motherhood and masculinity in the global economy: Reconfiguration of personal and economic life*. Brighton: Institute of Development Studies.

Kadioglu, A. (1994). Women's subordination in Turkey: Is Islam really the villain. *Middle East Journal, 48*, 645–660.

Kadioglu, A. (1998). Republican epistemology and Islamic discourse in Turkey in the 1990s. *The Muslim World, 88*, 1–21.

Kagitcibasi, C. (1986). Status of women in Turkey: Cross-cultural perspectives. *International Journal of Middle East Studies, 18*, 485–499.

Kagitcibasi, C. (1990). Family and socialization in cross-cultural perspective: A model of change. In J. Berman (Ed.), *Cross-cultural perspectives: Nebraska symposium on motivation* (pp. 135–200). Lincoln: Nebraska University Press.

Kagitcibasi, C., & Ataca, B. (2005). Value of children and family change: A three-decade portrait from Turkey. *Applied Psychology: An International Review, 54*, 317–338.

Kandiyoti, D. (1977). Sex roles and social change: A comparative appraisal of Turkey's women. *Signs, 3*, 57–73.

Kandiyoti, D. (1987). Emancipated but unliberated? Reflections on the Turkish case. *Feminist Studies, 13*, 317–338.

Kandiyoti, D. (1988). Bargaining with patriarchy. *Gender and Society, 2*, 274–290.

Kandiyoti, D. (1989). Women and the Turkish state: Political actors or symbolic Pawns? In N. Yuval-Davis, F. Anthias, & J. Campling (Eds.), *Woman-Nation-State* (pp. 126–149). New York: St. Martin's Press.

Kandiyoti, D. (1990). Rural transformation in Turkey and its implications for women's status. In F. Ozbay (Ed.), *Women, family and social change in Turkey* (pp. 91–104). Bangkok: UNESCO.

Kandiyoti, D. (2010). Gender and women's studies in Turkey: A moment for reflection. *New Perspectives on Turkey, 43*, 165–176.

Kandiyoti, D. (2011). Disentangling religion and politics: Whither gender equality? *IDS Bulletin, 42*(1), 10–14.

Karaomerlioglu, A. (1998). The village institutes experience in Turkey. *British Journal of Middle Eastern Studies, 25*, 47–73.

Kasaba, R. (1997). Kemalist certainties and modern ambiguities. In S. Bozdogan & R. Kasaba (Eds.), *Rethinking modernity and national identity in Turkey* (pp. 15–36). Seattle: University of Washington Press.

Kasaba, R. (2008). *Cambridge History of Turkey: Volume 4 Turkey in Modern World*. Cambridge: Cambridge University Press.

Kashyap, A. (2012). Maternal mortality: Ending endless deaths in childbirth. In M. Worden (Ed.), *The unfinished revolution: Voices from the global fight for women's rights* (pp. 231–238). New York: Policy Press.

Kaya, N. (2009). *Forgotten or assimilated? Minorities in the education system of Turkey*. Available online at: www.minorityrights.org/download.php?id=632. Accessed 25 May 2013.

Keyder, C. (2008). A brief history of modern Istanbul. In R. Kasaba (Ed.), *Cambridge history of Turkey: Volume 4 Turkey in modern world* (pp. 504–523). Cambridge: Cambridge University Press.

Kilic, A. (2008). The gender dimension of social policy reform in Turkey: Towards equal citizenship. *Social Policy & Administration, 5*, 487–503.

Kirdar, M. (2009). Explaining ethnic disparities in school enrolment in Turkey. *Economic Development and Cultural Change, 57*, 297–333.

Kirisci, K., & Winrow, G. (1997). *The Kurdish question and Turkey: An example of a trans-state ethnic conflict*. London: Frank Cass.

Kirk, J. (2004). Impossible fictions: The lived experiences of women teachers in Karachi. *Comparative Education Review, 48*, 374–395.

Kirk, J. (2006). *The impact of women teachers on girls education*. Thailand: UNESCO.

Kirk, J. (2008). *Women teaching in South Asia*. New Delhi: Sage Publications.

Knobloch, U. (2014). Questioning the gender-based division of labour: The contribution of the capabilities approach to feminist economics. In: *Capabilities, gender, equality: Towards fundamental entitlements* (p. 195). Cambridge: Cambridge University Press

Koca, C. (2004). Beden Egitimi Derslerinde Toplumsal Cinsiyet Rollerinin Yapilandirilmasi (Construction of Sex Roles in Physical Education). In: *Kadin Calismalarinda Disiplinlerarasi Bulusma, 3 (Interdisciplinary Meeting in Women's Studies, 3)* (pp. 186–194). Istanbul: Yeditepe Universitesi.

Koggel, C. (2003). Globalization and women's paid work: Expanding freedoms. *Feminist Economics, 9*, 163–184.

Koggel, C. M. (2013). A critical analysis of recent work on empowerment: Implications for gender. *Journal of Global Ethics, 9*(3), 263–275.

KSGM (Kadin Statusu Genel Mudurlugu). (2012). *Turkiye'de Kadinin Durumu*. TC Aile ve Sosyal Politikalar Bakanlığı, Kadın Statüs Genel Müdürlüğü Raporu, Ankaraç.

KSGM (Kadın Statüsü Genel Müdürlüğü). (2015, May 24). *Türkiye'de Kadına Yönelik Aile içi Şiddet Araştırması*. Retrieved from at: http://www.hips.hacettepe.edu.tr/KKSA-TRAnaRaporKitap26Mart.pdf

Kvale, S. (1996). *Interviews: An introduction to qualitative research interviewing*. London: Sage.

Landing, J. (2011). Bringing women to the table: European Union funding for women's empowerment projects in Turkey. *Women's Studies International Forum, 34*, 206–219.

Lukuslu, D. (2005). Constructors and constructed: Youth as a political actor in modernising Turkey. In J. Forbig (Ed.), *Revising youth political participation: Challenges for research and democratic practice in Europe* (pp. 29–36). Strasbourg: Council of Europe Publishing.

Manion, C., & Menashy, F. (2013). The prospects and challenges of reforming the world bank's approach to gender and education: Exploring the value of the capability policy model in the Gambia. *Journal of Human Development and Capabilities, 14*, 214–240.

Mardin, S. (2007). *Ideoloji.* İstanbul: İletişim Yayınları.

Marphatia, A., & Moussie, R. (2013). A question of gender justice: Exploring the linkages between women's unpaid care work, education, and gender equality. *International Journal of Educational Development, 33*, 585–594.

McClure, K. R. (2011). Turkey's eastern question: Education disparities and EU accession. The Washington Review of Turkish & Eurasian Affairs.

McClure, K. R. (2014). Education for economic growth or human development? The capabilities approach and the World Bank's Basic Education Project in Turkey. *Compare: A Journal of Comparative and International Education, 44*(3), 472–492.

McCowan, T. (2011). Human rights, capabilities and the normative basis of 'education for all'. *Theory and Research in Education, 9*(3), 283–298.

McCowan, T., & Unterhalter, E. (Eds.). (2015). *Education and international development: An introduction.* London: Bloomsbury Publishing.

Mills, A. (2007). Gender and Mahalle (Neighbourhood) in Istanbul. *Gender, Place & Culture, 14*, 335–354.

Monkman, K. (2011). Introduction: Framing gender, education and empowerment research. *Research in Comparative and International Education, 6*, 1–13.

Moreau, M. P., Osgood, J., & Halsall, A. (2007). Making sense of the glass ceiling in schools: An exploration of women teachers' discourses. *Gender and Education, 19*, 237–253.

Mosedale, S. (2005). Assessing women's empowerment: Towards a conceptual framework. *Journal of International Development, 17*(2), 243–257.

Muftuler-Bac, M. (2012). *Gender equality in Turkey. Report prepared for European Parliament.* Brussels: Directorate General for Internal Policies.

Murphy-Graham, E. (2008). Opening the black box: Women's empowerment and innovative secondary education in Honduras. *Gender and Education, 20*, 31–50.

Murphy-Graham, E. (2012). *Opening minds, improving lives: Education and women's empowerment in Honduras.* Nashville: Vanderbilt University Press.

Muscati, S. (2012). Women in Iraq: Losing ground. In M. Worden (Ed.), *The unfinished revolution: Voices from the global fight for women's rights* (pp. 79–92). New York: Policy Press.

Navaro-Yashin, Y. (2002). *Faces of the state: Secularism and public life in Turkey*. Princeton: Princeton University Press.

Neyzi, L. (2001). Object or subject? The paradox of 'youth' in Turkey. *International Journal of Middle East Studies, 33,* 411–432.

Nohl, A. (2008). The Turkish education system and its history. In A. M. Nohl, A. Akkoyunlu-Wigley, & S. Wigley (Eds.), *Education in Turkey* (pp. 15–48). Munster: Waxmann.

Nussbaum, M. (2000). *Women and human development: The capabilities approach*. Cambridge: Cambridge University Press.

Nussbaum, M. (2003a). Women's education: A global challenge. *Journal of Women in Culture and Society, 29,* 325–354.

Nussbaum, M. (2003b). Capabilities as fundamental entitlements: Sen and social justice. *Feminist Economics, 9*(2), 33–59.

Nussbaum, M. (2011). *Creating capabilities: The human development approach*. Cambridge: Harvard University Press.

Nussbaum, M., & Sen, A. (1993). *The quality of life*. Oxford: Clarendon Press.

O'Neill, O. (2000). *Bounds of justice*. Cambridge: Cambridge University Press.

Odhiambo, A. (2012). Fitsula: Giving birth and living death in Africa. In M. Worden (Ed.), *The unfinished revolution: Voices from the global fight for women's rights* (pp. 249–258). New York: Policy Press.

OECD. (2013a). *Better Life Index*. Retrieved from http://www.oecdbetterlifeindex.org/countries/turkey/. Accessed 2 Jan 2014.

Okcabol, R. (2005). *Turkiye'de Egitim Sistemi (The Education System of Turkey)*. Ankara: Utopya.

Okcabol, R. (2008). Secondary education in Turkey. In A. M. Nohl, A. Akkoyunlu-Wigley, & S. Wigley (Eds.), *Education in Turkey* (pp. 83–105). Waxmann: Munster.

Okin, S. M. (1989). *Justice, gender and the family*. New York: Basic Books.

Okin, S. M. (1999). *Is multiculturalism bad for women?* Princeton: Princeton University Press.

Okin, S. (2003). Poverty, well-being, and gender: What counts, who's heard? *Philosophy & Public Affairs, 31,* 280–316.

Öneş, U., Memiş, E. & Kızılırak, B. (2013). Poverty and intra-household distribution of work time in Turkey: Analysis and some policy implications. *Women's Studies International Forum, 41,* 55–64.

Ozbay, F. (1990). The development of studies on women in Turkey. In F. Ozbay (Ed.), *Women, family and social change in Turkey* (pp. 1–12). Bangkok: UNESCO.

Özkazanç, A., & Sayilan, F. (2008). Gendered power relations in the school: Construction of schoolgirl femininities in a Turkish High School. *International Journal of Social Sciences, 3*(1), 35–43.

Pateman, C. (1988). *The sexual contract.* Stanford: Stanford University Press.

Peristiany, J. (1966). *Honour and shame: The values of Mediterranean society.* Chicago: University of Chicago Press.

Phillips, A. (1998). *The politics of presence.* Oxford: Oxford University Press.

Phillips, A. (2007). *Multiculturalism without culture.* Princeton: Princeton University Press.

Prasso, S. (2012). A long march for women's rights in China. In M. Worden (Ed.), *The unfinished revolution: Voices from the global fight for women's rights* (pp. 277–286). New York: Policy Press.

Qizilbash, M. (2002). Development, common foes and shared values. *Review of Political Economy, 14*(4), 463–480.

Rankin, B., & Aytac, I. (2006). Gender inequality in schooling: The case of Turkey. *Sociology of Education, 79,* 25–43.

Rankin, B., & Aytac, I. (2008). Religiosity, the headscarf, and education in Turkey: An analysis of 1988 data and current implications. *British Journal of Sociology of Education, 29,* 273–287.

Rawls, J. (2013). *Political liberalism: Expanded edition.* New York: Columbia University Press.

Raynor, J. (2007). Education and capabilities in Bangladesh. In M. Walker & E. Unterhalter (Eds.), *Amartya Sen's capability approach and social justice in education* (pp. 157–176). New York: Palgrave Macmillan.

Raynor, J., & Unterhalter, E. (2008). Promoting empowerment? Contrasting perspectives on a programme to employ women teachers in Bangladesh, 1996–2005. In J. Kirk (Ed.), *Women teaching in South Asia* (pp. 149–172). India: Sage Publications.

Reay, D. (1997). Feminist theory, habitus and social class: Disrupting notions of classlessness. *Women's Studies International Forum, 20,* 225–233.

Reinharz, S., & Davidman, L. (1992). *Feminist methods in social research.* New York: Oxford University Press.

Robeyns, I. (2003a). Sen's capability approach and gender inequality: Selecting relevant capabilities. *Feminist Economics, 9,* 61–92.

Robeyns, I. (2003b). *The capability approach: An interdisciplinary introduction.* University of Amsterdam: Department of Political Science and Amsterdam School of Social Sciences Research.

Robeyns, I. (2005a). The capability approach: A theoretical survey. *Journal of Human Development, 6,* 93–114.

Robeyns, I. (2005b). Selecting capabilities for quality of life measurement. *Social Indicators Research, 74,* 191–215.

Robeyns, I. (2006). Three models of education: Rights, capabilities and human capital. *Theory and Research in Education, 4,* 69–84.

Robeyns, I. (2007). When will society be gender just? In J. Browne (Ed.), *The future of gender* (pp. 54–74). Cambridge: Cambridge University Press.

Robeyns, I. (2010a). Gender and the metric of justice. In H. Brighouse & I. Robeyns (Eds.), *Measuring justice: Primary goods and capabilities* (pp. 215–235). Cambridge: Cambridge University Press.

Robeyns, I. (2010b). Social justice and the gendered division of labour: Possibilities and limits of the capability approach. In T. Addabbo, M. Arrizabalaga, C. Borderias, & A. Owens (Eds.), *Gender inequalities, households and the production of well-being in modern Europe* (pp. 25–40). Surrey: Ashgate Publishing Company.

Sahin, I., & Gulmez, Y. (2000). Social sources of failure in education: The case in East and Southeast Turkey. *Social Indicators Research, 49,* 83–113.

Saleeby, P. W. (2014). Applying the capabilities approach to disability, poverty, and gender. In F. Comim & M. C. Nussbaum (Eds.), *Capabilities, gender, equality: Towards fundamental entitlements* (pp. 308–321). Cambridge: Cambridge University Press.

Sanal, M. (2008). Factors preventing women's advancement in management in Turkey. *Education, 128*(3), 380–391.

Sari, M. (2012). Exploring gender roles' effects of Turkish female teachers on their teaching practices. *International Journal of Educational Development, 32,* 814–825.

Sayilan, F. (2008). Gender and education in Turkey. In A. Nohl, A. Akkoyunlu-Wigley, & S. Wigley (Eds.), *Education in Turkey* (pp. 247–270). Munster: Waxmann.

Sen, A. (1985). Well-being agency and freedom: The Dewey Lectures. *Journal of Philosophy, 82,* 169–221.

Sen, A. (1987). *The standard of living.* Cambridge: Cambridge University Press.

Sen, A. (1990). *Individual freedom as a social commitment.* New York Review of Books.

Sen, A. (1993). Capability and well being. In M. Nussbaum & A. Sen (Eds.), *The quality of life* (pp. 30–53). Oxford: Clarendon Press.

Sen, A. (1999). *Development as freedom.* Oxford: Oxford University Press.

Sen, A. (2004). Capabilities, lists, and public reason: Continuing the conversation. *Feminist Economics, 10,* 77–80.

Sen, A. (2009). *The idea of justice.* London: Allen Lane & Harvard University Press.

Shorter, F. C. (1985). The population of Turkey after the war of independence. *International Journal of Middle East Studies, 17,* 417–441.

Skeggs, B. (1997). *Formations of class and gender.* London: Sage.

Skelton, C., Carrington, B., Francis, B., Hutchings, M., Read, B., & Hall, I. (2009). Gender matters in the primary classroom pupils' and teachers' perspectives. *British Educational Research Journal, 35*(2), 187–204.

Smits, J., & Gunduz-Hosgor, A. (2003). Linguistic capital: Language as a socio-economic resource among Kurdish and Arabic women in Turkey. *Ethnic and Racial Studies, 26,* 829–853.

Smits, J., & Gunduz-Hosgor, A. (2006). Effects of family background characteristics on educational participation in Turkey. *International Journal of Educational Development, 26,* 545–560.

Smulyan, L. (2000). Feminist cases of nonfeminist subjects: Case studies of women principals. *Qualitative Research in Education, 13,* 589–609.

Stacki, S. (2002). *Women teachers empowered in India: Teacher training through a gender lens.* New York: UNICEF.

Stacki, S., & Monkman, K. (2003). Change through empowerment processes: Women's stories from South Asia and Latin America. *Compare, 2,* 173–189.

Stivachtis, Y., & Georgakis, S. (2011). Changing gender attitudes in candidate countries: The impact of EU conditionality: The case of Turkey. *Journal of European Integration, 33,* 75–91.

Stromquist, N. (1995). The theoretical and practical bases for empowerment. In C. Medel-Anonuevo (Ed.), *Women, education and empowerment: Pathways towards autonomy* (pp. 13–22). Hamburg: UNESCO.

Stromquist, N. (2006). Gender, education and the possibility of transformative knowledge. *Compare, 36,* 145–161.

Stromquist, N. (2007). *The gender socialization process in schools: A cross-national comparison.* Paper prepared for the education for all global ,monitoring report 2008. Paris: UNESCO.

Subrahmanian, R. (2002). Engendering education: Prospects for a rights based approach to female education deprivation in India. In M. Molyneux & S. Ravazi (Eds.), *Gender justice, development and rights* (pp. 204–238). Oxford: Oxford University Press.

Sumer, S. (1998). Incongruent modernities: A common study of higher educated women from urban Turkey and Norway. *Acta Sociologica, 41,* 115–129.

Sumer, H. (2006). Women in management: Still waiting to be full members of the club. *Sex Roles, 15,* 63–72.

Sunderland, J. (2012). Damned if you do, damned if you don't: Religious dress and women's rights. In M. Worden (Ed.), *The unfinished revolution: Voices from the global fight for women's rights* (pp. 297–304). New York: Policy Press.

Sural, N. (2007). Legal framework for gender equality at work in Turkey. *Middle Eastern Studies, 43,* 811–824.

Syed, J., Ozbilgin, M., Torunoglu, D., & Alid, F. (2009). Rescuing gender equality from the false dichotomies of secularism versus shariah in Muslim majority countries. *Women's Studies International Forum, 32,* 67–79.

Tan, M. (2000). Eğitimde Kadın-Erkek Eşitliği ve Türkiye Gercegi (Gender Equality in Education and Turkish Reality). In M. Tan & Y. Ecevit (Eds.), *Kadın-Erkek Esitligine Doğru Yuruyus: Eğitim, Çalışma Yaşamı ve Siyaset* (pp. 21–116). Istanbul: TUSIAD.

Tan, M. (2005). Yeni Ilkogretim Programlari ve Toplumsal cinsiyet (New Curriculum and Gender in Education). *Egitim, Bilim, Toplum Dergisi, 3*(11), 68–77.

Tan, M. (2007). Women, education and development in Turkey. In M. Carlson, A. Rabo, & F. Gok (Eds.), *Education in multicultural societies: Turkish and Swedish perspectives* (pp. 109–124). Stockholm: Swedish Research Institute in Istanbul.

Tansel, A. (2002). Determinants of school attainment of boys and girls in Turkey: Individual, household and community factors. *Economics of Education Review, 21*, 455–470.

Tekeli, S. (1981). Women in Turkish politics. In N. Abadan-Unat, D. Kandiyotu, & M. B. Kiray (Eds.), *Women in Turkish society* (pp. 293–311). Leiden: E. J. Brill.

Tekeli, S. (1986). Emergence of the new feminist movement in Turkey. In D. Dahlereup (Ed.), *The new women's movement* (pp. 179–199). London: Sage Publications.

Tekeli, S. (1988). *Kadinlar Icin (For Women)*. Istanbul: Alan Yayincilik.

Tekeli, S. (1990). *Kadin Bakis Acisindan 1980'ler Turkiye'sinde Kadin*. Istanbul: Iletisim Yayinlari.

Tikly, L. (2011). Towards a framework for researching the quality of education in low-income countries. *Comparative Education, 47*(1), 1–23.

Tikly, L., & Barrett, A. (2011). Social justice, capabilities and the quality of education in low income countries. *International Journal of Educational Development, 31*, 3–14.

Tikly, L., & Barrett, A. M. (2013). *Education quality and social justice in the global south: Challenges for policy, practice and research*. Abingdon: Routledge.

Toksoz, G., & Gulay, A. (2004). Gender based discrimination at work in Turkey: A cross-sectorial overview. *Ankara Universitesi Siyasal Bilgiler Fakultesi Dergisi, 59*, 151–172.

Tomasevski, K. (2003). *Education denied*. London: Zed Books.

Toprak, B. (1990). Emancipated but unliberated women in Turkey: The impact of Islam. In F. Ozbay (Ed.), *Women, family and social change in Turkey* (pp. 39–49). Bangkok: UNESCO.

Toprak, B., Bozan, I., Morgul, T., & Sener, N. (2009). *Being different in Turkey: Religion, conservatism and otherization, research report on neighbourhood pressure*. Istanbul: Bogazici University Press.

TUIK (Turkiye Istatistik Kurumu). (2012). *Statistical indicators 1923–2012*. Ankara: Turkish Statistical Institute.

TUIK (Turkiye Istatistik Kurumu). (2013a). *Population of province 1927–2013.* Retrieved from http://www.tuik.gov.tr/UstMenu.do?metod=temelist. Accessed 4 Apr 2013.

TUIK (Turkiye Istatistik Kurumu). (2013b). Statistics about social security and health. Retrieved from http://www.tuik.gov.tr/. Accessed 4 Apr 2013.

TUIK. (2014a). İstatistiklerle Kadın, 2014. Retrieved from http://www.tuik.gov.tr/PreHaberBultenleri.do?id=18619. Accessed 23 Apr 2015.

TUIK. (2014b). Labour force statistics, November 2014. Retrieved from http://www.turkstat.gov.tr/PreHaberBultenleri.do?id=18634. Accessed 5 Mar 2015.

Turkey Central Statistics Office (TCSO). (1937). *Genel Nufus Sayimi 20 Ekim 1935 (General Population Census 20 October 1935).* Ankara.

UNDP. (2014). *Human development report 2014.* New York: United Nations Development Programme.

UNESCO. (2013). *Adult and youth literacy: National, regional and global trends, 1985–2015.* Retrieved from http://www.uis.unesco.org/Education/Documents/literacy-statistics-trends-1985-2015.pdf. Accessed 5 May 2014.

UNESCO. (2015). *Gender and EFA 2000–2015: Achievements and challenges.* Paris: UNESCO.

UNESCO & UNICEF. (2007). *A Human Rights-based approach to education for All.* New York: UNICEF.

UNICEF. (2003). *A gender review in education, Turkey: Analysis of results.* Ankara: UNICEF.

UNICEF & UNGEI. (2008). *Making education work: The gender dimension of the school to work transitions.* Bangkok: UNICEF and UNGEI.

Unluhisarcikli, O. (2008). Adult and further education: Systematic and historical apects of non-formal education in Turkey. In M. A. Nohl, A. Akkoyunlu-Wigley, & S. Wigley (Eds.), *Education in Turkey* (pp. 131–149). Munster: Waxmann.

Unterhalter, E. (2003a). The capabilities approach and gendered education: An examination of South African complexities. *Theory and Research in Education, 1*(1), 7–22.

Unterhalter, E. (2003b). *Education, capabilities and social justice.* Background paper for the EFA global monitoring report 2003/4. Paris: UNESCO.

Unterhalter, E. (2005a). Fragmented frameworks: Researching women, gender, education and development. In S. Aikman & E. Unterhalter (Eds.), *Beyond access: Developing gender equality in education* (pp. 15–35). Oxford: Oxfam.

Unterhalter, E. (2005b). Global inequality, capabilities, social justice: The millennium development goal for gender equality in education. *International Journal of Educational Development, 25,* 111–122.

Unterhalter, E. (2007a). *Gender, schooling and global social justice.* Oxon: Routledge.

Unterhalter, E. (2007b). Gender equality, education, and the capability approach. In M. Walker & E. Unterhalter (Eds.), *Amartya Sen's capability approach and social justice in education* (pp. 87–107). New York: Palgrave Macmillan.

Unterhalter, E. (2008). Global values and gender equality in education: Needs, rights and capabilities. In S. Fennel & M. Arnot (Eds.), *Gender education and equality in a global context: Conceptual frameworks and policy perspectives* (pp. 19–34). Abingdon: Routledge.

Unterhalter, E. (2009). Social justice, development theory and the question of education. In R. Cowen & A. M. Kazamias (Eds.), *International handbook of comparative education* (pp. 781–800). London: Springer.

Unterhalter, E. (2011). *How far does this go? Reflections on using the capability approach to evaluate gender, poverty, education, and empowerment*. A talk prepared for CIES gender committee symposium CIES conference, Montreal, May 2011. London: Institute of Education, University of London.

Unterhalter, E. (2012a). Poverty, education, gender and the millennium development goals: Reflections on boundaries and intersectionality. *Theory and Research in Education, 10*, 253–274.

Unterhalter, E. (2012b). Mutable meanings: Gender equality in education and international rights frameworks. *Equal Rights Review, 8*, 67–84.

Unterhalter, E. (2012c). Inequality, capabilities and poverty in four African countries: Girls' voice, schooling and strategies for institutional change. *Cambridge Journal of Education, 42*, 307–325.

Unterhalter, E., Kiko-Echessa, E., Pattman, R., N'Jai, F., & Rajagopalan, R. (2005). *Scaling up: Developing an approach to measuring progress on girls' education in commonwealth countries in Africa*. London: Commonwealth Secretariat.

UNWOMEN. (2012). *Progress of the world's women: In pursuit of justice*. Retrieved from http://progress.unwomen.org/pdfs/EN-Report-Progress.pdf. Accessed 4 May 2013.

Vaughan, R. (2010). Girls' and women's education within UNESCO and the World Bank, 1945–2000. *Compare: A Journal of Comparative and International Education, 40*(4), 405–423.

Velibeyoglu, J. (2013). Technical assistance for increasing enrolment rates especially for girls grant program compendium (2014, May 22). Retrieved from http://kizlarinegitimi.meb.gov.tr/files/img/hibeler_final_kitabi(1).pdf

Verick, S. (2014). Female labor force participation in developing countries. *IZA World of Labor*.

Vogler, C. (1998). Money in the household: Some underlying issues of power. *Sociological Review, 46*, 687–713. 288.

Vogler, C. (2005). Cohabiting couples: Rethinking money in the household at the beginning of the twenty first century. *The Sociological Review, 53*, 1–29.

Walker, M. (2006). Towards a capability-based theory of social justice for education policy-making. *Journal of Education Policy, 21,* 163–185.

Walker, M. (2007). Selecting capabilities for gender equality in education. In M. Walker & E. Unterhalter (Eds.), *Amartya Sen's capability approach and social justice in education* (pp. 177–196). New York: Palgrave Macmillan.

Walker, M., & McLean, M. (2013). *Professional education, capabilities and the public good: The role of universities in promoting human development.* New York: Routledge.

Walker, M., & Unterhalter, E. (2007). *Amartya Sen's capability approach and social justice in education.* New York: Palgrave Macmillan.

White, J. (2003). State feminism, modernization, and the Turkish Republican Woman. *NWSA Journal, 15,* 145–159.

White, J. (2008). Islam and politics in contemporary Turkey. In R. Kasaba (Ed.), *Cambridge history of Turkey: Volume 4 Turkey in modern world* (pp. 357–380). Cambridge: Cambridge University Press.

Yavuz, H. (2001). Five stages of the construction of Kurdish Nationalism in Turkey. *Nationalism and Ethnic Politics, 7,* 1–24.

Yavuz, H. (2003). *Islamic political identity in Turkey.* New York: Oxford University Press.

Young, I. (1990). *Justice and the politics of difference.* Princeton: Princeton University Press.

Young, I. (2002). *Inclusion and democracy.* Oxford: Oxford University Press.

Young, I. (2004). Structural injustice and the politics of difference. In K. Appiah, S. Benhabib, I. Young, & N. Fraser (Eds.), *Justice, governance, cosmopolitanism, and the politics of difference: Reconfigurations in a transnational world* (pp. 79–116). Humboldt: University of Berlin.

Zurcher, J. A. (1993). *Turkey: A modern history.* London: I.B.Tauris.

Index[1]

---

[1] Note: Page numbers with "n" denote notes.

Printed by Printforce, the Netherlands